Decolonizing "Prehistory"

ARCHAEOLOGY OF INDIGENOUS-COLONIAL INTERACTIONS IN
THE AMERICAS

Series Editors
Liam Frink
Aubrey Cannon
Barbara L. Voss
Steven A. Wernke
Patricia A. McAnany

Decolonizing "Prehistory"

Deep Time and Indigenous Knowledges

in North America

Edited by Gesa Mackenthun
and Christen Mucher

THE UNIVERSITY OF
ARIZONA PRESS

TUCSON

The University of Arizona Press
www.uapress.arizona.edu

ISBN-13: 978-0-8165-4229-1 (hardcover)

Cover design by Leigh McDonald
Cover art: Usufruct, 1995 by Lawrence Paul Yuxweluptun, courtesy of National Gallery of Canada
and Lawrence Paul Yuxweluptun

Publication of this book was made possible in part by financial support from the German Research
Foundation and the Jean Picker Fellowship Fund of Smith College.

Library of Congress Cataloging-in-Publication Data
Names: Mackenthun, Gesa, 1959– editor. | Mucher, Christen, editor.
Title: Decolonizing "prehistory" : deep time and indigenous knowledges in North America / edited
    by Gesa Mackenthun and Christen Mucher.
Other titles: Archaeology of indigenous-colonial interactions in the Americas.
Description: Tucson : University of Arizona Press, 2021. | Series: Archaeology of indigenous-
    colonial interactions in the Americas | Includes bibliographical references and index.
Identifiers: LCCN 2020046804 | ISBN 9780816542291 (hardcover)
Subjects: LCSH: Indians of North America—Historiography. | Archaeology and history—North
    America. | Nationalism and historiography. | North America—Historiography.
Classification: LCC E76.8 .D43 2021 | DDC 970.004/97—dc23
LC record available at https://lccn.loc.gov/2020046804

Printed in the United States of America
♾ This paper meets the requirements of ANSI/NISO Z39.48-1992 (Permanence of Paper).

To the memory of
Annette Kolodny (1941–2019)

Und meine Seele spannte
Weit ihre Flügel aus,
Flog durch die stillen Lande,
Als flöge sie nach Haus.

(And my soul extended
far its wings
and flew across the silent land
as if returning home.)

—JOSEPH FREIHERR VON EICHENDORFF,
"MONDNACHT" (*Moonlit night*)

Contents

Foreword

ONE OF THE PECULIAR FEATURES of historical consciousness among white Westerners is the shallowness of the underlying chronology. For all practical purposes, historical time rarely extends beyond some imagined point of national origins. The near side is the time of "we" and "us." On the other side lies the time of someone else and, still further back, the time of biology or nature. Genetic testing companies have made their peace with the shallowness of this particular historical consciousness. In a bizarrely neocolonial way, they make deep time comprehensible and accessible to their Western customers through the fiction of projecting nations back onto worlds that did not have them. A few years ago, for example, I learned that 60 percent of my ancestry is "British and Irish" and 23 percent "French and German." Wuh? How can my genetic ancestry be described by labels that don't even go back a thousand years? If I am allowed to slide the hashmark a little further back along the timeline, would the results now tell me that my ancestry is partly Turkish, Syriac, or Yemeni? The fiction makes sense only from a marketing point of view: no Europeanoid is going to pay to learn that they belong to the R-M269 or HV haplogroups. National labels provide customers with an illusory sense of understanding. But the fiction comes at a considerable cost, given how it naturalizes the nation and projects it backward in time.

The failure of the genetic testing companies to promote a framework of historical understanding that escapes the myth of nation is revealing. It demonstrates the profound degree to which historical consciousness is molded to suit the identity constructs of the present day. Different identities, different histories. White Westerners, a diverse people whose historical consciousness has long since been hollowed out by the shallow time of nations, are distinguished by their inability to think in terms of "we" across long time spans. Dipesh Chakrabarty has argued compellingly that the human inability to find meaning in a species-level history, a history projecting deep into the past, has become a serious liability in the era of the Anthropocene (*The Climate of History*). His diagnosis of the political stalemate is spot on. What he characterizes as a general human problem, however, may be something else. It may be, more specifically, a *Western* problem.

Over the past few years, I have had several opportunities to collaborate with scholars working in the Indigenous history of Australia and North

America. All these occasions, including the workshop in Schwerin that produced the contributions to this volume, have been intensely rewarding, even humbling experiences. Indigenous history has important political and legal dimensions, for its findings show how Western history and the epistemology on which it is based have been used to deny the rights of Indigenous and First Nations peoples. This social justice function, in turn, is grounded in a historical consciousness of mind-bending sophistication and profundity. Most important, Indigenous history is not bound by shallow time in the way that Western history is. As many of the contributions to this volume demonstrate, Indigenous history effortlessly projects the "we" deep into what Westerners think of as being the past. Long before the rise of Actor-Network Theory, moreover, Indigenous history grounded itself in a flat ontology that understands all actors—people, animals, volcanoes, rocks in a river, and so on—as participants in history. The "we" described in this way is generous and open.

Whenever I engage with Indigenous history, I am constantly challenged to reexamine my own thinking about time, identity, the nature of historical evidence, and the meaning of history itself. As a historian with a research interest in Europe before the sixteenth century, I find myself asking whether Europe too had (or has?) an Indigenous history, and if so, what that history might look like. The answer has to be yes, given how the Romans, at least in the circum-Mediterranean region, invented the practice of settler colonialism.[1] The political or epistemological framework that drives some scholarship in medieval Irish and Scottish historiography today, for example, has many parallels with the framework of Indigenous history. In some cases, the connections are explicit (see, among others, Smith, "Written Off the Map"). On some level, however, the answer also has to be no. Lithuanian history up to the early fifteenth century describes a people and a set of events that could easily be framed as an Indigenous history. The problem is that Lithuania became a nation, and along the way, Lithuanian national history became trapped in the shallow time of all such histories. In the process, the history lost some of the intangible qualities that make the Indigenous histories conveyed in this volume compelling on so many different levels.

On a more personal level, the opportunities I have had to exchange ideas with scholars of Indigenous history have taught me to question my prior understanding of the implications of deep history for Indigenous peoples. Deep history, as Andrew Shryock and various colleagues and I have conceived it, is an approach to the human past that seeks to transcend methodological specialization (Smail, *On Deep History*). Whatever history is, it cannot belong to historians and the texts upon which scholars in the discipline rely. Only in the late nineteenth century, as historians began to recoil from the deep abyss of human time that had been uncovered by geologists and archaeologists, did they insist that history be grounded in written documents. This reliance on writing allowed historians to continue conceiving of their subject in the short time frame allowed by Judeo-Christian history. Prehistory was invented in this process, and human history, as a result, was dismembered (Smail and Shryock, "History and the 'Pre'").

At the time, it seemed obvious to me that deep history ought to be enabling for Indigenous history. Indigenous time is invisible to the short chronology of Western historiography. This much is demonstrated by the existence of U.S. history textbooks that used to begin in 1492 and, following the convention of the time, rendered everything before that date as prehistory. Deep history also critiqued the textual methodology of conventional history. The approach assumes that human history transcends methodology, meaning that every bit of available evidence, including Indigenous storytelling, should be brought to bear on the past.

What became evident to me several years ago, during a conference in Australia, is that deep history is a gift that Indigenous peoples do not necessarily wish to receive (Smail, "Preface"). Part of the problem is that deep history accepts a Western understanding of time according to which the past is resolutely over and done with rather than being simultaneously here in the present. As several contributions to the present volume make clear, it also implies acceptance of Western ideas about what constitutes evidence for the past. Importantly, the forms of evidence valorized by Western epistemological systems distance the observer from the subject, making it impossible for any sense of we-ness to travel across time. In this way, the very technologies that have made the deep past visible to archaeologists, geneticists, and human evolutionary biologists have the paradoxical consequence of eroding historical consciousness. To put this differently, deep history, at least in the way that I have understood it, extends the chronology but does not offer any grounds for extending human identity deeper into the past. The approach hasn't fully come to terms with the idea that Indigenous storytelling is a way of knowing the past, and that the historical consciousness that emerges from Indigenous epistemology is something we could all learn from, given our current environmental and epistemological crises.

What I have come to realize is that the concept of deep history, at least in the way I have formulated it, is not necessarily relevant to Indigenous studies. Deep history offers a critique of the methodological and chronological framework of Western historical scholarship, but it is not clear that the approach challenges Western history's underlying epistemology. This is an unsettling realization, but unsettling in a good and thought-provoking way.

There is much that could be redone to reformulate deep history so that it becomes more relevant for Indigenous histories. Even so, I remain convinced that there are grounds for intellectual rapprochement and for shared work to be done. Among other things, deep history offers a sustained critique of history-as-usual. As I noted earlier, the approach has probably helped stretch historical time-space in ways that have been enabling for Indigenous history. I am also motivated to continue thinking about how I can bring Indigenous epistemology to bear on the many subjects I care about. Perhaps above all, the contributions to this volume bring great clarity to a subject on whose importance we all can agree, namely, that the past itself is a space in which colonial agendas are being played out, and that a major imperative for scholarship today is to decolonize our common past.

—Daniel Lord Smail

Note

1.   On Roman colonialism and its relevance for modern settler colonialism, see Dietler, *Archaeologies of Colonialism.* The classic work on the colonial enterprise of medieval Latin Christendom is Bartlett, *The Making of Europe.*

References

Bartlett, Robert. *The Making of Europe: Conquest, Colonization, and Cultural Change, 950–1350.* Princeton University Press, 1993.

Chakrabarty, Dipesh. *The Climate of History in a Planetary Age.* University of Chicago Press, 2021.

Dietler, Michael. *Archaeologies of Colonialism: Consumption, Entanglement, and Violence in Ancient Mediterranean France.* University of California Press, 2010.

Smail, Daniel Lord. *On Deep History and the Brain.* University of California Press, 2008.

Smail, Daniel Lord. "Preface: The Gift of History." *Long History, Deep Time: Deepening Histories of Place,* edited by Ann McGrath and Mary Anne Jebb, Australian National University Press, 2015, pp. xi–xvi.

Smail, Daniel Lord, and Andrew Shryock. "History and the 'Pre.'" *American Historical Review,* vol. 118, no. 3, June 2013, pp. 709–37.

Smith, Angèle. "Written Off the Map: Cleared Landscapes of Medieval Ireland." *Landscapes of Clearance: Archaeological and Anthropological Perspectives,* edited by Angèle Smith and Amy Gazin-Schwartz, Routledge, 2008, pp. 49–70.

Acknowledgments

WHILE THE WORLD SEEMS TO be sliding from one man-made catastrophe into the next, this book joins a conversation about how humans imagine the beginnings of their presence on this planet—more particularly, how Americans have imagined the pre-Columbian past. American "prehistory," it turns out, is a highly political topic—associated with and expressive of cultural struggles about firstness, ethnic identity, territory, and American societies' attitudes toward the nonhuman world.

Our group of scholars from various disciplines first discussed the meanings of America's deep past, and how to "decolonize" it, at a symposium in Schwerin, Mecklenburg (Germany)—the home state of archaeologist Heinrich Schliemann as well as the ancient homeland of Germans and Slavs who were written about by their enemies the Romans and Christian Knights. We would like to thank the German Research Foundation for financing the symposium (and the research project from which it grew). We would also like to thank Stefan Livo (Krause) and Alexander Bräuer for their diligent and competent preparation of the conference, as well as Susanne Lachenicht, Hartmut Lutz, John Munro, and Astrid Windus, who shared with us their expertise as discussants.

We are grateful to the anonymous readers of the manuscript for their suggestions and for the series editors' very generous endorsement of our book. We thank Sheila McMahon for her meticulous and competent copyediting. The series Archaeology of Indigenous-Colonial Interactions in the Americas—represented by Liam Frink, Aubrey Cannon, Barbara L. Voss, Steven A. Wernke, and Patricia A. McAnany—is indeed the perfect place for this volume. We thank the Jean Picker Fellowship Fund and the Kahn Institute at Smith College for their support.

Last not least, we thank Allyson Carter for guiding us through the stony trail of the publishing process.

Decolonizing "Prehistory"

Introduction

Gesa Mackenthun and Christen Mucher

IN 2017 THE REMAINS OF the Ancient One—also known as Kenne-wick Man—were laid to rest on the territories of the Confederated Colville Tribes (Rosenbaum; see also Meltzer). Since the surfacing of his bones in 1996, the Ancient One had been the subject of archaeological, jurisdic-tional, and epistemological debates that superficially pitted representatives of "Western science" against "Native Americans" (Colwell 243–48). Kinship and property claims to the remains were mediated through narratives of be-longing, research, and biological essentialism. Yet the strongest narrative about the Ancient One was not about him—or the Colville Tribes—at all; instead, it was the story about uses of the deep past in present-day identity and sovereignty politics.[1]

In the current day, controversies about ancestor repatriation, DNA-based population theories, and debates over historical migrations continue to serve as flash points that illuminate the colonial ideology according to which Amer-ican "prehistory"—whether ancient or precolonial—has been narrativized and rendered a singular subject for collective consumption.[2] Constructions of America's ancient past—or the "invention" of American "prehistory"—occur in national and international political frameworks that are characterized by struggles over racial and ethnic identities, access to resources and environ-mental stewardship, the commodification of culture for touristic purposes, and the exploitation of Indigenous knowledges and histories by industries ranging from education to film and fashion. The past's ongoing appeal reveals the relevance of these narratives to current-day concerns about individual and collective identities, pursuits of sovereignty and self-determination, and questions of the origin—and destiny—of humanity. While scholars and publics in the Global North have sought to understand America's past for five hundred years, this volume argues that these narratives matter today, perhaps more deeply than before.

In bringing together experts across disciplines—from American studies, archaeology, and anthropology to legal studies, history, and literary studies—*Decolonizing "Prehistory"* combines a critical investigation of the "making" of the American deep past with perspectives from Indigenous traditional knowledges, multispecies histories, and attention to ongoing systems of intellectual colonialism. The volume's various contributions share assumptions about the complexity and ambivalence of colonial encounters and their impact on scientific discourse; they reveal how anthropology, archaeology, and cultural heritage partake in the collective ideological construction of Indigenous cultures even while storing away precious and reliable information; and they share a concern for empowering counterhegemonic voices that disrupt conventional tropes and narratives of "prehistory." This collection thus forwards a critical stance toward the paradoxical role that modern scholarship—archaeological, historical, and other—plays in adding legitimacy to, but also delegitimizing, contemporary colonialist practices (Matthews 33, after Oland et al. 4).

Crucially concerned with deconstructing the distinction between "history" and "prehistory," this volume analyzes the production of historical knowledge about the ancient American past and ongoing conflicts over land, sovereignty, the environment, historicity, and identity. Racially inflected origin stories, for example, frequently obscure socioeconomic conflicts over access to land and water in the present. The volume thus particularly reflects on the political significance of American antiquity at the present historical moment, with its resurgence of racist and identitarian ideologies reformulated in the face of global ecological catastrophe (see Kolodny and Deloria in this volume). It insists that the ongoing debates over ancient America—geological, cultural, biological—are highly political. Identifying "land" as the common referent of archaeological excavation and socioeconomic conflict, the volume's contributors pay particular attention to the "topological" aspects of knowledge—that is, place-based logics and poetics—that reach back to the times before colonialism but whose significance continues into the present (Thrush, Budhwa, Carlson and Naxaxalhts'i [McHalsie], and Mackenthun in this volume).[3] As Keith Basso, Julie Cruikshank, Roger Echo-Hawk, Ruth S. Ludwin, Coll Thrush, and others have shown, North America has been a storied land filled with historical landmark knowledge long before the arrival of the first white settler. Topological knowledges are especially important in current-day articulations of indigeneity (Christie and Picas in this volume) because they call attention to the critical necessity of the long-neglected spatial dimension as the Earth—suffocating under the burden of its fossilized past—is increasingly in need of both new and ancient imaginaries and strategies for survival.

Next to problematizing the key term *prehistory*, the volume wants to contribute to the ongoing project of "decolonizing" scientific knowledge about the American deep past, following new paths toward a transcultural epistemology that acknowledges the value of Indigenous knowledges—long marginalized and delegitimized within the dominant episteme (Cajete; Kimmerer)—within and beyond the colonial historical record.[4] *Decolonizing "Prehistory,"* therefore, builds on vital postcolonial, decolonial, and Indigenous critiques of the coloniality of Western scientific knowledge, working to situate the topological and political aspects of these analyses front and center to emphasize how the notions of an American *vacuum domicilium* or *terra nullius* run counter to Indigenous "grammars of place" (Goeman) that upend settler colonial property relations by asserting that "wisdom sits in places" (Basso; see also Nichols).

One of the volume's most important inspirations is the groundbreaking—if controversial—polemic against the myths of colonial science written by the eminent American Indian scholar Vine Deloria Jr., *Red Earth, White Lies: Native Americans and the Myth of Scientific Fact* (1995). "Western science today," Deloria writes in the final chapter,

> is akin to a world history which discusses only the Mediterranean peoples. . . . We are living in a strange kind of dark ages where we have immense capability to bring together information but when we gather this data, we pigeonhole it in the old familiar framework of interpretation, sometimes even torturing the data to make it fit. (211)

Deloria arrives at this gloomy conclusion after examining multiple "scientific" assumptions about the American past that have been taken as truth: from the Bering Strait and Clovis First theories, to the Pleistocene Overkill and Solutrean hypotheses (about an alleged mass slaughter of megafauna and an Ice Age migration from Europe to America, respectively), to the battle over the Ancient One / Kennewick Man. Like Vine Deloria Jr., contributors to *Decolonizing "Prehistory"* find in these theories the same predictable narratives of savagery and civilization that have increasingly gained a following in the age of "alternative" facts and "fake news." Although many of the volume's contributions are inspired by Deloria's bravery in questioning these powerful narratives, it is not our intention to join in accusations or defenses of Deloria's book. Nevertheless, his critique of the provinciality of Western scholarship and its refusal to commit to an ethically responsible increase of knowledge has stood the test of time.

"Prehistory": Decolonizing the Past

Drawing from the Danish "three-ages system" of the 1830s (and the term *forhistorisk*) and coined in English by the Scottish Canadian antiquarian-archaeologist Daniel Wilson in 1851 before being popularized by Sir John Lubbock in his 1865 book *Pre-Historic Man* (Rowley-Conwy 119; Kehoe, *Land of Prehistory* xiii), "prehistory" is a nineteenth-century scientific concept that serves to disarticulate the epistemic claims of colonized societies over and against the claims of European colonizers. In positing Indigenous peoples and most non-European cultures as "prehistorical," the colonial episteme also denies them what Lynn Hunt calls "historicality": the right to have a history in the first place (124).

Conventionally, the term *prehistory* has been used to refer to societies that did not use alphabetic writing. This is because Europeans assumed that the basis of historical recordkeeping was located in European-style literacy (Ong 1); thus any period preceding European contact (the beginning of "history"), the logic follows, was prehistorical. This link between history and writing also evokes the centrality of writing to the establishment of colonial regimes (Cheyfitz, *Poetics*): from the Spanish Requerimiento to Anglo colonialism's treaties, federal Indian law, and reeducation in boarding schools, colonial dispossession has been effected both physically and intellectually through both writing and the suppression of orally transmitted knowledge (Cheyfitz, "[Post]colonial" 55–56).

The taxonomy of *history* and *prehistory* rests on a global hierarchy in which Western societies have arrogated to themselves the right to study non-Western "others," thereby turning the othered peoples and cultures into scientific objects. Anthropologist Johannes Fabian refers to this monological approach as a temporal and political "denial of coevalness" (1, 32). In their edited volume, *The Death of Prehistory* (2013), anthropologists Peter R. Schmidt and Stephen A. Mrozowski follow Fabian in identifying the labeling of Indigenous and precolonial societies as "primitive, prehistorical, or mythological" as a cultural trope within the larger discursive formation of empire. They explain the harmful effects of continuing to use *prehistory* on the political realities of Indigenous societies, writing that it "is often an oppressive reminder of their political, cultural, and economic disenfranchisement," and they optimistically hope for a "future without prehistory" (3, 1). Philip J. Deloria shows in this volume that this oppressive attitude is exhibited with particular force in the discourse of "big histories" such as Yuval N. Harari's *Sapiens* (trans. 2014)—which was itself inspired by an earlier generation of popular historical accounts such as Jared Diamond's extremely successful *Guns, Germs, and Steel* (1997)—those indefatigable best sellers whose principal cultural work seems to consist of "explaining the global dominance of Europe" and the world order that emerged with European expansion (Deloria in this volume). In his chapter here, Deloria investigates the "supposedly neutral science-based narratives of the deep past" that inhere in concepts such as "prehistory," while also examining "the various historicities and knowledge productions" in which such long-form "big histories" are embedded.

In the nineteenth century, the Hegelian division of humanity into peoples with history and those without (Wolf) coincided with the notion that physical journeys to remote places were akin to sojourns into the ancient past: into, as feminist anthropologist Alice Beck Kehoe summarizes, the "Land of Prehistory" (208). This is the intellectual substrate from which the discipline of anthropology grew. Indeed, Kehoe argues that the denial of cultural equivalence (or coevalness) provided the epistemic framework for American "prehistoric" archaeology (227).

While archaeologists and anthropologists created their objects of study in the nineteenth and twentieth centuries, orally transmitted Indigenous knowledges were frequently dismissed as irrelevant. In response, Schmidt and Mrozowski propose that Indigenous histories be regarded as a counterarchive to the imperial written record (13–14). As archives of the past in their own right, Indigenous oral traditions exceed—and survive—colonial efforts at replacement and destruction.[5] Archaeologists Maxine Oland, Siobhan Hart, and Liam Frink write in *Decolonizing Indigenous Histories* (2012) that because these traditional histories have more often than not been "lost in translation" (2), the work of "decolonizing archaeology" is all the more necessary to address and correct those losses.

The present volume emphatically embraces Oland et al.'s decolonizing project, agreeing that such an effort "is fundamentally about restructuring power relations in the present and for the future" (4).[6] Indeed, Indigenous archaeology itself, suggests Ojibwe archaeologist Sonya Atalay, is a "decolonizing practice" ("Indigenous"), and this growing field is restructuring power relations and bringing the "future without prehistory" into the present. In this volume, Jeff Oliver addresses the promise of Indigenous archaeology but also elaborates the challenges that a commitment to criteria such as equity, responsibility, and inclusion poses to conventional archaeological methodology and practice.

The purpose of a decolonial approach, then, is to "make visible, open up, and advance radically distinct perspectives and positionalities that displace Western rationality as the only framework and possibility of existence" (Walsh 17). As both a theory and a practice—inside and outside academia—decoloniality

> denotes ways of thinking, knowing, being, and doing that began with, but also precede, the colonial enterprise . . . It implies the recognition and undoing of the hierarchical structures of race, gender, heteropatriarchy, and class that continue to control life, knowledge, spirituality, and thought, structures that are clearly intertwined with and constitutive of global capitalism and Western modernity. (Walsh 17)

Across the Americas, decoloniality or decolonial practices have largely been formed by scholars and activists critiquing "the control of labor and subjectivity, the practices and policies of genocide and enslavement, the pillage of life and land, and the denials and destruction of knowledge, humanity, spirituality, and cosmo-existence" that, in postcolonial theorist Catherine E. Walsh's words, became the "modus operandi" of the "colonial matrix of power" (Walsh 16; Mignolo and Walsh; see also Quijano). These have emerged not only from analyses of disciplines traditionally accompanying colonial dispossession—namely anthropology and archaeology—but also from the hemispheric analysis of colonial capitalism: the practices of war, forced displacement, and the brutal trade in enslaved humans, as well as enforced labor and kleptocratic property regimes.[7]

For years now, postcolonial, decolonial, and Indigenous intellectuals have been pushing to revise Western accounts of historical and scientific development, including intellectual history. This decolonization of knowledge would include, as Sujit Sivasundaram writes, "think[ing] beyond categories of colonized and colonial and to fragment traditions of knowledge on all sides" (155). Such decolonial fragmentation would necessitate the disentangling of time, temporality, and history from the forces of coloniality. In this spirit, historian Daniel Lord Smail, writing about deep history, proposes including histories of Neolithic and Paleolithic peoples in these "deep" accounts, thereby abolishing the distinction between "historical" and "prehistorical" altogether (*On Deep History* 2). But, as Smail suggests in his foreword to this volume, perhaps even a critical theorization of "deep time" cannot account for Indigenous pasts that are also "simultaneously here in the present."

Following the guidelines laid out by Māori scholar Linda Tuhiwai Smith in her seminal *Decolonizing Methodologies* (1999), this volume seeks to challenge the ubiquitous colonial narratives by exposing power imbalances and recentering Indigenous knowledges of the ancient American past, by centering "the landscapes, images, themes, metaphors and stories in the indigenous world" and producing "deconstructed accounts of the West" (146, 149). As social scientists Eve Tuck and K. Wayne Yang have cautioned, decolonizing work insists on a territorial counterpart to intellectual efforts. Decolonization, they write, "is necessarily unsettling" (7). That is, while always tied to the repatriation and recognition of land, decolonization also requires a structural commitment to undoing the ongoing effects of coloniality on bodies and minds, which includes a demystification of the scientific categories and hierarchical structures that underlie the discourse of American "prehistory."

The Racial Subtexts of American "Prehistory"

Considering the construction of the American past in terms of "deep time" has the particular benefit of denaturalizing the durability of colonial structures and calling the entire enterprise of colonial history making into question (Smail and Shryock). In particular, the notion of "deep time" calls the bluff of "race" as an inherent or inevitable category. Along these lines, the "advantage of using geological time as a human measure," according to literary scholar Wai-Chee Dimock, "is that it compels us to rethink the phenomenology of race itself, against the history of the planet" (177). Dimock writes,

> The planet did not begin with these [racial] divisions, and there is no reason why they should persist as a taxonomic bedrock, a rationale for carving up the world's populations into discrete units. There is such a thing as a preracial planet. Its reference point is geological time, at the tail end of which Homo sapiens emerged, a small, tawdry band, its survival uncertain, standing or falling as a species, and only as a species. (177)

The imposition of racial categories on the distant global past seriously challenges the notion, expressed here by Dimock and in this volume by Christen Mucher, that there was something like a "preracial planet" and humanity is one common species among others. And yet these "new biofictional lineages" (Wilcox 126) do not tell us anything about the "racial" or ethnic composition of humans, nor are they historical measuring rods. Indeed, geneticists and cultural theorists alike have in recent years struggled to explain the relative value of "race" and geography on time scales of tens (if not hundreds) of thousands of years (Reich, "Genetics").

Racialized narratives of American "prehistory" began with the first European settlers and gained speed in the eighteenth and nineteenth centuries (as Roger G. Kennedy, Annette Kolodny, Christen Mucher, and Robert Silverberg have demonstrated). They are a product of colonialism, and their current resurgence in narratives of "white genocide" and ethnonationalism are alarming. Thus, to reject, as Smail does, any division between "prehistory" and "history"—a colonial arrangement of the "tail end"—is an important step toward mitigating the influence that "race" holds over traditional historical narratives of human history, including those about the distant past.

While the racialization of American "prehistory" has been a constant fact on various levels of representation (Gniadek in this volume), the rise of ancient DNA analysis in particular has caused the ghostly return of scientific racism in revived insinuations—especially in the digital arena—that the American continent must originally or anciently have been peopled *not* by the biological ancestors of today's Native Americans but by peoples with racial links to Europe (TallBear, *DNA*). As with the case of the Ancient One / Kennewick Man, these imaginary racial lineages produce outcomes that frequently define rights of intellectual property, restitution, and reburial, all while reasserting white colonial power.

Observing, with worry, that many narratives of the peopling of the Americas are still saturated with latent racialist assumptions, anthropologist Michael Wilcox explains that "the geneticist controls the means, methods, and modes of racial authenticity, supported by an older scientific logic of research inherited from nineteenth- and early twentieth-century kinship anthropology" ("Colonizing" 126; see also TallBear, "Narratives"; Tsosie and McGregor). Readings of genetic sequences exhibit what Jodi A. Byrd has called modern "blood logics" (xxiii), which ultimately invite new forms of racial hierarchies and racial supremacism, as Annette Kolodny argues in this volume. Writing in the 1990s, a time when the supposedly infallible DNA tests began entering the field of archaeology, David Lowenthal warned that they "echo[ed] the magical power of sacred relics" (*Heritage* 204). The "cult of genes, like that of blood, is overwhelmingly deterministic," he adds (206). The assumed power of genetic testing to definitively identify ancestors and descendants exists within a matrix of colonial desires for empirical knowledge, and it is here in particular where Vine Deloria's caution against pigeonholing new data "in the old familiar framework of interpretation" finds its latest object lesson.

The intensity with which DNA-based ancestry detection is currently conducted, especially in the United States, is symptomatic of a larger problem: that of a pervasive crisis of individual and collective identity, growing from the theoretical deconstruction of essentialist assertions of ethnic groups and

the social hierarchies connected with such essentialist notions. More specifically, the *querelle* over ancient American genes is a symptom of a categorically
weak conceptualization of identity that has been gaining new traction in recent years: identity as inherited and inevitable (in accordance with the social
deterministic narrative in circulation since the late nineteenth century) rather
than something accomplished through work, education, and social commitment. Such biologically fixed, antisolidarity constructions of the human past
and present rest on the belief that, as Lowenthal writes, "we attribute what
we are to *being*, which cannot be changed, rather than to *doing*, which can"
(*Heritage* 196). These claims also have their roots in those same old-fashioned
Enlightenment constructions of "civilization" and "progress" from which colonial science long ago rendered whole populations exempt by also rendering
them extinct.

From the beginning, reflections on the massive reduction of Indigenous
peoples led settler writers to anticipate Native Americans' imminent extinction. As Gesa Mackenthun argues in this volume, "extinction" is, to use Wilcox's phrase, a "terminal narrative" that looms large again today with reference to nonhuman species and whose cultural function lies in opting out of
alternative behaviors to prevent further loss of life. It is part of the same idiom
that speaks of "populations" instead of human beings, as Christen Mucher
argues in her chapter. Indeed, narratives of extinction, as various chapters
in this volume suggest, accumulate new mileage from genomic acrobatics
while their ideological function—as naturalizations of social inequality, as
antihumanist counternarratives—remains the same.

Topological Knowledges

In a different way, essentialist definitions of identity also rest on dubious ground
in that settlers have seldom learned the stories of the lands on which they live.
One could say, with the Mexican philosopher Edmundo O'Gorman, that settler
colonial societies, while passionately "inventing" America, have so far shown
relatively few signs of actually having "discovered" its real meanings. As Keith
Thor Carlson and Naxaxalhts'i (Sonny McHalsie) show in this volume, while
settler colonial cultures may cherish what Deloria calls the "Mediterranean"
heritage, they show little respect or understanding for the topological wisdom
of America's Indigenous peoples. What is more, colonial mythology conventionally holds that Indigenous peoples did not leave a lasting trace upon the
land but instead lived upon it in a (frequently nonsedentary) "state of nature,"
leaving it "virgin soil" in senses both physical and epistemological (Oliver 26).

"If we accept the grand narrative of first contact and European colonialism," writes Jeff Oliver with reference to the Pacific Northwest, "the marginality of the landscape and its [alleged] lack of human agency—in short, its domination by nature not culture—represent the region's most salient plotline" (26). This assumption looms large in American environmentalist discourse from the writings of John Muir to present wilderness conservationism and national park management. But the "wilderness ideal," as Mark Spence argues (5), depends on the absence of Aboriginal inhabitants as well as the rejection of Indigenous knowledges as an extension of the disavowal of Indigenous occupation. Coll Thrush argues that this destructive mythology is driven by "the divorce of deep time from the colonial past" (this volume), and he calls vital attention to the necessary link across tradition, history, and land in accounts of Indigenous inhabitance in the Pacific Northwest.

In her 1999 essay "Landscape, History, and the Pueblo Imagination," Laguna Pueblo writer Leslie Marmon Silko explains how land itself can function as an archive.

> Location, or "place," nearly always plays a central role in the Pueblo oral narratives. Indeed, stories are most frequently recalled as people are passing by a specific geographical feature or the exact place where a story takes place. The precise date of the incident often is less important than the place or location of the happening. "Long, long go," "a long time ago," "not too long ago," and "recently" are usually how stories are classified in terms of time. But the places where the stories occur are precisely located, and prominent geographical details recalled. . . . It is impossible to determine which came first: the incident or the geographical feature which begs to be brought alive in a story that features some unusual aspect of this location. (36)

The data-driven precision demanded by colonialism's empiricist narratives is completely contrary to the archival function of land in Silko's account; here, the story is determined by place, not by timelines; events are relational and instructive rather than documentary.

Referring to Aboriginal topological (or space-related) knowledge in Australia, philosopher Yi-Fu Tuan writes:

> Landscape is personal and tribal history made visible. The native's identity—his place in the total scheme of things—is not in doubt, because the myths that support it are as real as the rocks and waterholes he can see and touch. He finds recorded in his land the ancient story of the lives and deeds of

the immortal beings from whom he himself is descended, and whom he reveres. The whole countryside is his family tree. (157–58)

Tribal peoples possess vast archives of topological knowledge; their history is inscribed in widely visible landmarks as well as inconspicuous (or hidden) sites, giving the lie to colonial assertions that America's indigenes did not *have* writing, records, or history. While the colonial regime of writing worked in conjunction with the political mythology of Native nomadism in disarticulating non-Western senses of history and homeland—implying a lack of territorial attachment—Indigenous oral traditions contain innumerable landmark narratives, stories that, in the words of the Confederated Colville Tribes, "witness our ancestral claim to the land . . . and to the resources found here. These landmark legends define our home" (Ferguson 6). Ceremonial and sacred lands are imbued with the stories that root Native identities in place and hold histories for their peoples.[8]

Several chapters in this volume are dedicated to exploring Indigenous topological knowledges as avenues to understanding the distant past. Contributions by Rick Budhwa, Keith Thor Carlson and Naxaxalhts'i (Sonny McHalsie), Annette Kolodny, Gesa Mackenthun, Jeff Oliver, Mathieu Picas, and Coll Thrush reflect how Indigenous oral traditions were and are vehicles for the transmission of historical, geological, and spiritual knowledges that are also inextricably tied to the land. Concerning knowledge of ancient events, Carlson writes, "our focus cannot only be on trying to determine if stories of the Great Flood, for example, can be linked to a geological reality; what matters more is appreciating how belief in the historical legitimacy of the contents of such stories shapes people's subsequent historical behavior" (*Power of Place* 112).[9] And as Nimachia Howe explains, land-based stories re-create homelands, encode Indigenous metaphysics, and "contribute to the sense of *who* the People are" (16, xiii).

The Present Uses of Indigenous Topological Knowledges

The preservation of ancient Indigenous knowledges, however, has been difficult as one of its primary media, the land itself, has been appropriated, transformed, and often destroyed by settler colonial societies in search of farmland, commodity resources, and transportation highways. Likewise, Indigenous ways of knowing homelands have been systematically disarticulated through a scientific episteme that has reduced Native cultures to mappable kinship systems and collectible material artifacts, Native bodies to racial

stereotypes and exploited labor, and Indigenous intellectual worlds to folkloric collections of "myths and legends." In their contribution here, Carlson
and McHalsie show how the destruction of culturally significant landmarks
(especially stones and rocks)—frequently due less to a lack of good will than
to a lack of cultural sensibility—nonetheless deprives Stó:lō and other peoples
of parts of their cultural moral script. Yet the hope that settler society would
preserve these landmarks if they better understood their cultural meanings
also demands an end to extractive capitalism and the technologies of uneven
power that sustain the settler colonial state.

This includes the use of the past as a technology of power. Indeed, knowledges about place and the American deep past are critical in the context of
legal struggles over territory, artifacts and remains, and natural resources
and environmental management. Under the rule of neoliberalism, topological
knowledges are sometimes evoked as evidence in land rights litigation, as
court cases, especially in Canada, demonstrate. Writing about the Australian
Aboriginal Lands Act, anthropologist Elizabeth Povinelli explains how even
well-intentioned legislation remains impeded by incorrect assumptions about
the nature of Indigenous knowledge transmission. By this act, the Crown
admits landmark knowledge as evidence only if it "*retained* a specific kind of
totemic imaginary . . . a trace from a period of time anterior to the violence of
settler colonialism" (Povinelli 80). For this, claimants and witnesses have to
embody and give evidence of their "prehistorical"—coded as non-Western—
epistemologies in the language of Western rationalism, a requirement that
ignores the fact that colonized peoples have long been forced to adjust their
lives and languages to the rule of colonizing societies to survive. Similarly,
the landmark Canadian Supreme Court Delgamuukw ruling of 1997, while
authorizing oral traditions as evidence, requires proof of the unbroken land
tenure of Indigenous claimants, which ignores the severe disruptions enacted
upon First Nations and Métis people under colonial and Dominion rule. In
these instances, Indigenous claimants are called upon to act in accordance
with fossilized, romantic, and harmfully simplified views of Indigenous character and history (see the discussion by Oliver in this volume), forced to operate strategically within the hermeneutic field of colonial power.

Moreover, various legal scholars point to the strong link that exists between Indigenous interests for cultural preservation and environmental concerns. Legal scholar John Borrows, for example, contends that there is a need
to reformulate settlement planning in the light of Indigenous environmental
knowledge, which has a legality of its own (54), and he encourages American and Canadian societies to act more respectfully toward Indigenous conceptions of land. Due to the extreme importance of court rulings in settler

societies, the cultural knowledge of legal agents (lawyers and judges) is essential. As various cases mentioned in this volume show (Kolodny, Kirsten Carlson), legal decisions go in both directions and courts are not necessarily sympathetic to environmental and Indigenous concerns.

Likewise, archaeological evidence has been used in conflicts over land ownership and stewardship, lending empirical support to the claims of continuous cultural presence in the embattled territory. Picas and Jessica Christie explore the complicated legacies of extraction upon which current-day articulations of heritage rest in current-day Maya communities in Mexico (this volume), but they also demonstrate the ways in which archaeological and heritage knowledge is being used for the community members' benefit, a key commitment of community-based and Indigenous archaeologies (Atalay, *Community-Based Archaeology*).

Structure of the Book

The North American geographical scope of *Decolonizing "Prehistory"* extends from the Pacific Northwest to the Yucatán Peninsula. After the foreword by Daniel Lord Smail reflecting on "prehistory" and "deep history," and this introduction, the volume opens with a chapter by the late Annette Kolodny. In addition to the influence of Vine Deloria Jr., detailed in the beginning of this introduction, Kolodny's work has galvanized academic conversations around the topic of "prehistory" and the culpability of anthropologists, writers, and the public in maintaining understandings of the past that enable operations of colonial violence in the present. Kolodny's chapter triangulates the reemergence of white ethnonationalism and narratives of racial ancestry drawing on colonial discourses of human antiquity with the denial of environmentally relevant ancient knowledges as epitomized in the Penobscot Nation's legal battle for recognition of their river rights. Kolodny's powerful evocation of the entanglements between academic and nonacademic reconstructions of the deep past with present-day racialist identity politics and the legal struggle of Indigenous nations for territorial sovereignty and respect was inspired by the 2016 U.S. presidential election of Donald J. Trump. Her searing analysis of his and his followers' actions and rhetoric discloses their deep ideological roots, which will exceed his executive tenure and continue to demand democratic vigilance.

Kolodny's chapter is followed by two contributions tracing the genealogy of these conflicts. Christen Mucher and Melissa Gniadek examine progenitors to current-day discussions about antiquity and coloniality in "romantic" aesthetics and Indigenous versus "scientific" origin stories. These are followed by five chapters with a geographical focus on the Pacific Northwest that examine discourses on the distant past from quite different theoretical and epistemic perspectives but united by their awareness of the power of the different kinds of evidence and stories used in imagining the American deep past in conjunction with deep space. First among these, Rick Budhwa and Gesa Mackenthun continue Kolodny's and Mucher's arguments about epistemically embattled uses of Indigenous stories. Budhwa stresses the significance of oral traditions for reconstructing seismic events in the Pacific Northwest, while Mackenthun discusses the colonial narrative of extinction, countering it with a rereading of the Indigenous and "scientific" narrative archives on Crater Lake, Oregon. Next, Keith Thor Carlson and Stó:lõ knowledge-keeper Naxaxalhts'i (Sonny McHalsie) offer cross-cultural reflections on Stó:lõ topology and identity, followed by archaeologist Jeff Oliver's self-reflective examination of the ideological implications of the current transcultural transformation in the field of American archaeology.

Coll Thrush shows that today's scientific reconstructions of ancient cultures and practices affect the way we imagine the future by assessing Indigenous and colonial tales of creation and topological transformation from the peoples of the Southern Salish Sea. Thrush's poetic evocation of placemaking is followed by two chapters describing the cultural productivity and performativity of (re)constructions of the ancient past in present-day heritage politics in a quite different geographical area, the Maya country of the Yucatán. In these contributions, Jessica Christie and Mathieu Picas explore the implications of heritage making and tourism on collective identity formation among current-day Maya communities. Philip J. Deloria's chapter then adds to the critique of scientific discourse with a review of popular "Big History" accounts of the ancient human past and their tendency to reactivate older colonial narratives and mythologies, and thereby continue to epistemologically colonize the distant past. The volume concludes with an epilogue by legal scholar Kirsten Matoy Carlson, who reflects on constructions of American antiquity through legal discourses about territorial sovereignty and ecological stewardship, reminding us of the distant past's relevance to contemporary legal practice—returning us to Kolodny's example from the Penobscot Nation—and recalling the material consequences of the past in the present.

The authors dedicate this book to Annette Kolodny, who accompanied this project with great enthusiasm and encouragement from its early beginnings and, in spite of her failing strength, almost to its end. Her contribution demonstrates her unique critical approach, one that insisted on identifying the deep historical layers of the contemporary discourses of discrimination.

Annette understood well that the distant past is not exempt from ideological inscription, and that these inscriptions have a powerful impact today. She deserves our admiration for standing up to a patriarchal academic world, for telling truth to power within and outside academia, and for staying active even during her last challenges. It was important to Annette that these words and conversations continue, for all our sakes.

Notes

1. See the controversial 2014 book *Kennewick Man: The Scientific Investigation of an Ancient American Skeleton*, edited by Douglas Owsley and Richard Jantz, and the 2015 *Nature* article by Morten Rasmussen et al. for contrast.

2. Recent developments in Light Detection and Ranging (LiDAR) and other remote-sensing technologies have called into question previous population counts altogether (Clynes). Contributors to a recent volume published by the University of Arizona Press (Cameron et al.) have pointed to the precariousness of all empirical data used to quantify the pre-Columbian era as well as the ideological implications of posthumanist, catastrophic narratives that downplay the deadliness of direct and structural colonial violence and divest America's Indigenous peoples of agency or resilience (Reséndez).

3. *Merriam-Webster* defines "topology" (besides its meaning in mathematics) as the "topographic study of a particular place, specifically the history of a region as indicated by its topography" (merriam-webster.com/dictionary/topology, accessed 16 Nov. 2019).

4. Empirical and epistemic imperialism is related to the "academic silencing" of alternative approaches to the distant past as well as the silencing of what Michel de Certeau calls the "unspoken conditions" that enable scientific discourse in the first place (Schmidt and Mrozowski 12; de Certeau 62–63).

5. Colonial cultures also wrote themselves into the history before Columbus, as Annette Kolodny shows in her magisterial study of the construction of Viking heritage, *In Search of First Contact*.

6. Less interested in "ancient" history than in the transition from the precolonial to the colonial period, Oland et al. attend to "the complexities of Indigenous lives that are neither 'prehistoric' nor 'historic,' 'precolonized' nor fully 'colonized,' and both 'continuous' and 'changed'" (3).

7. Postcolonial and subaltern studies scholars connected to the Indian subcontinent, Africa, and Latin America have prioritized critiques of language and literature in the maintenance of colonial power. For example, to Kenyan writer Ngũgĩ wa Thiong'o, decolonization must take place through a reappropriation of language, as colonial power was imposed through linguistic control, the "biblical message of subservience," and colonial administration, labor, and property regimes (66–67).

8. In *Red Earth, White Lies*, Vine Deloria Jr. used Dorothy Vitaliano's term *geomyth* to refer to those story traditions using land as an archive for historical knowledge (168–69), a term taken up by some subsequent scholars such as Adrienne Mayor but rejected by others for its folkloric association.

9. Carlson's statement reflects an understanding of history, "prehistory," and historicity in the Indigenous oral tradition that fundamentally differs from that of the modern Western episteme with its dogma of authenticity and written verifiability. Indigenous stories about the past, without neglecting the importance of accurate memory, are told in ways that reflect the present of storytelling and prepare the community for the future. Western historical narratives, of course, do the same—as historians such as Hayden White and Dominick LaCapra have sufficiently shown—but are usually less honest about their own constructions and provinciality (Chakrabarty).

References

Atalay, Sonya. *Community-Based Archaeology: Research with, by, and for Indigenous and Local Communities*. University of California Press, 2012.

Atalay, Sonya. "Indigenous Archaeology as a Decolonizing Practice." *American Indian Quarterly*, vol. 30, nos. 3 & 4, Summer & Fall 2006, pp. 280–310.

Basso, Keith. *Wisdom Sits in Places: Landscape and Language Among the Western Apache*. University of New Mexico Press, 1996.

Borrows, John. *Recovering Canada: The Resurgence of Indigenous Law*. University of Toronto Press, 2002.

Byrd, Jodi A. *The Transit of Empire: Indigenous Critiques of Colonialism*. University of Minnesota Press, 2011.

Cajete, Gregory. *Native Science: Natural Laws of Independence*. Clear Light, 2000.

Cameron, Catherine M., et al., eds. *Beyond Germs: Native Depopulation in North America*. University of Arizona Press, 2015.

Carlson, Keith Thor. *The Power of Place, the Problem of Time: Aboriginal Identity and Historical Consciousness in the Cauldron of Colonialism*. University of Toronto Press, 2010.

Chakrabarty, Dipesh. *Provincializing Europe Postcolonial Thought and Historical Difference*. Princeton University Press, 2000.

Cheyfitz, Eric. *The Poetics of Imperialism: Translation and Colonization from "The Tempest" to "Tarzan."* University of Pennsylvania Press, 1991.

Cheyfitz, Eric. "The (Post)colonial Construction of Indian Country: U.S. American Indian Literatures and Federal Indian Law." *The Columbia Guide to American Indian Literatures of the United States Since 1945*, edited by Eric Cheyfitz, Columbia University Press, 2006, pp. 1–124.

Clynes, Tom. "Exclusive: Laser Scans Reveal Maya 'Megalopolis' Below Guatemalan Jungle." *National Geographic Magazine*, 1 Feb. 2018.

Colwell, Chip. *Plundered Skulls and Stolen Spirits: Inside the Fight to Reclaim Native America's Culture*. University of Chicago Press, 2017.

Cruikshank, Julie. *Do Glaciers Listen? Local Knowledge, Colonial Encounters, and Social Imagination*. University of British Colombia Press, 2005.

Cruikshank, Julie. "The Social Life of Texts: Editing on the Page and in Performance." *Talking on the Page: Editing Aboriginal Oral Texts*, edited by Laura L. Murray and Keren Rice, University of Toronto Press, 1999, pp. 97–119.

de Certeau, Michel. *The Writing of History*. Columbia University Press, 1988.

Deloria, Vine, Jr. *Red Earth, White Lies: Native Americans and the Myth of Scientific Fact*. Scribner, 1995.

Diamond, Jared. *Guns, Germs, and Steel: The Fate of Human Societies*. W. W. Norton, 1997.

Dimock, Wai-Chee. *Through Other Continents: American Literature Across Deep Time*. Princeton University Press, 2008.

Echo-Hawk, Roger C. "Ancient History in the New World: Integrating Oral Traditions and the Archaeological Record in Deep Time." *American Antiquity*, vol. 65, no. 2, 2000, pp. 267–90.

Fabian, Johannes. *Time and the Other: How Anthropology Makes Its Object*. Columbia University Press, 1983.

Ferguson, Jennifer K., comp. *Upper Columbia River Book of Legends*. Confederated Tribes of the Colville Reservation, 2007.

Goeman, Mishuana. *Mark My Words: Native Women Mapping Our Nations*. University of Minnesota Press, 2013.

Harari, Yuval Noah. *Sapiens: A Brief History of Humankind*. Translated by the author with the help of John Purcell and Haim Watzman, Harvill Secker, 2014.

Howe, Nimachia. *Retelling Trickster in Naapi's Language*. University Press of Colorado, 2019.

Hunt, Lynn. *Measuring Time, Making History*. Central European University Press, 2008.

Kehoe, Alice Beck. *The Land of Prehistory: A Critical History of American Archaeology*. Routledge, 1998.

Kennedy, Roger G. *Hidden Cities: The Discovery and Loss of Ancient North American Civilization*. Penguin, 1994.

Kimmerer, Robin Wall. *Braiding Sweetgrass: Indigenous Wisdom, Scientific Knowledge and the Teachings of Plants*. Milkweed, 2013.

Kolodny, Annette. *In Search of First Contact: The Vikings of Vinland, the Peoples of the Dawnland, and the Anglo-American Anxiety of Discovery*. Duke University Press, 2012.

LaCapra, Dominick. *History and Criticism*. Cornell University Press, 1985.

Lowenthal, David. *The Heritage Crusade and the Spoils of History*. Cambridge University Press, 1996.

Matthews, Christopher N. "Public Dialectics: Marxist Reflection in Archaeology." *Historical Archaeology*, vol. 39, no, 4, 2005, pp. 18–36.

Mayor, Adrienne. *Fossil Legends of the First Americans*. Princeton University Press, 2005.

Meltzer, David J. "Kennewick Man: Coming to Closure." *Antiquity*, vol. 89, no. 348, 2015, pp. 1485–93.

Mignolo, Walter, and Catherine E. Walsh. *On Decoloniality: Concepts, Analytics, Praxis.* Duke University Press, 2018.

Mucher, Christen. *Before American History.* University of Virginia Press, forthcoming.

Ngũgĩ wa Thiong'o. *Decolonising the Mind: The Politics of Language in African Literature.* James Currey / Heinemann, 1986.

Nichols, Robert. "Theft Is Property! The Recursive Logic of Dispossession." *Political Theory*, vol. 46, no. 1, 2018, pp. 3–28.

O'Gorman, Edmundo. *The Invention of America: An Inquiry into the Historical Nature of the New World and the Meaning of Its History.* Indiana University Press, 1961.

Oland, Maxine, et al., eds. *Decolonizing Indigenous Histories: Exploring Prehistoric/Colonial Transitions in Archaeology.* University of Arizona Press, 2012.

Oliver, Jeff. *Landscapes and Social Transformations on the Northwest Coast: Colonial Encounters in the Fraser Valley.* University of Arizona Press, 2010.

Ong, Walter. *Orality and Literacy.* Methuen, 1983.

Owsley, Douglas W., and Richard L. Jantz, eds. *Kennewick Man: The Scientific Investigation of an Ancient American Skeleton.* Texas A&M University Press, 2014.

Povinelli, Elizabeth. *Geontologies: A Requiem to Late Liberalism.* Duke University Press, 2016.

Quijano, Aníbal. "Coloniality of Power, Eurocentrism, and Latin America." *Nepantla: Views from the South*, vol. 1, no. 3, 2000, pp. 533–80.

Rasmussen, Morten, et al. "The Ancestry and Affiliations of Kennewick Man." *Nature*, vol. 523, 2015, pp. 455–58.

Reich, David. "How Genetics Is Changing Our Understanding of 'Race.'" *New York Times*, 23 Mar. 2018.

Reséndez, Andrés. *The Other Slavery: The Uncovered Story of Indian Enslavement in America.* Johns Hopkins University Press, 2017.

Rosenbaum, Cary. "Ancient One, Also Known as Kennewick Man, Repatriated." *Tribal Tribune*, 18 Feb. 2017, tribaltribune.com/news/article_aa38c0c2-f66f-11e6-9b50–7bb1418f3d3d.html.

Rowley-Conwy, Peter. "The Concept of Prehistory and the Invention of the Terms 'Prehistoric' and 'Prehistorian': The Scandinavian Origin, 1833–1850." *European Journal of Archaeology*, vol. 9, no. 1, Apr. 2006, pp. 103–30.

Schmidt, Peter R., and Stephen A. Mrozowski. *The Death of Prehistory.* Oxford University Press, 2013.

Silko, Leslie Marmon. "Landscape, History, and the Pueblo Imagination." *At Home on the Earth: Becoming a Native to Our Place*, edited by David Landis Barnhill, University of California Press, 1999, pp. 30–42.

Silverberg, Robert. *Mound Builders of Ancient America: The Archaeology of a Myth.* New York Graphic Society, 1968.

Sivasundaram, Sujit. "Sciences and the Global: On Methods, Questions, and Theory." *Isis*, vol. 101, no. 1, 2010, pp. 146–58.

Smail, Daniel Lord. *On Deep History and the Brain.* University of California Press, 2008.

Smail, Daniel Lord, and Andrew Shryock. "History and the 'Pre.'" *American Historical Review*, vol. 118, no. 3, June 2013, pp. 709–37.

Smith, Linda Tuhiwai. *Decolonizing Methodologies: Research and Indigenous Peoples*. Zed Books, 1999.

Spence, Mark David. *Dispossessing the Wilderness: Indian Removal and the Making of the National Parks*. Oxford University Press, 1999.

TallBear, Kim. "Narratives of Race and Indigeneity in the Genographic Project." *Journal of Law, Medicine & Ethics*, vol. 35, no. 3, Aug. 2007, pp. 412–24.

TallBear, Kim. *Native American DNA: Tribal Belonging and the False Promise of Genetic Science*. University of Minnesota Press, 2013.

Thrush, Coll, and Ruth S. Ludwin. "Finding Fault: Indigenous Seismology, Colonial Science, and the Rediscovery of Earthquakes and Tsunamis in Cascadia." *American Indian Culture and Research Journal*, vol. 31, no. 4, 2007, pp. 1–24.

Tsosie, Rebecca, and Joan L. McGregor. "Genome Justice: Genetics and Group Rights." *Journal of Law, Medicine & Ethics*, vol. 35, no. 3, Aug. 2007, pp. 352–55.

Tuan, Yi-Fu. *Space and Place: The Perspective of Experience*. University of Minnesota Press, 1977.

Tuck, Eve, and K. Wayne Yang. "Decolonization Is Not a Metaphor." *Decolonization: Indigeneity, Education and Society*, vol. 1, no.1, 2012, pp. 1–40.

Walsh, Catherine E. "Decoloniality in/as Praxis." *On Decoloniality: Concepts, Analytics, Praxis*, edited by Walter Mignolo and Catherine E. Walsh, Duke University Press, 2018, pp. 13–32.

White, Hayden. *Tropics of Discourse: Essays in Cultural Criticism*. Johns Hopkins University Press, 1978.

Wilcox, Michael V. "Colonizing the Genome: DNA and the New Raciology in American Archaeology." *Entangled Knowledge: Scientific Discourses and Cultural Difference*, edited by Klaus Hock and Gesa Mackenthun, Waxmann, 2012, pp. 115–29.

Wolf, Eric. *Europe and the People Without History*. University of California Press, 1982.

I

Competing Narratives of Ancestry in Donald Trump's America and the Imperatives for Scholarly Intervention

Annette Kolodny

Thoreau's Amnesia

IN THE LAND INHABITED BY the Wabanaki, including the Passamaquoddy, Mi'kmaq, and Penobscot Tribes, "there is no place which is not marked by the hand of the Master. And it is to be seen on hills and rivers and great roads, as well as mighty rocks, which were in their day living monsters" (Leland 62). Charles Godfrey Leland makes this observation in *The Algonquin Legends* (1884), referring to place-related stories of the Indigenous people he had met in Maine, Nova Scotia, and New Hampshire. One story tells how the mythical hero Glooskap (Klose-kur-beh) frees the people from a giant bullfrog who had egotistically stopped up the river, leaving the people thirsty. His slain body is transformed into a mighty river and the people turn into river creatures (114–19). A Penobscot woman tells him a similar story, about how Glooskap liberates the Penobscot River from a dam built by a gigantic beaver. At "Moose-tchick," his interlocutor continues, Glooskap killed a moose whose "bones may be seen at Bar Harbor turned to stone. . . . He threw the entrails of the Moose across the [Penobscot] bay to his dogs, and they, too, may be seen there to this day, as I myself have seen them" (65). In a note, Leland refers to Henry David Thoreau's rendition of a similar landmark story, now geographically related to Mount Kineo near Moosehead Lake further north.[1] In *The Maine Woods* (1864), Thoreau mentions how he was only half listening to his Penobscot guide, who, referring to the moosehead-like shape of the mountain,

repeated the tradition respecting this mountain's having been anciently
a cow moose,—how a mighty Indian hunter, whose name I forget, succeeded in killing this queen of the moose tribe with great difficulty, while
her calf was killed somewhere among the islands in Penobscot Bay. (qtd.
in Leland 65n)

Leland continues quoting Thoreau's comment that the story "did not amount
to much" and that his guide was trying to make up for the lack of contents
with "a drawling tone, long-windedness, and a dumb wonder which he hopes
will be contagious" (66n)—a remark that, together with his forgetting of
the hero's name, is indicative of the colonizing culture's disrespect for the
storytelling cultures of Native America. Quipping at Thoreau's own "nasal
stories about Nature," Leland assures his readers of the liveliness of native
storytelling to which he has often been a witness, and adds: "This writer [Tho-
reau] passed months in Maine, choosing Penobscot guides expressly to study
them, to read Indian feelings and get at Indian secrets, and this account of
Glooskap, whose name he forgets, is a fair specimen of what he learned" (66n).
Referring to Thoreau's complaint that "the Anglo-American . . . grub[s] up"
all the forest trees without being able to "converse with the spirit of the tree
he fells" (66n), Leland retaliates:

> If Mr. Thoreau had known the Indian legend of the spirit of the fallen
> tree—and his guide knew it well—he might have been credited with
> speaking wisely of the poetry and *mythology* which he ridicules the poor
> rural Yankees for not possessing. Such a writer can, indeed, peep and bot-
> anize on the grave of Mother Nature, but never evoke *her* spirit. (66n–67n)

Thoreau's amnesia and lack of intercultural empathy illustrate a pervasive
disregard for Indigenous stories as historically relevant information about
America's recent and ancient past. Colonial scientific discourse translated this
inattention into a general dismissal of orally transmitted knowledge, which
was mostly effaced from the field of anthropology and relegated to the field
of folklore studies following the massive antiquarian work of nineteenth- and
early twentieth-century collectors of "Native lore." Thus banished from the
realm of scientific knowledge to the realm of the imagination, Indigenous
stories were not regarded as relevant archives containing information about
ancient territorial relations and historical events. Colonial termination and
relocation policies further interrupted the transmission of an Indigenous epistemic counterarchive. As early as the late nineteenth century, Leland mentions
how the majority of stories had already been lost.

Today the stories, collected by non-Indian figures such as Leland as well as Indigenous storytellers such as Joseph Nicolar, whose *Life and Traditions of the Red Man* contains a whole chapter on the extensive river journeys of Klose-kur-beh throughout the area of today's Maine and Nova Scotia, are precious elements of cultural knowledge that form the general epistemic background of legal motions to retain Indigenous control over ancient riverine territory.

This chapter focuses on two seemingly unconnected sets of recent events with deep historical roots. Because of Donald J. Trump's intentionally disruptive presidency, the political implications of both sets of events present themselves more clearly than they would otherwise have done. The first concentrates on assertions of historically derived racial purity and racial superiority promoted by the globally active alt-right movement, which includes white supremacist "manifestos" circulated online by its militant terrorist arm.[2] The increasing verbal and physical brutality of male Anglo-Saxon supremacism coincides with popular advertisements for home DNA test kits promising to reveal an individual's previously unknown multilayered ethnic and racial heritage. These seemingly competing cultural narratives are in the process of replacing historically grown and collectively remembered narratives of cultural migration, conflict, and interaction, and they raise disturbing questions about the future of the American experiment of forging a nation out of diversity and difference.

A second set of events emanates from a lawsuit first filed in 2012 by the Penobscot Indian Nation against the State of Maine. This lawsuit represents the Penobscots' effort to retain the Penobscot River as part of their legally and historically designated reservation. Inadvertently, however, this lawsuit coincides with the revival of a long-discredited scholarly narrative about superior ancient peoples who predated the ancestors of modern Indian groups in North America and then mysteriously disappeared. In this instance, that narrative forms part of the ideological substrate of non-Indian attempts to undermine the Penobscot Nation's claim to have inhabited their river, as they claim, "since time immemorial." Simultaneously, among non-Native citizens of Maine sympathetic to the Penobscots' claim to their river, there has emerged the narrative of the ecological Indian, the image of Native peoples as traditionally close to nature and therefore historically protective of its complex living systems.

What ties these two very different sets of events and their related narratives together is the opportunity each offers for scholarly intervention as well as the wider societal implications of each. In the first set, those implications impinge upon the future of liberal democracy in the United States. In the second, the critical role of Indigenous nations in the environmental protection of America's "natural resources" (more specifically the Penobscot Nation's entitlement to protect the Penobscot River watershed) as well as the future of Native American sovereignty rights are at stake.

Race Wars and Genome Fever: White Supremacy Versus DNA Narratives

What most Americans remember about the August 2017 Unite the Right rally in Charlottesville, Virginia, is the violence. That violence has a history. It began with the assumption by white Europeans who first invaded and then settled North America that they were superior to the Indigenous peoples they encountered here, an attitude that was also extended to the Africans kidnapped and brought in bondage as enslaved peoples. Originating in the eighteenth century, these hierarchies of humankind were expressed in a scientific "racial" taxonomy that placed white Christians of Western and Northern Europe at the top of its hierarchy. The belief in immutable racial differences contributed to the emergence of the Ku Klux Klan at the end of the Civil War and, in subsequent decades, the emergence of white nationalists (largely Anglo-Saxon protestants) who opposed the immigration of ethnically divergent people. Spurred by the nation's changing demographics, that history continues today.

Advocating America's return to its supposedly dominant white European past, well-funded and well-organized white nationalists and white supremacists have again become both more vocal and more visible. The propaganda of the National Policy Institute (NPI), for example, is tailored to bolster an increasing sense of precarious social and economic status within the shrinking middle class and the disappearing blue-collar working class, both of which regard themselves as the victims of globalization. In a foreword to a new edition of racist eugenicist Madison Grant's 1933 book, *The Conquest of a Continent*, NPI representative Richard Bertrand Spencer raises the specter of a "thoroughly miscegenated and thus homogenated and 'assimilated' nation, which would have little resemblance to the White America that came before it" (qtd. in SPLC, "Richard Bertrand Spencer"). The evocation of white firstness speaks to an aggrieved sense of pure white European manhood that supposedly founded and built this nation and that is now losing its privileges, being replaced by undeserving affirmative action recipients, globalist Jews, scheming feminists, and criminal brown hordes invading the country from the south.

Some white supremacists and white nationalists identify as Christians, while others—such as those who claim a Nordic Viking heritage—prefer a pagan identity. Both groups advocate a future white-dominated "ethnostate" and frequently style themselves after armed militias in preparation for a future race war. Under the Trump presidency, their racist terminology has entered mainstream discourse (Spencer qtd. in Wood). A white nationalist who goes by the Twitter handle @TheNordicNation "approvingly proclaimed, 'You can say #WhiteGenocide now, Trump has brought it into the mainstream'" (qtd. in Weisman 29).

After posting on social media pictures of himself draped in a Confederate flag, on 17 June 2015, hoping to spark a race war, twenty-one-year-old white supremacist Dylann Roof shot twelve African Americans attending a prayer service in the Mother Emanuel African Methodist Episcopal Church in Charleston, South Carolina. In response to that horrific event, several southern states began to remove from public spaces those monuments that honored so-called Confederate heroes and to rename streets and parks that honored their memory.

By early spring 2017, the City Council of Charlottesville, Virginia, had renamed the park previously named for Confederate general Robert E. Lee from Lee Park to Emancipation Park. After a few smaller rallies, the Unite the Right rally on 12 August 2017 was intended to bring together the full spectrum of the alt-right and, in the words of former Ku Klux Klan imperial wizard David Duke, to initiate "a turning point for the people of this country. We are determined to take our country back. We're going to fulfill the promises of Donald Trump" (qtd. in Cohen).[3] The events that followed will enter the history books. Swarms of angry, tiki-torch-wielding white men shouted ugly slogans, including "Jews will not replace us." During that rally—one of the most ghastly demonstrations of violent white male supremacism since the 1920s—one of the alt-right demonstrators deliberately drove his car into a crowd of lingering counterprotestors, injuring nineteen, some seriously, and killing thirty-two-year-old Heather Heyer, a paralegal from Charlottesville. All of it was caught on camera. Just two hours after Heyer's death, President Trump addressed the media from his vacation home in Bedminster, New Jersey, condemning "in the strongest possible terms this egregious display of hatred, bigotry and violence *on many sides, on many sides*" (emphasis added). He repeated this statement three days later, additionally laying blame on the campaign to remove Confederate statues, which was in his view an attempt to "change history" (Merica).

Taken together, Trump and his father's longtime refusal to rent or sell units in their buildings to people of color; Trump's continued condemnation and public persecution of the Central Park Five, a group of Black and Latino teenagers falsely accused of raping and assaulting a white woman in Central Park in 1989 and later found innocent; Trump's insistent promotion of "birtherism," the lie that Barack Obama was not born in the United States and therefore could not be a legitimate president; Trump's coded anti-Black rhetoric and disdain for immigrants from "shit-hole countries"; Trump's eagerness to build a wall along the border with Mexico; Trump's cruel treatment of asylum seekers from Mexico, Central America, and South America; Trump's attempted Muslim ban; Trump's stated preference for immigrants from Norway; Trump's repeated refusal to condemn the neo-Nazi chants of Charlottesville; and his declaration at a rally in Houston, Texas, on 23 October 2018 that he was himself a "nationalist" (which his white supremacist followers heard as "*white* nationalist" [@DrDavidDuke])—all of these combined to confirm that on the crucial matter of race, Trump stood with them. More than any other president in recent memory, Trump's policies and pronouncements seemed to be moving the nation closer to the alt-right's much-desired ethnostate.[4]

Three months later, the same Nationalist Front coalition organized two "White Lives Matter" rallies in Tennessee. The ultimate aim of their activities, explained one of the rally leaders, was the creation of a "white ethnostate" or "white homeland" in America. Attempting to soften their public image, they pronounced themselves to be "white civil rights advocates" (qtd. in Mathias). Among the counterprotestors were several young people who offered free genetic testing. Under the spell of the advertisements for home DNA test kits promoted everywhere online and on television, these counterprotestors believed they were offering the white supremacists an opportunity to discover how racially mixed they really were. As might be expected, none of the assembled white supremacists accepted that offer.

Had the youthful counterprotesters in Shelbyville, Tennessee, been able to persuade the white supremacists to take up their offer of free DNA testing, they may well have found themselves disappointed by the results. According to an August 2016 article in the *New York Times*, the DNA of only 3.5 percent of those 160,000 DNA-kit customers who agreed to participate and who identified as "white" contained "African" elements. If the majority of the white supremacists in Shelbyville came from the South, however, then their chances of having African ancestry might have been higher, especially so if any of them hailed from South Carolina, "where at least 13 percent of those who said they were white had African ancestors" (Kolata). DNA test kits, while generally refuting the ideology of racial homogeneity, do not always deliver the extreme cultural diversity their advertisements promise.[5]

Given the uniformity of the stories told in these advertisements, we can hardly fault the young counterprotesters for their confidence that DNA testing would surely disprove the white supremacists' belief in their own racial purity. Nor should we fault them for their (equally naïve) hope that the white supremacists might actually have welcomed the discovery of more complicated heritages. For even if misleading in their totality, those advertisements offer the narrative of diversity and intermixture as a ubiquitous and welcome feature of today's America. For many U.S. citizens, taking the DNA test is an adventure of self-discovery, a welcome revelation of more complicated backgrounds, and a sign of an enhanced identity. Many DNA advertisements reiterate the cultural story of America's collective multiethnic identity. They confirm a cosmopolitan narrative of one large, genetically interconnected family.

Three premises appear to undergird the advertisements for DNA test kits: that most Americans have more complex family backgrounds than they know; that most Americans will welcome the discovery of this new knowledge; and that worldwide, all human beings are genetically interrelated. Of the three, only the last stands up to scientific scrutiny. The 2016 analysis of test-kit users and their DNA results demonstrated that the vast majority of those who identified as white learned that they did not in fact have any African, Native American, or Hispanic intermixture. Whether those who receive different results now or in the future will always welcome that information remains uncertain. All we really can say at the moment is that, in a flagrant distortion of the meaning of genetic evidence, some white supremacists are now "flaunting DNA ancestry test results indicating exclusively European heritage as though they were racial ID cards" (Harmon).

What confuses the issue in both the DNA narratives and in the narratives of white racial superiority is the murky meaning of the word *race*. The word has some saliency within zoology but when applied to human beings it makes no sense because, as a species, whatever the superficial differences in our physical appearance or the geographical differences in our place of family origin, we are far more genetically alike than we are different (Keita et al.). In the DNA narratives, to their credit, "race" is rarely used, even if some *idea* of race silently hovers in the background. The word itself is instead subsumed by more accurate terms such as *ethnicity*, *nationality*, or *place of family origin*.

DNA ancestry discourse clearly deviates from white supremacist discourse that is permeated with the view of race as "a biological fact," which no society dares ignore (SPLC, "Jared Taylor"). Genetically based data reveal the fallacy of the notion of racial Anglo-Saxonism as the unifying premise underlying the entire movement. In addition, recent research on the evolution and genetics of pigmentation offers a serious challenge to white supremacists' dependence on skin color as the defining characteristic of race. The research of University of Pennsylvania geneticist Sarah A. Tishkoff on the genetic imprint of skin color in Africans "dispels a biological concept of race" and renders racial classification according to skin color "essentially meaningless" (qtd. in Zimmer). In 2017 Tishkoff and her colleagues identified "eight genetic variants in four narrow regions of the human genome that strongly influence pigmentation—some making skin darker, and others making it lighter." Their research shows that skin-color-related genes "are shared across the globe. . . . One of them, for example, lightens skin both in Europeans and hunter-gatherers in Botswana" (Zimmer). Equally significant is the revelation that these "gene variants were present in humanity's distant ancestors, even before our species evolved in Africa 300,000 years ago. The widespread distribution of these genes and their persistence over millenniums" provides clear evidence that white people do not possess any special or "racially" unique genetics for their skin color, nor do Black people possess any particular "racially" specific genetic variants for their pigmentation (Zimmer). Variation in pigmentation appeared to be caused by a combination of environmental impact and population mixing and matching over many generations (Zimmer). The findings are confirmed by Harvard geneticist David Reich, whose team sequenced ancient human genomes and found that "'whites' represent a mixture of four ancient populations that lived 10,000 years ago and were each as different from one another as Europeans and East Asians are today" (Reich). The alt-right response to this research is to dismiss it as knowledge produced by a "liberal scientific establishment" committed to concealing the "truth about biological racial differences" (SPCL, "Jared Taylor," qtd. in Harmon).

"Prehistoric" Education

The remedy for white supremacists' inability (or refusal) to comprehend recent genetic research, grasp the fundamentals of human evolution, and absorb the contributions of many different groups to American history and culture would seem to be *education*. But that proposition rests on the assumption that the choice of textbooks and the design of curricula are in the hands of scholarly experts and trained teachers. In the United States today, this is not always the case.

Too often, the selection of K–12 textbooks in our public schools is in the hands of locally elected school boards or politically appointed state-wide school boards. For good or for ill, both are subject to pressures from organized community groups and from special interests, including white supremacist segments of the alt-right. In recent years, members of the Texas State Board of Education have increasingly bowed to the influence of political conservatives and evangelical Christians. Thus, in 2014, ideas promoted in textbooks proposed by the board included "the notion that Moses and Solomon inspired American democracy, that in the era of segregation only 'sometimes' were schools for black children 'lower in quality,' and that Jews viewed Jesus Christ as an important prophet." That same year, reviews of more than forty history, geography, and government textbooks for grades 6–12 found "a number of U.S. history textbooks [which] evidence a general lack of attention to Native American peoples and culture and occasionally include biased or misleading information" and at least "one world history textbook [that] includes outdated—and possibly offensive—anthropological categories and racial terminology in describing African civilization" (Strauss).[6]

The continuity of racist assumptions attached to African Americans may have something to do with the way in which slavery, its many legacies, and the Civil War are taught, or not taught, in our schools—and not just in Texas. Educators generally complain about "unclear state content standards and inadequate curricular resources. The net result: High school students are virtually illiterate on the subject [of slavery and its aftermath], and this has had severe consequences for our national life" (Muhammad). A 2007 report from the National Science Teachers Association "indicated that 1 in 8 public high school biology teachers presented creationism as being scientifically credible, and 6 in 10 were teaching evolution in a way that misrepresented its scientific soundness" (Norman).[7]

Given all this, and despite several generations of research showing race to be a social construct, how can we expect future generations to grasp ancient and modern population movements and mixtures? What will tomorrow's citizens understand about pre-Columbian Indigenous civilizations? How will they appreciate the cultural heritages and remarkable survival skills of today's Native peoples? If we cannot trust the accuracy of our school teaching, how can we expect to eradicate beliefs in racial hierarchies as "biological fact" and dislodge the notion of genetically determined white racial superiority? We have to concede that, while the understanding of race as a social construct has certainly permeated college and university education, it has hardly been understood by society at large where it continues to be challenged by the crude political mythology of white supremacy. It is becoming urgent for academics and intellectuals to directly intervene with these developments, inside and outside the university classroom.[8]

Reading Old Bones

Latent ideas about white priority, combined with amnesia about the "prehistory" of Indigenous Americans, featured in the discussion about the provenance
of an ancient Paleoamerican male skeleton discovered in 1996 on the banks of
the Columbia River in Kennewick, Washington. After two decades of vicious
controversy, in February 2017 the skeletal remains were finally returned to a
coalition of Columbia Basin Native American tribes and quietly reburied at an
undisclosed location. This reburial of "the Ancient One," as his Native descendants refer to him, received significantly less media coverage than the original
mistaken report that the "Kennewick Man" skull had "Caucasoid" features, a
report generally interpreted as meaning he had been Caucasian and white. Various archaeologists lobbied in favor of the view that the ancient man was racially
distinct from Indigenous Americans (e.g., Ainu, from Japan). These theories
revived the long-discredited belief that Native peoples had been preceded on
this continent by superior white races, presumably from Europe (Kolodny, *In
Search* 24–26, 31–40, 126–31). But when more definitive genetic analysis was
completed in June 2015, the research team found that "Kennewick Man is
closer to modern Native Americans than to any other population worldwide,"
and his DNA demonstrated "continuity with Native North Americans"—just
as the Columbia Basin tribes had claimed all along (Rasmussen).

More recently, the study of ten-thousand-year-old skeletal remains from
England (first discovered in 1903 and nicknamed "Cheddar Man") "went
viral" in both the UK and the United States when DNA analysis revealed
that the ancient man "would have had black hair, blue eyes—and dark skin"
(McKie). This contradicted common assumptions that the English had always
been white and gave rise to many speculations about ancient migrations and
the phenotypes of "prehistorical" peoples.

One archaeological narrative relates to the ancestors of today's Indigenous
inhabitants of Maine and New Brunswick. According to this narrative, well
before the advent of any Algonquian peoples, an ancient "Red Paint People"
had occupied the area and then disappeared. In an unpublished paper titled
"Late Archaic Change on the Maine Coast: Population Replacement or Continuity?," the prominent archaeologist and longtime Maine resident William
A. Haviland explains that the theory of a Red Paint People dates back to
the excavations of ancient burial sites by Warren K. Moorehead in 1922. By
Red Paint, Moorehead was referring to a powdered form of iron oxide called
red ocher used in these burials. As Haviland further explains, "The idea that
these were the graves of a pre-Algonquian people gained widespread popularity" because later burials by peoples known to be Algonquians—like the

Penobscots—contained either little red ocher or none at all. "Supposedly," continues Haviland, "these early people mysteriously disappeared, to be replaced by people ancestral to the region's historically known Indians" ("Late Archaic Change" 9). Although this notion was strongly disputed "in the 1940s and '50s by archaeologists Wendell Hadlock and Douglass Byers," writes Haviland, "by then the idea of a 'lost Red Paint people' was so deeply entrenched that it lived on in the public mind, eventually resurfacing in professional archaeological circles" ("Late Archaic Change" 9).

Among those who helped "resurface" that idea was Bruce J. Bourque, who, until his resignation in 2017, had served as the state's chief archaeologist and curator of ethnography at the Maine State Museum. In his book *Twelve Thousand Years: American Indians in Maine* (2001), Bourque writes of the "Red Paint culture," which "disappeared abruptly around 3800 B.P. and seem to have left no trace in the cultures that succeeded them locally" (61). Its elaborate technology vanished, and the cemeteries were abandoned. All of this, Bourque contends, happened very quickly, and the Red Paint culture was replaced by the Susquehanna culture, "a new and quite distinct culture" that "suddenly appeared across the Northeast" (62).

Bourque's language presents "prehistory" as a drama of sudden displacement. Rather than the area being simply reinhabited by a succeeding population, the region is suddenly overrun. These word and phrase choices suggest sympathy for a preceding, superior culture violently driven out by immigrants from the south, somewhat like ancient Rome by barbarian hordes or, for that matter, today's United States by demonized southern Latinos.[9]

The drama continued in 2012, when Bourque published *The Swordfish Hunters: The History and Ecology of an Ancient American Sea People*, a multilayered book combining the history of archaeology as a developing discipline with the gradual refinement of scientific methods in lifting the veil from the mystery of the Red Paint burials. Wrapped in a personal narrative of Bourque's archaeological quest, *The Swordfish Hunters* further elaborates Bourque's theories about Red Paint history and culture.

In a 2017 synopsis of his argument, Bourque acknowledges, "Humans around the world have used red ocher in rituals for a long time" ("Ancient Swordfish Hunters"). But he insists that the large amounts of the brilliant red powder found in these graves is "unequalled anywhere." Moreover, the graves (but only rarely the village sites) also contained "beautiful and exotic artifacts," including

figurines of sea birds, seals, porpoise-like creatures, and beavers, the earliest such sculpted forms known in North America. The graves also held

objects from far away: beautifully polished slate spear tips from the eastern Great Lakes, over 700 miles to the west, and graceful spear points of
a translucent stone called quartzite, commonly known as Ramah chert,
which is found only on a single mountaintop 1,000 miles to the north in
Labrador. Even the ocher itself must have come from outside Maine, for
none occurs within the state. ("Ancient Swordfish Hunters")

"Taken together," Bourque argues, "the ocher, the artifacts, the graves, and
the cemeteries themselves set the Red Paint People far apart, not only from
those who came before them, and those who followed, but from every other
known hunter-gatherer group in northern North America" ("Ancient Swordfish Hunters").

What most caught Bourque's attention in the excavations of Red Paint
village sites and cemeteries, however, was "the abundance of swordfish bone."
Especially in the grave sites, much of the bone found there had been fashioned
into "daggers, fish hooks, and even harpoons suited for swordfish hunting."
It was this last item that persuaded Bourque that, "unlike other prehistoric
coastal occupants," the Red Paint People had "practiced a dangerous form
of maritime hunting"—swordfish hunting. "What I suspect 'explains' this
remarkable culture is that, around 5,000 years ago," writes Bourque, "young
male social entrepreneurs began to experiment with the dangerous sport of
swordfish hunting, gaining great prestige by returning to their communities
with this wonderful fish for all to enjoy." But, he explains, "Marine hunting
usually requires hierarchically organized groups comprised of boat crews led
by a high-status boat captain—a social entrepreneur who has amassed the material wealth and social skill needed to build a boat and command the loyalty
of its crew. When not hunting, these men can use their boats for other self-
aggrandizing purposes, such as to trade in distant places for valuable goods"
("Ancient Swordfish Hunters"). This hierarchical arrangement set the Red
Paint People apart from other, generally egalitarian hunter-gatherer groups.

Still, only about sixty cemeteries with burials marked by the significant
use of red ocher have been discovered, all of them located "from the An-
droscoggin River [in Maine] to the St. John in New Brunswick [Canada]."
Bourque accepts that "we have probably found nearly all the Red Paint cemeteries that exist and, while they are numerous," he also admits that "they are
not numerous enough to have included all the souls who were a part of this
culture over perhaps as much as a millennium." As a consequence, Bourque
speculates that "these cemeteries were for just boat captains and shamans," as
a recognition of their special status and an additional sign of social hierarchy
("Ancient Swordfish Hunters").

In archaeological terms, their culture did not last long. "Radiocarbon dating tells us that the Red Paint People first appeared no earlier than 5,000 years ago," Bourque explains, reiterating the language of his earlier book, "and then suddenly vanished about 1,200 years later, replaced by a wave of immigrants from the southern Appalachians." What may have been their "undoing," speculates Bourque, was the swordfish hunting itself, in his words a "risky" and "maladaptive behavior" that caused the loss of too many "young men in their prime." For, as Bourque describes in vivid detail, "swordfish hunting is . . . not for the faint-hearted. . . . Once struck by a harpoon, . . . [swordfish] often unleash their devastating power upon their assailants, darting away, then arcing back to drive their sword through even the thickest wood ship planking. Small boats like the dugouts used by the Red Paint People risked being overturned or even pierced by the sword." And even if the hunters believed that their risks could be "lessened by the spiritual protection provided by the shamans," as Bourque makes clear, those risks were nonetheless very real ("Ancient Swordfish Hunters").

Thus the drama of this story centers on those brave, audacious, slightly suicidal young men who once took "life-threatening risks to bring rewards to the community" but whose numbers, in evolutionary terms, were diminished because of their "maladaptive" practice. Here, the discourse of social Darwinism mingles with romantic heroism. After all, as Bourque points out, "the more sensible course would have been to ignore the swordfish and to focus upon the immense cod that lived in the same waters, and could be caught with little effort or danger using only a hook and line" ("Ancient Swordfish Hunters"). The Red Paint youngsters, we may conclude, were not just a bit too daring but also quite irrational in their hunting choices. They were too heroic to survive as a people (which, to Bourque, apparently hinges on the survival of young men, not young women).

In his eagerness to set the Red Paint People apart from any group that either preceded or followed them, Bourque ignores a great deal of fairly well-established archaeological data. For example, during the period when Bourque claims the Red Paint People first appeared—"no earlier than 5,000 years ago"—and through their subsequent, relatively brief, duration of "about 1,200 years," most archaeologists agree with Haviland and Marjory W. Power that Algonquian peoples were moving into or already permanently inhabiting Maine and maritime Canada. After successive population influxes—most from the southwest—by at least six thousand years ago (and possibly even twice that), "speakers of Proto-Algonquian dialects probably lived in a belt stretching from the Great Lakes across New York and New England into the Atlantic Provinces of Canada to southern Labrador" (Haviland and Power

67, 201–2). Some of these groups occupied homelands stretching from the Kennebec to the St. John River, while others occupied homelands extending from the Kennebec to the Merrimack River and west to Lake Champlain (Haviland, "Who Was Here First?"). This time frame encompasses Bourque's entire timeline for the Red Paint People and more than covers all the geographical areas in which Bourque locates the sixty significant Red Paint cemeteries.

There are some additional facts to consider. Even the earliest Algonquian groups maintained active trade with one another and with other far-flung trading networks; this is confirmed by their geographically precise story traditions. Therefore, it would not be surprising for them to have secured what Bourque characterized as "exotic" trade materials originally sourced from great distances, even as far as a mountaintop in Labrador. And because the manufacture and use of chipped stone tools was abandoned soon after the arrivals of Europeans, archaeological excavations of precontact sites in Maine identified as Algonquian provide evidence that cherts, Kineo felsite, and quartzite were once both available and heavily used for knapping. None of these materials appear to have been in any way "exotic" or restricted to the use of a distinctive Red Paint culture. We also know that the earliest Europeans who fished for cod off the Grand Banks of Newfoundland repeatedly marveled at the seaworthiness of Algonquian (birchbark) canoes and the intrepid skillfulness of those who used them to hunt for whales in the waters off Newfoundland and Labrador (Kolodny, *In Search* 259, 261, 265). This suggests a long tradition of Algonquian maritime skills that might certainly have once included swordfish hunting. Yet it is also possible that the same swordfish bone harpoons that Bourque assumes were used exclusively by Red Paint People to hunt swordfish might also have been used by ancestral Algonquians to hunt whales, as did their descendants. When all these facts and possibilities are brought together, the Red Paint People no longer seem quite so unique or "far apart . . . from every other known hunter-gatherer group in northern North America" ("Ancient Swordfish Hunters").

Climate change also had its impacts. "The first Native Americans who entered [Maine] around 12,000 years ago almost certainly walked on the last remnants of the huge Laurentide [glacial] ice sheet that once extended from the Canadian Arctic across the Gulf of Maine," write scientists who have studied the state's climate history (Jacobson et al. 18). While "the first half of that period had warmer, drier summers," other scientists add, "conditions along the east coast of Maine became cooler and moister some time between 6,000 and 5,000 years ago" (Schauffler and Jacobson 235). This corresponded "with the timing of rapid increases in tidal amplitude and diurnal mixing of cold water in the Gulf of Maine" (235). In other words, following the recession of the glaciers, Maine gradually experienced significant warming, a warming that affected both the climate and the water temperatures in the Gulf of Maine. At some point, therefore, those waters became warm enough to attract species that thrive in warmer waters—like swordfish. But as Maine began to cool again between six thousand and five thousand years ago, coastal sea levels rose rapidly and, with that, higher tides drew colder waters into the Gulf of Maine. In turn, these "marine effects" also helped further cool the climate (Schauffler and Jacobson 235). Since swordfish prefer warmer waters, the gradual cooling of the Gulf of Maine eventually drove them to seek warmer waters elsewhere.

It is thus reasonable to conclude that it was not the Red Paint People who disappeared around 3,800 years ago (as Bourque believes) but the swordfish. Indeed, in this climatological-based model, there is no need to invent a mysterious Red Paint People in the first place. Climate change explains the relatively brief duration of swordfish hunting as well as its disappearance. After that, the Indigenous coastal inhabitants turned—or *returned*—their attention to other species.[10]

For Bourque, aside from their swordfish hunting, what singularly distinguishes the Red Paint People is their ample use of red ocher in burials clustered together in cemeteries. When red ocher is not present, or is only minimally present, he assumes the disappearance of the Red Paint People and their replacement by others. Indeed, Haviland challenges the thesis of a wholly new replacement population migrating "from southern New England into coastal Maine." Such a migration seems doubtful, "given that the supposed migration came at a time when the climate of down east Maine was becoming cooler than it had been." In Haviland's view, it is highly unlikely for people "adapted to a relatively warmer climate [to] move into a cooler one" ("Late Archaic Change" 4).

To better scrutinize the population replacement thesis, Haviland examines the linguistic and oral traditions of Maine's Algonquian peoples, their "material culture" (i.e., artifacts and technology), their subsistence practices, and their mortuary practices. Based on this evidence, he develops a persuasive argument for continuity over long expanses of time rather than disruption or displacement. With regard to the use of red ocher in burials, Haviland argues that this practice waxed and waned with changing climatic conditions and related changing trade routes. He notes that there is evidence of "the sporadic use of red ochre both before and after the Moorehead phase" (which Bourque equates with the Red Paint People), something that even Bourque acknowledged in his first book, *Twelve Thousand Years*. "If, as Bourque suspects," continues Haviland, "the red ochre was an import from the north, we would expect that its use would be most common when contacts with the northerners were most intense. With the redirection of most trade to the south, a return to the earlier sporadic use would make sense." Changes in material culture and in burial practices, Haviland suggests, "came as people along the down east coast were dealing with climate change in their homeland," and, as a consequence of those changes, "earlier elements of indigenous culture reasserted themselves"—including a reduced use of red ocher in burials. Finally, he concludes, "the weight of the evidence favors continuity over population replacement" ("Late Archaic Change" 10).

The theory of violent and disruptive population replacements in the "prehistorical" past is well known since late eighteenth-century U.S. archaeology; it has been used for explaining the "mysterious" disappearance of the Maya as well as that of the "Mound Builders." Its cultural work consists in making the European conquest of America and genocidal policies toward the Indigenous population seem less unprecedented, perhaps even a matter of historical justice. Its similarity with the alt-right's ideological narrative of population replacement and "white genocide" is uncanny.

"The River Is Who We Are"

In early August 2012, the Penobscot Nation was shocked to receive the copy of a directive sent out by Maine state attorney general William J. Schneider asserting that the State of Maine retained exclusive regulatory and enforcement authority over all activities on the Penobscot River. Previous treaties made between the Penobscots and the colony and state of Massachusetts remained in force when the State of Maine was established in 1820 from what had been a portion of Massachusetts. These treaties always included—implicitly and explicitly—the river in their understanding of the territory to be used by the Penobscots. The Maine Indian Claims Settlement Act of 1980 expressly states in the section "Definitions":

> "Land or other natural resources" means any real property or other natural resources, or any interest in or right involving any real property or other natural resources, including, but without limitation, minerals and mineral rights, timber and timber rights, *water and water rights and hunting and fishing rights*. ("An Act to Implement" § 6203, 3, emphasis added)

Given the fact that the Land Claims Settlement, tacitly and implicitly like all the treaties before it, recognized the Penobscot River as part of the Penobscot Reservation, the Penobscots were able to establish a trust of $24 million to help improve the water quality of the river. The members of the Penobscot River Restoration Project patiently negotiated with the industrial plants responsible for some of the pollution; the trust purchased and removed two hydropower dams that had blocked the natural development of marine life in the lower part of the river (the Great Works Dam in 2012 and the Veazie Dam in 2013); and it accomplished the restoration of sea-run fisheries in the river (NRCM, "Penobscot River Restoration Project").

The attorney general's directive cut right into these collaborative efforts to restore the quality of the river. Schneider's argument was based on his reading of the meaning of the word *solely* in the Claims Settlement Act of 1980, where it states that "Penobscot Indian Reservation" means "the islands in the Penobscot River reserved to the Penobscot Nation . . . consisting *solely* of Indian Island, also known as Old Town Island, and all the islands in said river northward" ("An Act to Implement" § 6203, 8, emphasis added). Schneider asserted that *solely* excluded the waters of the river from the reservation. But his reading deviated from all former understandings of the status of the river and completely ignored the cultural knowledge about its centrality in Penobscot epistemology. In sum, the directive threatened the Penobscot Nation's territorial sovereignty, its shared ecological stewardship of the river, and access to its major food resource.

In 2012 the Nation filed a lawsuit in the U.S. District Court for the District of Maine, litigated by Schneider's successor as attorney general, Janet T. Mills. Finally, in May 2019, after six years of uncertainty and a massive campaign to retain tribal sovereignty and the newly achieved ecological standards, Mills, now governor of Maine, proposed an "Act to Protect Sustenance Fishing" that was signed into law on 18 June 2019. The law includes an upgrade of legal protections for more than four hundred miles of rivers and streams for the Penobscot Nation and the other riverine tribes ("New Laws Deliver Landmark Protections").[11] This legal act ends an extensive conflict that centers on the definition of territory and on the cultural significance of the river to the Penobscot Nation.

The Penobscot reservation is located in the middle of the Penobscot River; its members depend on the river culturally as well as for their daily sustenance. In protecting Penobscot "sustenance fishing," the law respects the Native Americans' ancestral tradition of taking only a *sufficiency*, that is, the fish (and game) required to sustain an individual and his family, as opposed to the Euro-American habit of mass harvesting for commercial purposes. Like their ability to monitor the river itself, the Penobscots view these hunting and fishing rights as inherent to their retained legal status as a sovereign nation. The new law also protects the free-flowing character of the Penobscot River, which had been ecologically restored over the past fifteen years as a result of the Penobscot River Restoration Project (NRCM, "New Laws Deliver").

The success came after a long struggle, which included the intervention of the federal Department of Justice and various members of Congress in support of the Penobscots as well as massive support from the non-Indian communities along the river, with whom they had established good long-term working relations.[12] Over decades of patient intercultural communication, negotiation, and ecological collaboration, the Penobscots won the confidence of their local neighbors and demonstrated that fears that the tribe might deprive them of property or access to river recreation were unfounded.

The tribe's legal success was also the result of Appeals Court judge Juan Torruella's minority opinion, written in June 2017. It states that previous legal agreements had been "enacted against the backdrop of an unextinguished and 'sacred' right of the Indians inhabiting Maine to . . . the uncontested proposition that this aboriginal title included the Penobscot River and its bed" (United States, Court of Appeals for the First Circuit 51). Contrary to the two majority judges from whose opinion Torruella dissented, he read all prior documents as part of an interconnected continuity and, as such, with the "understanding that the Nation's rights to hunt and fish were both 'expressly retained sovereign activities,' and that the tribes have the 'permanent right to control hunting and fishing within . . . their reservations.'" In further support, Torruella provided a "deep" historical reading of the case within "the relevant history commenc[ing] with the epic of the American Revolution, a time when the Nation had aboriginal title to land which was 'centered on the Penobscot River'" (39, 36).

In all the court filings related to *Penobscot Nation v. Janet T. Mills*, nowhere has there been any reference as to why, in 2012, Maine's state attorney general suddenly chose to declare that the waters of the Penobscot River were no longer part of what had, until then, been legally defined as within the Penobscots' reservation. Sherri Mitchell, a member of the Penobscot Nation and an Indigenous rights attorney, traced the story to July 2012, when former Republican governor Paul LePage "met with Canadian officials and representatives of Exxon Mobil" to discuss a controversial project to pump tar sands oil from western Canada to the Atlantic Ocean.

"They needed a way to get from Canada to the coast so they could ship it out to foreign markets," said Mitchell. "Immediately after that meeting the state Attorney General's office issued a memorandum stating that the tribe did not have jurisdiction over any of its territorial waters." (Flisiuk)

According to Mitchell, "the Governor of the State of Maine in collusion with the Attorney General's office was working to benefit industry to allow them to cross the Penobscot River unimpeded by tribal rights." She added: "They're trying to pave the way for dirty industry to come through here'" (qtd. in Flisiuk). The proposed tar sands corridor, explained the article,

> would cut through both the Penobscot and Kennebec Rivers, potentially jeopardizing the fisheries and water quality there while consuming 13,500 acres of land. . . . The Penobscot River is a critical focal point for these energy projects, and Mitchell believes that the state sought to take away the Nation's rights to the river so they'd be able to launch these long-disputed energy projects unobstructed. She says this poses major concerns for both Natives and non-Natives in the area, as all the proposed construction, mining, fracking, and truck traffic, not to mention potential oil spills (of which Exxon Mobil does not have a good track record of avoiding or cleaning up), could tarnish the health of the Penobscot River Watershed, Maine's largest at 8,750 square miles. (Flisiuk)

As both this article and the documentary film *The Penobscot: Ancestral River, Contested Territory* (Sunlight Media Collective, 2019) make clear, there will have to be significant cleaning of the river even though the worst environmental devastation has probably been prevented for the time being. Penobscot Nation chief Kirk Francis says that, although his people have done a good job of cleaning up a century of degradation, he nonetheless remains concerned about lingering and future pollution from chemicals dumped into the river over four decades, resulting in nine tons of mercury deposits sitting at the river's bottom, phosphorous overloads leading to toxic algal blooms, and high levels of dioxin from the bleaching process of the adjacent paper mills (Flisiuk; Sunlight Media Collective).

With the help of "thousands of allies," including "the good citizens of Maine" (as tribal members state in the film) but mainly also due to their own ecological effectiveness and communicative skill, the Penobscot Nation will be able to continue its work of healing the river. The Penobscots successfully dispelled fears promoted by popular narratives circulating among uninformed citizens: that "the Indians want to take it all back and exclude everyone else"; that the Penobscots were falsely regarded as "ecological" because the "ecological Indian" was invented by white romanticists (Krech; cf. Kolodny,

"Rethinking"); and that the Penobscots and their Wabanaki relatives had not inhabited the river since time immemorial but had violently replaced an earlier population in "prehistorical" times—the so-called Red Paint Culture. A belief in Bourque's ancient and displaced Red Paint People lingers on.

Haviland offers his speculation as to why: "Not only did this [scenario] appeal to the public's love of a mystery, but there was another reason for this theory's popularity. Probably unconsciously in many cases, it was . . . thought that, if the later Indians had disposed of an earlier people, then current citizens of Maine, whose ancestors came from Europe, did not have to feel so guilty about displacing Wabanaki peoples from their lands" ("Late Archaic Change" 9).[13] In a posting on his blog on 2 August 2015 (updated on 13 August 2015), Bourque expresses almost precisely this sentiment as his own.

> Is it reasonable to argue that more recent arrivals to the Penobscot River region thereby have weaker ties to it? Does the fact that my ancestors, for example, arrived in New England in the 1890s mean that my ties to the region are less strong than descendants of, say, Pilgrims bearing names like Alden, Bradford, Carver, or Winslow? . . . Don't the people who work in river-powered industries and who guide sporting clients on the Penobscot River . . . have ties to it that are arguably as strong as the descendants of people who "traditionally" fished in it?

In 2014 Bourque's written opinion had been admitted as part of the State of Maine's countersuit against the Penobscots, yet it is nowhere quoted or even alluded to in the summary judgment. Thus it remains unclear what influence Bourque's testimony wielded. In an oral deposition taken on 15 October 2014, Bourque had explained that no one, not even the Penobscots themselves, "had a competent grasp on what the real history of the indigenous people of this region was" (Bourque, "Deposition" 5, 6).

Without any mention of a prior Red Paint People, and based solely on his own readings of both French and English primary historical sources, Bourque argues, "The concept of a Penobscot Tribe solely residing upon and occupying the Penobscot River for thousands of years is grossly and demonstrably inaccurate" ("The Penobscot Nation" 3).[14] Bourque writes that the "Penobscot Tribe did not exist as a politically or ethnically distinct people until Massachusetts effectively forced that identity upon them in order to create a negotiating partner in a European model" during the French and Indian Wars (1755–63) to facilitate land transactions ("The Penobscot Nation" 3–4). After 1760, he claims, the tribe was militarily so diminished that "it is inconceivable that the Penobscots could have secured treaty terms that left the

River in Indian control." Bourque appears to regard the Penobscots not as a sovereign nation but as quasi supplicants—first to the British settler-invaders who could have annihilated them and later to the federal government that allowed them to continue using their river and inhabiting their islands. Native American sovereignty, in his reading, is based on the generosity of the colonizer. He therefore concludes that "the Penobscots had no such claim to the Penobscot River, did not believe they had such a claim, and understood that the River was a public resource available to all" ("The Penobscot Nation" 3–5, 69). With his statements, Bourque challenged the current prevailing view of most archaeologists and anthropologists as well as the self-representations of the Penobscots themselves: that the Penobscots had always been predominantly a riverine people.

The Indigenous knowledge behind the Penobscots' self-representations as a riverine people, however, appears to be an area that Bourque never studied firsthand. When deposed by lawyers for the Penobscot Nation, he acknowledged that he had never interviewed any Penobscot Nation member and had never pursued ethnographic fieldwork among the Penobscots (Bourque, "Deposition" 12). Nonetheless, entirely dismissing the Penobscots' assertion that they had never ceded sovereignty over the river to anyone, Bourque insisted that they never "claimed exclusive use of the River or its resources" ("The Penobscot Nation" 3–5).

His reasoning follows colonial logic, essentializing Penobscot culture as hunter-gatherers while simultaneously forcing upon them an alien understanding of land ownership. It translates the fact that, in the conceptual framework of the Penobscots, the river had always been a shared resource into a denial of their ownership and stewardship under present capitalist conditions.

During the trial, expert testimonies such as Bourque's, but also those of scholars invited by the Penobscot Nation claimants, quickly made their way into the public arena in the form of blog postings, letters to the editor, and op-ed articles. In February 2015, an early supporter of the Penobscot Nation reminded readers of the *Portland Press Herald* that "Bourque has stirred controversy among his fellow anthropologists and local historians" because he "hypothesizes that the 'Red Paint People' are a lost tribe that existed thousands of years ago and mysteriously vanished, and that the Penobscots and other tribes of the Wabanaki Confederation . . . are relatively recent arrivals to the region" (Sekera). Nickie Sekera speculates that Bourque, as museum curator, acted out of self-interest, "as it allows the Maine State Museum . . . to hold on to any artifacts, bones or other relics that are over a thousand years old" on the grounds that they do not belong to the ancestors of any of today's Indigenous inhabitants. In April 2015, Maria Girouard, a member of the Penobscot Nation, went as far as accusing Bourque of complicity in "committing genocide against indigenous peoples by stealing all that defines their culture—in this case, [taking] the Penobscot River away from the Penobscots" (qtd. in Daugherty).

In the blog post "The Genocide Card," posted on 10 August 2015, Bourque reproves Penobscot commentators for "playing" the "genocide card" although both the British and the early U.S. governments had granted them limited sovereignty in spite of their military weakness. And in an entry titled "We Have Been Here Forever!," Bourque directly attacks Native Americans' claims of continuous occupation. The real issue, he suggests, is that the Indians were determined to regulate the river beyond the control of non-Indian Maine residents and taxpayers: "In fact, the case turns out to be about who controls a major river and all that this implies for the economy of the region and indeed of the whole state" ("My Role as Expert Witness"). His reiteration of the myth that the Indians want to take it all back and exclude everyone else is coupled with his refutation of his antagonists' apparent claim "that the Penobscot Nation has been in existence for 4,000 years" ("We Have Been Here Forever!"). In a 2017 issue of *Maine Boats, Homes & Harbors*, Bourque repeats his earlier narrative of ancient and sudden population exchange and asserts that the swordfish hunters had been "replaced" by a "wave of immigrants from the southern Appalachians" ("Ancient Swordfish Hunters"). The verbal and structural similarities with the alt-right's racist story of population replacement are striking. But populations are not "exchanged" or "replaced" unless as a result of genocidal planning. Rather, they are subject to adaptation and change.

In March 2015, Joseph Hall, who teaches Native American history at Bates College in Lewiston, Maine, entered the public debate with several articles in local newspapers. In these articles, Hall alerts readers to the cultural rights of the Penobscots as well as the rights of non-Natives living along the river to their own clean environment. He regards the Penobscots as reliable protectors of the river. Hall quotes Penobscot chief Kirk Francis: "'This river is simply who we are. It's the very core of our identity as a people and it's simply the most important thing in the Penobscot Nation's life'" ("Joseph Hall"). He also insists that the tribe's right to sustenance fishing will be much weaker than tribal jurisdiction over the river: "The state does not interfere with sustenance fishing. Poisonous chemicals in the river already do," he drily adds, concluding that "Mills and the state need to do more than not interfere with sustenance fishing rights; they need to help make those rights safe to exercise" ("Joseph Hall").[15]

∴

In Joseph Nicolar's account, Klose-kur-beh is sent on his journey down the river and toward the seashore by seven pine trees who choose him for this task because of his beautiful and cheerful singing (123). At the end of his journey, the trees announce, he will have found "that there is a spirit in all things, and where there is a spirit there is knowledge, and where there is knowledge there is power" (124). They also tell him that he must not use the river for his own convenience alone "because this swift water was made for the convenience of three men,—one red, one white, and one black" (124). Wisdom sits in ancient places (Basso). And in peoples' ancient stories.

Notes

This chapter was revised and edited by Gesa Mackenthun. Annette would also like to thank Abigail Dockter for her invaluable assistance.

1. The lake's name signals the survival of the Indian story into colonial times.

2. Such statements were published in connection with the mass murders in Utøya (Norway, 2010), Christchurch (Aotearoa / New Zealand, 2019), and El Paso (United States, 2019).

3. The major organizers included Spencer's NPI, the Ku Klux Klan, various clubs associated with the neo-Nazi website *The Daily Stormer*, and four groups that form the Nationalist Front: the neo-Confederate League of the South, the Traditionalist Worker Party, Vanguard America, and the National Socialist Movement. Other groups included the Fraternal Order of Alt-Knights, Identity Evropa, the Rise Above Movement, the American Guard, the Detroit Right Wings, True Cascadia, and Anti-Communist Action.

4. Trump still insisted on the guilt of the Central Park Five in statements made to CNN in October 2016 (Burns).

5. In one ad, when a woman uncertain of her ethnic and geographical origins receives her DNA results, she gleefully exclaims, "I'm everything! I'm from all nations!" (Ancestry, "Livie"). In another ad, a woman says she is excited about being "26 percent Native American." The camera then focuses on her pie chart, which shows her to be 26 percent Native American, 23 percent Other, 23 percent Iberian Peninsula, 15 percent Italy/Greece, 5 percent African, and 8 percent Asian. In a voice-over, she says: "This is what I'm made of, this is where my ancestors came from, and I absolutely want to know more about my Native American heritage. It's opened up a whole new world for me." We last see her surrounded by a display of traditional southwestern Puebloan pottery (Ancestry, "Kim").

6. One notorious example was revealed in 2015, when Texas adopted McGraw-Hill's *World Geography*. Omitting any reference to the horrors of the Middle Passage or the many cruelties of enslavement, *World Geography* contained the following sentence:

"The Atlantic Slave Trade between the 1500s and 1800s brought millions of workers from Africa to the Southern United States to work on agricultural plantations" (qtd. in Schaub). Embarrassed by the nationwide adverse publicity, McGraw-Hill agreed in a Facebook posting "that our language . . . did not adequately convey that Africans were both forced into migration and to labor against their will as slaves." The publisher promised "to communicate these facts more clearly" in the book's digital version and in the "next print run" (qtd. in Schaub). Not surprisingly, Brian Belardi from McGraw-Hill Education admitted that this textbook "will not be used for the company's clients in other states" (Isensee). In September 2018, when the Texas State Board of Education attempted to streamline standards for the social studies curriculum, a special review board composed of teachers, professors, and curriculum experts suggested "removing evangelist Billy Graham from the curriculum, revising sections describing the Civil War as a states' rights issue, and removing mentions of Moses' influence on the nation's founding documents." Despite the review board's recommendations, "the State Board voted to keep these elements of the curriculum" intact (Hess). "In an op-ed published in *The Washington Post*, Donna Bahorich, chair of the Texas State Board of Education . . . defend[ed] the board's decision to keep references to Moses' influence over founding American documents, pointing to artistic representations of the biblical lawmaker at the U.S. Supreme Court building and in the U.S. Capitol Building" (Hess).

7. Several years ago, when my husband and I last visited the North Rim of the Grand Canyon and headed toward one of our favorite viewing areas, we passed a group of schoolchildren listening in rapt silence as a park ranger explained the antiquity of the canyon and pointed to the differently colored stratified layers everywhere lining the canyon walls. Each layer, he explained, had been separately deposited over eons of geological time. Having heard these ranger talks during several previous visits, my husband and I walked over to where we could look down into the vast expanse of the gold and pink hues of the canyon. A few moments later, a young father with a son of about six or seven years of age came and stood next to us. Prompted by a question from his father, all excited, the little boy said, "That's the canyon made by Noah's flood." "Good boy," replied his father approvingly, after which he proceeded to describe how the canyon had been carved out in a matter of hours by the force of the receding waters from Noah's Flood, then, as though reciting some lesson from a book, he explained how the canyon's fossil imprints of now-extinct animals represented remnants of creatures that died 4,300 years ago in that biblical Great Flood. The curious boy understood nothing of the canyon's true geological history, nor did he learn anything about the Indigenous Havasupai, whose historic lands surround the park and members of whose community make their home part-time on the canyon's floor. After this incident, I began to look for children's books that offered an accessible and illustrated version of geological history, early hominid development, and the branching of the human family tree but found precious few for younger children. I also searched in vain for children's books that focused on the peopling of the Americas, or a larger historical overview through deep time. And there was certainly no

discussion comparing traditional Native views of their history with Euro-American (mis)constructions of that same history. Due to the provisionality of our constantly increasing knowledge about these issues, digital media would be the ideal way of communicating this knowledge to the youth.

8. I am thinking of interventions in the form of op-ed pieces, adult education, and, of course, the education of children.

9. Bourque's theory has been widely disseminated all across Maine. In addition to his two books and several articles in local magazines, Bourque has also promoted his ideas through public lectures, online videos, and exhibits designed by him for the State Museum. As the former state archaeologist, his views were—and continue to be—influential.

10. In an email dated 30 December 2018 from William Haviland to the author, Haviland writes that, to the best of his knowledge, "swordfish bones do not show up in middens after about 3,800 BCE." He adds, "As far as the 'Red Paint' burials go, many (most?) are concentrated where spring fishing would have been especially good. This suggests people gathering for the resource, bringing the remains of relatives who have died over the winter."

11. The others are the Passamaquoddy Tribe, the Houlton Band of Maliseets, and the Aroostook Band of Micmacs.

12. This is impressively shown in the Sunlight Media Collective documentary *The Penobscot: Ancestral River, Contested Territory* (2019).

13. "Wabanaki" refers to the Wabanaki Confederacy of Algonquian tribes from Canada and the United States, including the Penobscots, Passamaquoddy, Mi'kmaq, Abenaki, and Maliseet. "Wabanaki" itself is derived from the Algonquian word for dawn, meaning the eastern seaboard where the sun first rises. Wabanaki peoples are thus often called "People of the Dawnland."

14. Instead, he insisted, they had been a hunter-gatherer people dependent on coastal resources and had been driven into the Penobscot River Valley only when "crowded off the coast by Anglo settlements" in the second half of the eighteenth century (Bourque, "Deposition" 19).

15. While the act protecting sustenance fishing is in force, the lawsuit over jurisdiction on the river is still pending.

References

"An Act to Implement the Maine Indian Claims Settlement." Senate, 26 Mar. 1980, lldc .mainelegislature.org/Open/LDs/109/109-LD-2037.pdf. Accessed 11 Aug. 2019.

Ancestry. "AncestryDNA TV Commercial, 'Testimonial: Livie.'" *iSpot.tv*, Ad ID 1613583, 2016, ispot.tv/ad/wDMp/ancestrydna-testimonial-livie. Accessed 14 June 2018.

Ancestry. "Ancestry Stories: Kim." *YouTube*, actor Kim Trujillo, 28 Jul. 2016. youtube .com/watch?v=lexegLWPIHg. Accessed 24 June 2018.

Basso, Keith. *Wisdom Sits in Places: Landscape and Language Among the Western Apache*. University of New Mexico Press, 1996.

Bourque, Bruce J. "Ancient Swordfish Hunters." *Maine Boats, Homes & Harbors* 149, Nov./ Dec. 2017, maineboats.com/print/issue-149/ancient-swordfish-hunters.

Bourque, Bruce J. "Deposition of Bruce J. Bourque, Ph.D." 15 Oct. 2014. Offices of the Attorney General *re* Penobscot Nation v. Janet T. Mills, et al. Civil Action No.1:12-cv-00254-GZS. Included as Document 8B in "My Role as Expert Witness," *Bruce's Blog*, 27 Jul 2015, updated 13 Aug. 2015, sites.google.com/a/bates.edu/bruces-blog/home/myroleasexpertwitness.

Bourque, Bruce J. "The Genocide Card." *Bruce's Blog*, 10 Aug. 2015, updated 13 Aug. 2015, sites.google.com/a/bates.edu/bruces-blog/home/thegenocidecard.

Bourque, Bruce J. "My Role as Expert Witness." *Bruce's Blog*, 27 July 2015, updated 13 Aug. 2015, sites.google.com/a/bates.edu/bruces-blog/home/myroleasexpertwitness.

Bourque, Bruce J. "The Penobscot Nation and the 1796, 1818 and 1820 Treaties: An Anthropological and Historical Analysis." 15 Sep. 2014. Included as Document 8a in "My Role as Expert Witness," *Bruce's Blog*, 27 Jul. 2015, updated 13 Aug. 2015, sites.google.com/a/bates.edu/bruces-blog/home/myroleasexpertwitness.

Bourque, Bruce J. *The Swordfish Hunters: The History and Ecology of an Ancient American Sea People*. Bunker Hill, 2012.

Bourque, Bruce J. *Twelve Thousand Years: American Indians in Maine*. University of Nebraska Press, 2001.

Bourque, Bruce J. "We Have Been Here Forever!" *Bruce's Blog*, 2 Aug. 2015, updated 13 Aug. 2015, sites.google.com/a/bates.edu/bruces-blog/home/wehavebeenhereforever.

Burns, Sarah. "Why Trump Doubled Down on the Central Park Five." *New York Times*, 19 Oct. 2016.

Cohen, Zachary. "Trump's Mixed Messaging Sparks Concerns of 'Emboldened' White Supremacists." *CNN*, 19 Aug. 2017, cnn.com/2017/08/19/politics/trump-remarks-alt-right/index.html.

Daugherty, Alex. "Penobscot Community Organizer Cuts Ties with Bates." *Bates Student*, 6 Apr. 2015, thebatesstudent.com/2015/04/06/penobscot-community-organizer-cuts-ties-bates/.

@DrDavid Duke. "Trump Embraces Nationalism in a Massive JamPacked 99.9 % White Venue in Houston! Zio Journalists asked him if this is White Nationalism! Of course fundamentally it is as, there is no ethnic or racial group in America more Nationalist than White Americans . . . So What's the Problem?" *Twitter*, 23 Oct. 2018, 1:45 p.m.

Flisiuk, Francis. "'Maine Has Its Own Standing Rock'—The Penobscot River Fight Explained." *Portland Phoenix*, 1 Oct. 2017, conwaydailysun.com/portland _phoenix/news/maine-has-its-own-standing-rock—-the-penobscot/article_5a1679fa -a800–5f89–9e71-c5a7b63222c2.html.

Grant, Madison. *The Conquest of a Continent, or, The Expansion of Races in America*. Scribner, 1933.

Hall, Joseph. "Joseph Hall: The Penobscots are Fighting for Their Culture." *Sun Journal*, 15 Mar. 2015, sunjournal.com/2015/03/15/joseph-hall-penobscots-fighting-culture/.

Harmon, Amy. "Why White Supremacists are Chugging Milk (and Why Geneticists are Alarmed)." *New York Times*, 17 Oct. 2018.

Haviland, William A. "Late Archaic Change on the Maine Coast: Population Replacement or Continuity?" Unpublished paper on file in the archives of the Deer Isle-Stonington Historical Society, Maine. Quoted by permission of the author.

Haviland, William A. "Who Was Here First?" Guest column, *Island Advantages*, 17 Apr. 2008, 4.

Haviland, William A., and Marjory W. Power. *The Original Vermonters: Native Inhabitants, Past and Present*. Rev. ed., University Press of New England, 1994.

Hess, Abigail. "The Texas Board of Education Voted to Remove Hillary Clinton and Helen Keller from School Curriculum." *CNBC*, 20 Sep. 2018, cnbc.com/2018/09/20/texas -votes-to-remove-hillary-clinton-helen-keller-from-curriculum.html.

Isensee, Laura. "How Textbooks Can Teach Different Versions of History." *NPR*, 13 Jul 2015, npr.org/sections/ed/2015/07/13/421744763/how-textbooks-can-teach-different -versions-of-history.

Jacobson, George L., et al. "Maine's Climate Yesterday, Today, and Tomorrow." *Maine Policy Review*, vol. 17, no. 2, 2008, pp. 16–23.

Keita, S. O. Y., et al. "Conceptualizing Human Variation." *Nature Genetics*, vol. 36, 2004, pp. S17–S20.

Kolata, Gina. "With a Simple DNA Test, Family Histories Are Rewritten." *New York Times*, 28 Aug. 2017.

Kolodny, Annette. *In Search of First Contact: The Vikings of Vinland, the Peoples of the Dawn-land, and the Anglo-American Anxiety of Discovery*. Duke University Press, 2012.

Kolodny, Annette. "Rethinking the 'Ecological Indian': A Penobscot Precursor." *Interdisciplinary Studies in Literature and Environment*, vol. 14, no. 1, Winter 2007, pp. 1–23.

Krech, Shepard, III. *The Ecological Indian: Myth and History*. W. W. Norton, 1999.

Leland, Charles Godfrey. *The Algonquin Legends of New England*. Boston, 1898.

Mathias, Christopher. "'White Lives Matter' Rally Cancelled After Meeting Heavy Resistance in Tennessee." *Huffington Post*, 28 Oct. 2017, huffingtonpost.com/entry/white -supremacist-rallies-tennessee_us_59f48222e4b07fdc5fbe7286.

McKie, Robin. "Cheddar Man Changes the Way We Think About Our Ancestors." *The Guardian*, 10 Feb. 2018.

Merica, Dan. "Trump Condemns 'Hatred, Bigotry and Violence on Many Sides' in Charlottesville." *CNN*, 13 Aug. 2017, https://www.cnn.com/2017/08/12/politics/trump -statement-alt-right-protests/index.html.

Muhammad, Khalil Gibran. "Were the Founders Against Slavery All Along?" *New York Times*, 18 Oct. 2018.

Natural Resources Council of Maine (NRCM). "New Laws Deliver Landmark Protections for Sustenance Fishing and Clean Rivers." News release, 21 June 2019, nrcm.org/ maine-environmental-news/landmark-protections-tribal-sustenance-fishing-clean -rivers/. Accessed 10 Aug. 2019.

Natural Resources Council of Maine (NRCM). "Penobscot River Restoration Project." nrcm.org/projects/waters/penobscot-river-restoration-project/. Accessed 11 Aug. 2019.

Nicolar, Joseph. *The Life and Traditions of the Red Man*. 1893. Edited, annotated, and introduced by Annette Kolodny. Duke University Press, 2007.

Norman, Abby. "The Battle to Teach Evolution in Public Schools Is Far from Over." *Futurism*, 21 May 2017, futurism.com/battle-teach-evolution-public-schools-far-from -over/.

Penobscot Nation, Plaintiff v. Janet T. Mills et al. "Second Amended Complaint (Injunctive Relief Requested)." Filed Feb. 2013. *Re* Civil Action No.1:12-cv-00254-GZS.

Rasmussen, Morten, et al. "The Ancestry and Affiliations of Kennewick Man." *Nature*, vol. 523, 2015, pp. 455–458.

Reich, David. "How Genetics Is Changing Our Understanding of 'Race.'" *New York Times*, 23 Mar. 2018.

Schaub, Michael. "Texas Textbook Calling Slaves 'Immigrants' to Be Changed, After Mom's Complaint." *Los Angeles Times*, 5 Oct. 2015.

Schauffler, Molly, and George L. Jacobson Jr. "Persistence of Coastal Spruce Refugia During the Holocene in Northern New England, USA, Detected by Stand-Scale Pollen Stratigraphies." *Journal of Ecology*, vol. 90, 2002, pp. 235–50.

Sekera, Nickie. "Maine Voices: State Should Drop Lawsuit That Would Grab River from Penobscot Nation." *Portland Press Herald*, 17 Feb. 2017, pressherald.com/2015/02/ 17/maine-voices-state-should-drop-lawsuit-that-would-grab-river-from-penobscot -nation/.

Southern Poverty Law Center (SPLC). "Jared Taylor." Extremist Files database, splcenter .org/fighting-hate/extremist-files/individual/jared-taylor. Accessed 18 Sep. 2018.

Southern Poverty Law Center (SPLC). "Richard Bertrand Spencer." Extremist Files database, splcenter.org/fighting-hate/extremist-files/individual/richard-bertrand-spencer -0. Accessed 31 May 2018.

Strauss, Valerie. "Proposed Texas Textbooks Are Inaccurate, Biased and Politicized, New Report Finds." *Washington Post*, 12 Sep. 2014.

Sunlight Media Collective. *The Penobscot: Ancestral River, Contested Territory*. Documentary, 2019, sunlightmediacollective.org/index.php/our-projects/the-penobscot-ancestral -river-contested-territory. Accessed 10 Aug. 2019.

Thoreau, Henry David. "The Allegash and East Branch." *The Maine Woods*. Boston, 1864, pp. 161–304.

United States, Court of Appeals for the First Circuit. *Plaintiffs v. Janet T. Mills et al.* Docket nos. 16–1424, 16–1435, 16–1474, and 16–1482, 30 June 2017. Appeals from the United States District Court for the District of Maine, media.ca1.uscourts.gov/pdf .opinions/16–1424P-01A.pdf.

Weisman, Jonathan. *(((Semitism))): Being Jewish in America in the Age of Trump*. St. Martin's, 2018.

Wood, Graeme. "His Kampf." *The Atlantic*, June 2017.

Zimmer, Carl. "Genes for Skin Color Rebut Dated Notions of Race, Researchers Say." *New York Times*, 12 Oct. 2017.

2

"Born of the Soil"

DEMOGRAPHY, GENETIC NARRATIVES, AND AMERICAN ORIGINS

Christen Mucher

This. No that. This. No.
They debate decades, millennia,
then give in to some subtle pull,
a strand of maternal code, thinner than hair,
stronger and lasting long as humanity.

—HEID ERDRICH, "MITOCHONDRIAL EVE"

The Ancient DNA Revolution

SINCE 2001, WHEN THE FIRST map of an entire human genome became publicly available, the technology for splicing, recombining, and reading genetic material has invigorated fields from molecular biology and anthropology to statistics. In recent years, even "prehistoric" human teeth and bones have been transformed into a slurry of Cs, Gs, As, and Ts, into data limited only by provenience and processing capacity. Unsurprisingly, then, American prehistory—or, to use Pawnee scholar Roger C. Echo-Hawk's preferred term, "ancient American history"—has also been rocked by the "ancient DNA revolution" (267, 268). Almost every day, new "discoveries" confirm or upend long-held certainties; and as newer technologies emerge, so do new theories of the "global dispersal of modern humans" (Raff; Hoffecker et al.).[1] While high-throughput sequencing may be cutting-edge technology, however, geneticists are ultimately using new tools to pursue an old question that has occupied minds on either side of the Atlantic for at least four hundred years (Hofman and Warinner). As Thomas Jefferson put it in 1782: "From whence came those aboriginal inhabitants of America?" (162). Like so many of his contemporaries, Jefferson wanted to pinpoint Indigenous origins and confirm the peopling of the Americas in order to locate the continent's initial occupants on the received chronology of world history. Today, ancient genomic studies in academic journals such as *Nature, Evolutionary Anthropology*, and the *Proceedings of the National Academy of Sciences (PNAS)* continue Jefferson's centuries-old demographic work.

By the late eighteenth century, the scholarly consensus held that the Americas' Indigenous peoples had originated elsewhere; while Atlantic scholars were willing to explore hypotheses of migration from many directions, few would entertain claims of American autochthony, of America's peoples being "born out of the earth" of Turtle Island (North America).[2] For his part, Jefferson believed that Americans' origins ultimately derived from the Old World because in the model of prehistory provided by Genesis, all Creation's peoples originated in the lands and events documented in the Bible. To him, the question was not whether or how the original Americans were (or were not) autochthones but whether they had migrated to the New World via the Atlantic or the Pacific (Jefferson 163). After the validity of the sixteenth-century Bering Strait hypothesis was seemingly confirmed by Captain James Cook's mapping of the fifty-odd-mile-wide strait between Capes Dezhnev (Siberia) and Prince of Wales (currently Alaska) in 1778, the "Asiatic hypothesis"—meaning the earliest American ancestors had come from Siberia or neighboring Great Tartary in Asia—became the most popular model for explaining the Americas' original population.

In 1798, when Jefferson's acquaintance Mihšihkinaahkwa (Little Turtle)—the Miami leader who was rumored to resemble the group of "Tartars" visiting Philadelphia—was pressed about the likeness and his own origins, he reportedly volleyed: "Should not these Tartars, who are like us, have gone first from the American side? Are there any proofs to the contrary? Why should not their fathers and our's [*sic*] have been born in our country?" (Volney 362–63).[3] Little Turtle rejected the claim that his ancestors were Asian immigrants, especially because it contradicted what he knew to be true: the Miami word for "people"—*mihtohseeniaki*—meant "born of the soil" (Volney 363). And because Miami people had emerged from the waters of Saakiiweesiipi (St. Joseph's River) onto Kihcikamionki (the Land of the Great Lake), which became Myaamionki, Miami Land, they became Myaamiaki, the Miami people, on that land (Ironstrack; Sutterfield 2).[4] If Tartars were related to Miamis, Little Turtle countered, then why couldn't they "have been born in our country," migrating afterward to Asia?

More than two centuries later, Western scientists are still locating Indigenous Americans' origins across the Bering Sea, denying—as British science writer Adam Rutherford does in *A Brief History of Everyone Who Ever Lived* (2016)—Indigenous traditions of autochthony in favor of the "scientifically valid notion of the migration of people from Asia into America" (142). By contrast, only recently has there been much interest in establishing the "scientifically valid" origins of ancient Europeans—whose projection as a primordial "pure race" has long supported white supremacy—outside Europe, even though the mosaic migration model locates all origins in Western Asia and Northeastern Africa (Curry; Genesis 1–3; Lazaridis et al.). The centuries-old uneven desire to locate "foreign" origins for some *Homo sapiens* but not for all means that even the most well-meaning deployment of DNA-driven historic demography proffers the threat of displacement.

"Like many tribes of the Americas," writes Rutherford, "the Taíno believed that they had always lived on those lands. In their religious traditions, their ancestors emerged from a sacred cave on what we now call Hispaniola" (129–30). However, Rutherford avers, "the indigenous people *hadn't* always been there, as some of their traditions state, but they *had* occupied these American lands for at least 20,000 years" (130). Alluding to traditional Taíno knowledge only to dismiss it, Rutherford defers instead to a date—one more debatable than he acknowledges—for the real truth of Taíno origins. Ultimately, Rutherford asserts the supremacy of settler worldviews in the guise of epistemological difference: Taíno stories are situated *belief*, whereas Rutherford's interpretation of the DNA evidence is *knowledge* (Cruikshank 248; TallBear 12). Refusing a narrative in which Indigenous peoples emerged on Turtle Island time out of mind, he embraces instead one in which they trekked across the mammoth steppe during the scientifically named and calculated "Upper Paleolithic" (Williams and Madsen). His truth is held by numbers and artifacts, not stories.

While numerous North American traditions contain remembrances of stars, ice, water, and the surfacing of Earth, several also posit specific sites of emergence—such as mountains, caves, or in the case of the Miami, rivers—that illustrate the connection of peoples to homelands.[5] Indeed, as Mohawk and Anishinaabe sociologist Vanessa Watts asserts, "Our truth . . . [for] a majority of Indigenous societies, conceives that we (humans) are made from the land; our flesh is literally an extension of the soil" (27). Many teachings assert Indigenous autochthony, though few insist on a singular presence: instead, traditional origin narratives overwhelmingly recall the coming of the present world and describe successive worlds past; they frequently explain how a people—a group, a family, a band, and so forth—came to be, and they teach of the reciprocal relations between *the People* (humans) and other more-than-human beings. In fact, as Tewa scholar Gregory Cajete (Santa Clara Pueblo) asserts, these teachings are integral to the workings of Native science, which "is connected to the origins and migrations of people through the American landscape" (70). Some traditions indeed recall periods of movement as essential to the process of coming-to-be, although others—such as Klamath and Modoc traditions from the Pacific Northwest—maintain no such migration memories (Budhwa in this volume). For years, settler scholars have sought to use emergence and migration traditions to substantiate "scientifically valid" claims about Indigenous origins, remaining skeptical as to whether they hold ancient knowledge but approving when they seem to locate a peoples' homeland elsewhere (Deloria in this volume).[6]

Although Rutherford recognizes, in his words, that the "scientifically valid notion of the migration of people from Asia into the Americas may challenge Native creation stories," and this may in turn have "the effect of undermining indigenous claims to land and sovereignty"—*and* although he proposes a "new model of engagement" with Indigenous communities and geneticists with more trust building—the "scientifically valid" accounts he propounds nonetheless minimize the potentially dire stakes of narrating land and life in such an authoritative, universalist fashion (Rutherford 10).

Yet paradoxically Rutherford's search for quantifiable, verifiable, totalizing knowledge refuses the truth of Indigenous stories in favor of the supposedly self-evident "stories in our genes." For many Western scientists and science writers, when faced with genetically generated hypotheses about the human past, it can be hard to remember that the "prehistories" enabled by ancient DNA are still, also, *stories*.[7] Unlike the traditional narratives told by Indigenous elders, which are about *existence*, those told by geneticists are about *evidence*. Indigenous stories are told in words, images, landscapes, and relationships; scientific ones use alphanumeric codes, the numbers of the balance sheet, and colonial epistemic paradigms. One requires an unfolding of knowledge hierarchies that moves toward the decolonial; the other upholds a violent tradition of Enlightenment expertise and Discovery Doctrine land claims (W. Echo-Hawk 18, 20).

This chapter looks to the stories of ancient American history as told by popular science outlets in order to argue that the implicit (or explicit) rejection of Indigenous oral tradition enacted by genomic migration stories reenacts past instances of dispossession in the present. It traces connections across those research impulses driving current-day paleogenomics and earlier technologies for the transformation of human bodies into data points and type specimens, asking about, as Philip J. Deloria has formulated it, "the political consequences of deep-time historical narration and the various historicities and knowledge productions embedded in both stories and critiques" of human origins for the past and present age (in this volume). Ultimately, the chapter argues that the tools and motivations of eighteenth- and nineteenth-century "state science" bear a family resemblance to the "ancient DNA revolution" of today, all of them part of an intellectual genealogy that refuses Indigenous humanity and historicality.

Origin Stories

In *Who We Are and How We Got Here: Ancient DNA and the New Science of the Human Past* (2017), Harvard geneticist David Reich discusses how mapping the Neanderthal genome exposed his own "strong bias against the possibility of Neanderthal interbreeding with modern humans," which we now know did happen (36). This revelation led him to question the fundamental "African origins" model of human evolution, one that was supposedly confirmed in 1987 when the "most deeply splitting human mitochondrial DNA lineages" were traced to one female relative—"Mitochondrial Eve"—in Ethiopia (Reich 5, 10). The theory held power not just because of this genetic evidence but because it was a culturally palatable story: it tracks with Abrahamic traditions placing human genesis in or near the biblical "Holy Lands" (further implied by the reference to Eve). Reich's Neanderthal research, however, showed him that Africa may not, *exactly*, have been the origin of all *human beings*, even if it is the place of origin for most of the *DNA* within current-day "anatomically modern humans" (49).

For Reich, "Out of Africa" had long limited his imagination of evolution; to him, the Neanderthal experience was a warning tale about the dangers of dominant paradigms and the influence that origin stories about the past can hold over the present. Reich's lesson also reveals the banal frequency with which scientists search for human origins in terms of purity and differentiation instead of adaptation and continuity ("interbreeding"); of geographic migration ("*Out* of Africa"); and of ontic rather than cultural emergence. Reich's account reveals the background assumptions and less overt choices that go into narrating for *ourselves* a common past, even for those at the very edge of technology's blade. As such, beginning accounts of human history with "two feet," that is, with our earliest bipedal ancestors—as Rutherford does in his book—is an interpretive choice rather than a given (20).

To Western scientists, the family to which we current humans belong—and where "we" began—is unknown and constantly changing.[8] According to present scientific consensus, the Earth has been populated by the bipedal, ambulatory human beings classified as *Homo sapiens* for roughly 300,000 years, a mere fraction of the 3.9 billion years estimated for the planet's multicellular life (Rutherford 2). Other bipedal hominoid relatives, such as chimpanzees, *Australopithecus africanus*, and *Ardipithecus* "Ardi" *ramidus*, are millions of years old.[9] Among our many ancient relatives, "anatomically modern humans" or *Homo sapiens* (sometimes called *Homo sapiens sapiens*)—humans like us—are thought to be only about 100,000 years old (Rutherford 36). "Anatomically modern," however, includes only those humans with *majority* genomic heritage tracing to Africa from roughly 300,000 years ago—that is, all of us now, but not all hominids ever (Rutherford 22).[10]

Homo sapiens themselves did not exist—conceptually as such—until 1758. That was the year the great Swedish taxonomist Carl Linnaeus included the taxonym in his *Systema Naturae*, the first instance of the genus-and-species concept being applied to humans (Linnaeus took himself—the "wise man"—as type specimen). For almost a century afterward, following Linnaeus all human creatures were classed as *Homo sapiens* and subsequently subdivided into six quasi-racial "subspecies" (*Ferus* ["Wildmen"], *Americanus, Europaus, Asiaticus, Afercanus, Monstruosus*), placed into what Kim TallBear, the Sisseton Wahpeton Oyate scholar of science and technologies, has called "continental-level race categories" (6). This categorization persisted until a skull uncovered in Westphalia's Neander Valley received the name *Homo neanderthalensis* in 1864. The species-level change retains a sense of the era's scientific racism in its effort to create a "pure" type: *neanderthalensis* versus *sapiens* implies that there could have been no reproduction between the two hominid groups. Despite difficulties in accounting for Neanderthal Man's beginnings, the discovery led to no revision of Europeans' "Holy Land" origins mythology (Allentoft; Sample, "Piece of Skull").

Despite Linnaeus's *sapiens*-centrism, multiple groups of humans—some of whom are now called Neanderthals, Denisovians, and Flores Islanders, and who are cousins to "anatomically modern humans"—populated the Earth until about 40,000 years ago. Over one million years ago, we all shared common ancestors. Recent research has shown that present-day humans still carry fractional amounts of genetic material from these allegedly extinct *Homo* species as well as genetic traces of our other, more-than-*Homo*, ancestors. If we consider ourselves connected to the beings with whom we share ancestral ties—through shared genetics as well as shared narratives and memories—and we recall that scientists do not yet understand the way that intergenerational memory works or the extent to which "our" DNA is exclusive to "us," then the scientific quest for "origins" is doubly interpretive rather than empirical. And as of yet it has resulted in accounts that depend on teleological narrative conventions to structure beginnings, middles, and ends.

Gene Flow

The Pleistocene Epoch (from about 2.5 million to 12,000 years ago) saw at least twenty cycles in which the planet froze and warmed, causing enormous change and rearranging earth, ice, and water. Scientists believe that during the Last Glacial Maximum (LGM)—when the global sea level was at its lowest and the Laurentide and Cordilleran Ice Sheets covered western North America—one million square acres of now-submerged land they call "Beringia" hosted a complex group of anatomically modern humans (Raghavan et al., "Upper"). Once a diverse landmass stretching from the high Arctic of current-day Siberia to Alaska's Mackenzie River, Beringia spanned what is now the Bering Sea (Goebel and Graf 21; Llamas et al.; Moreno-Mayar et al., "Early"; Pinotti et al.). Near Mal'ta in south-central Siberia, genetic material has been identified from a 24,000-year-old "ancient North Eurasian" boy (MA-1) (Rahgavan et al., "Genomic"), while fecal biomarkers uncovered at a lake in far northern Athabaskan Gwazhał (Brooks Range, Alaska), may imply an ancient human presence in Western Beringia up to 32,000 years ago (Vachula et al.).

Using previously collected sets of Indigenous American genotypes—in other words, portions of blood, tissue, and bone abstracted into alphanumeric patterns and statistical data—geneticists have determined the relationship of this "Ancient Beringian" population to present-day Indigenous Americans (Moreno-Mayar, "Terminal"). A 2016 analysis of "222 Native American and relevant Eurasian Y chromosomes"—the former of which included 16 "ancient samples"—has seemingly, to the point, "rule[d] out occupation of the Americas before 19,500 years ago" (Pinotti et al. 149). The current consensus is that, around 20,000 year ago, some members of the steppe group moved away—to "occupy" the Americas—while others stayed behind in Beringia (Hoffecker et al; Moreno-Mayar et al., "Terminal"; Rasmussen et al.; Reich et al.; Skoglund and Reich). Most geneticists and archaeologists alike hypothesize that, about 16,000 years ago, the melting ice sheets opened migration corridors down the Pacific Coast and into what is currently western Canada via the Yukon and Mackenzie River valleys (Braje et al.; Bortolini et al.; Froese et al.). Migrants arrived over water and land (Dillehay et al.; Raff and Bolnick). As the ice melted, Beringia flooded; consequently, Asia and the Americas became separate geographical entities, even if this division is more prevalent in topological than biological narratives.

From all this data, geneticists and paleoanthropologists have developed different population models for the Americas, variously called "out-of-Beringia," "Two-Components," and "Beringian-American" (González-José et al. 182; Pinotti et al. 157). Later groups of human arrivals—euphemistically called "streams of Asian gene flow" (Reich et al. 372, 375)—are unironically referred to as "colonization models," terminology revealing the deep settler colonial inclination to automatically assume that the continent's earliest peoples were "early settlers" of a "final frontier" (Callaway; O'Rourke and Raff R202). These models trace what TallBear calls "the migration of particular nucleotides via human bodies across time and space" (TallBear 12; see also Raghavan et al., "Upper"). TallBear, of course, recalls that "such bounded ethnic or racial descriptions of certain nucleotide sequences would not have any salience were it not for the established idea within genetic science that 'Native America' . . . is a distinct genetic or biological category" (12).

In 1968 an ancient toddler was unearthed from the Anzick family farm in Montana. His body was found surrounded by more than one hundred stone and ivory tools, some of which were covered in red ocher, and these burial objects were identified by archaeologists as belonging to the "Clovis" material culture complex. The carefully prepared interment site signifies that, to someone, at some point at the horizon of peoples' memory, this toddler was counted as special. The ancient child—now renamed Anzick-1—is still one of the oldest humans uncovered in North America. At the time, the 13,000- to 12,600-year-old time stamp of "Clovis complex" tools—grave goods—entombed with him confirmed a familiar migration chronology for the continent.

In 2014 scientists announced that the genetic data extracted from the toddler's 13,000-year-old bones was compatible with the hypothesis that Anzick-1 belonged to a population directly ancestral to many contemporary Native Americans (Rasmussen et al.).[11] The specific Y-chromosome clade "discovered" in Anzick-1's DNA was given the code Q-CTS1780 (the emergence of the Q haplogroup has been traced to Central Asia 32,000 years before the present) and identified as "one of the two clear founding lineages in Beringia" (the other is Q-M3) (Pinotti et al.; Rasmussen et al.). The mapped sequences of mutations revealed that "the gene flow from the Siberian Upper Palaeolithic Mal'ta population into Native American ancestors is also shared by the Anzick-1 individual and thus happened before 12,600 years b[efore] p[resent]" (Raghavan et al., "Upper"). Recently, a group of geneticists interpreted "three to four independent lineages as autochthonous [to Beringia] and likely [population] founders: the major Q-M3 and rarer Q-CTS1780 present throughout the Americas, the very rare C3-MPB373 in South America, and possibly the C3-P39/Z30536 in North America" (Pinotti et al. 149; see also González-José et al. 176). This is all to say that the DNA results connected "Anzick-1" to Beringian ancestors and descendants in Central and

South America, calling—if nothing else—the Clovis First hypothesis into question.[12]

Rutherford wrote that Anzick-1 was once "a very special child who had been ceremonially buried in splendor. Now he's special because we have his complete genome" (137). The uncomfortable image of grieving relatives alongside lab techs betrays the difficult reality that in plotting the ancient American past, "we" raise the dead not to mourn them but instead to abstract them into proof for "our" genetic narratives. "We" employ statistical models to compensate for uncertainties, measuring standard deviation, LRT distribution, F3-statistics, and weighted coefficients of variation to construct story-telling whisker plots and phylogenetic trees. Living and ancient tissue samples have become data points "converging to tell a *new* and *consistent* story of the first Americans" (Waters 38, emphasis added). And although in these newer migration narratives "Beringia" is marked off from "Asia," "Eurasia," and "Tartary," the "out-of-Beringia" model remixes lines of genetic, cultural, and racial difference into a new, alphanumeric articulation of the old Asian-origins hypothesis, one that still refuses to credit Little Turtle's knowledge that his ancestors were "born of the soil" of Miami, not "Tartar," lands (Pinotti et al. 149). Ironically, the origin story that geneticists are now telling, that of the phylogenetic expansion of Q-M3, Q-CTS1780, C3-MPB373, and C3-P39/Z30536, began in the earth, water, and ice that resemble some of the topographies maintained in Indigenous traditions.[13]

In *Red Earth, White Lies* (1995), the eminent Yankton Dakota scholar and activist Vine Deloria Jr. outlined the damage done when non-Natives assume the basic validity of the Bering Strait theory—both in terms of its limited "Clovis First" chronology and its epistemic contempt—and went as far as to call it "scientific folklore" that "exists and existed only in the mind of scientists" (70, 91). He argued that Indigenous oral traditions contain knowledge about the history of the continent and its original peoples, and that ignoring this knowledge had impoverished Western accounts of the Earth's history (Deloria, *Red Earth* xiv).[14] When non-Natives assume the Bering Strait theory as a given, Deloria asserts, it renders them incapable of entertaining any other origin accounts. Moreover, the refusal to engage Indigenous knowledges translates into an implicit denial of Indigenous existence. Until Indigenous peoples were fully connected to early human history, he later wrote, "we will never be accorded full humanity" (Deloria, "Indians, Archaeologists" 597). By introducing skepticism, doubt, and multiplicity into areas formerly closed off to discussion, Deloria aimed to show that there is room—and even an ethical necessity—for maintaining multiple stories of ancient America.

Demographics of Removal

Demography is the analysis of populations, and, linguistically and rhetorically, the association of "population" with "depopulation" has never been far
off. Literary scholar Molly Farrell has argued that the very understanding of
a group of people as a "population" is tied up with colonialism and violence,
and specifically that "representing individuals as numbers was a central element of colonial projects" (6, 2; see also Nelson 17). In Europe's early modern
era, scholars and political advisors who believed humanity was recovering
from a great decimation estimated that repopulation would require more
space than the continent's crowded cities allowed. Those doing the crowding
began to be conceptualized (by those doing the enclosing) as a countable—
and thereby discountable—popular body: a population.

"Population science" and the question of sizing were taken up by early
English demographer John Graunt, in his *Natural and Political Observations
upon the Bills of Mortality* (1663), and by William Petty in *Political Arithmetick*
(1690). Colonial projectors used it to tout overseas colonies as an opportunity
for controlled depopulation—as a mechanism for discarding "waste" bodies in
order to encourage "proper growth"—at home (Bauman). As both Farrell and
anthropologist Diane M. Nelson point out, the classic reference text *Political
Arithmetick* was written to help England solve its "Irish problem" (Farrell
7; Nelson 25–26). According to Graunt's contemporary Charles Davenant,
the foundation for controlling population, he wrote in *Discourses on the Public
Revenues, and on Trade* (1698), was "to be laid in some competent knowledge
of the numbers of the people" (qtd. in Hoppit 525).[15] For Davenant and his
colleagues, "political arithmetic" referred to "the art of reasoning by figures,
upon things relating to government," that is, accounting by and for the state
(qtd. in Hoppit 517). Unsurprisingly, the record-keeping technologies and
mathematical models used to estimate this growth were derived from the
trade in enslaved laborers and the fruits of unfree labor (Rosenthal).

In the eighteenth century, discourses of ancient and modern demographics
directly influenced the ways in which past, living, and future populations
were used for political calculations (Farrell 212). Scottish minister Robert
Wallace's influential *A Dissertation on the Numbers of Mankind in Antient and
Modern Times* (1753) continued to argue for the "superior populousness of
Antiquity," but philosophers such as David Hume and Montesquieu blamed
bad governance for the paucity of past populations, bolstering contemporary
calls for reform. In *Histoire Naturelle* (1749–89), the Comte de Buffon argued
that differences in climate caused birth rates to rise or decline; Thomas Jefferson famously included a discussion of American populations in his *Notes on*

the State of Virginia (1787) in response (Farrell 201, 212). Thomas Malthus's *Essay on the Principle of Population* (1798), in which he suggested arresting population growth for social benefit, triggered even more attention to what was increasingly being called "statistics"—from the German *Statistik*, for its connection to the state—as an intrinsic component of population analysis.[16]

As the United States developed a decennial census to appropriate government representation and estimate tax liability, American scholars were also taking up the problem of estimating past populations for which there were no census records.[17] Benjamin Franklin, in his 1751 essay "Observations Concerning the Increase of Mankind," had projected colonial population growth from Philadelphia's Bills of Mortality (Houston 109). Using a similar formula in the 1780s, Yale College president Ezra Stiles had predicted a U.S. population of 200 million by 2020 (Stiles 36). While forecasts such as Franklin's and Stiles's extrapolated *future* numbers, abstracting historical information about migration, settlement, or climate patterns also helped propose hypothetical sizes and chronologies for humans of the *past*.

In the eighteenth and nineteenth centuries, establishing how many people had once lived in a place was believed to be a reliable predictor of how many people the continent could be expected to sustain. Franklin believed that the size of population was regulated by its means of subsistence, or its "carrying capacity," and because large populations required vast amounts of food, he assumed that agriculture—rather than hunting—was the best way to support numerous people (Aldridge 37). Small populations, per Franklin, resulted from insufficient provisions and, relatedly, an insufficient land base from which to provide them. Agriculture had the benefit of requiring less land than hunting and thus he believed that convincing Native peoples to practice European-style agriculture was necessary to "free up" more land for the projected British American population. "The hunter, of all men, requires the greatest quantity of land from whence to draw his subsistence," Franklin wrote in 1751 (224). Enumerating past and present Native "hunters," therefore, was a way of estimating the potential acreage available for future white "husbandm[e]n," "gardener[s]," and "manufacturer[s]" (224).

As treaties proliferated and agents were called to oversee annuities and the factory system in the early nineteenth century, they were also expected to collect information about the size and history of resident populations (Prucha 89–178). Indeed, attention to Indigenous origins thus increasingly focused on issues of sustenance, birth rates, and warrior counts in order to approximate not only the current population size but also its size before the European invasion. The crucial issue was not only documenting, and lauding, the growth of the United States but also in keeping track—through a coordinated system of

Indian agents—of its Indigenous neighbors, many of whom were perceived as threats to the new nation. In 1820, for example, Michigan territorial governor Lewis Cass published pamphlets meant to assist Indian agents with "collecting materials to illustrate the past and present condition of the Indians" (*Inquiries* 2). Among the questions distributed to traders and Indian agents in Ohio, Indiana, and Michigan Territory, Cass asked about the diplomatic processes of war and peace, about birth, marriage, and divorce rates, and about funeral rites and customary celebrations (*Inquiries* 5–10). He wanted to know the count of men, women, and children as well as villages, and whether these numbers were "increasing or decreasing" (*Inquiries* 31). Thus, inquiries into human origins were connected not only to the contemporary destabilization of Judeo-Christian cosmology in the wake of colonialism—as is usually explained—but also to the concurrent development of technological and administrative tools to quantify and control Indigenous populations.

Despite its clearly "statistical" focus, Cass's guidelines, which he published as *Inquiries Respecting the History, Traditions, Languages, Manners, Customs, Religion, &c. of the Indians, Living Within the United States* in 1823, began with the category of "traditions": "What is the original Indian name of the tribe . . . ? What is the earliest incident they recollect in their history? Whence did they come? What migration have they made, and when, and why? What memorable events in their history have been transmitted to them?" (3). This connection of demography to origin traditions would have made perfect sense to Cass: as territorial governor, he was interested in documenting migration patterns so as to provide a historical precedent for the displacement of Great Lakes and Ohio Valley Indigenous groups and thereby to ensure the success of Michigan's bid for statehood. If Indigenous groups were shown to be mere occupants—not aboriginal possessors of their homelands—then Cass could consider them lacking valid title to defend, sell, or cede those lands for compensation. The information Cass collected was also sent to Washington, where politicians such as James Monroe and Andrew Jackson were concurrently debating how to justify deporting Native groups to "Indian Territory."

The same year that Cass published his *Inquiries*, 1823, U.S. Supreme Court justice John Marshall delivered the unanimous decision in the now infamous *Johnson v. M'Intosh* case.[18] The suit was over land, and specifically whether Thomas Johnson's heirs—recipients of acreage near the confluence of the Wabash and White Rivers purchased from Piankashaw sellers fifty years before— were able to clarify their title and eject William M'Intosh, who claimed that same land by Congressional patent. Declaring that the Piankashaw had no right to sell or convey—only to occupy—their land, the court found Johnson's original purchase invalid and thereby vacated Native landholding rights across the board. Marshall rested the decision on the Discovery Doctrine, by which the Catholic Church conferred sovereignty to the "discoverers" of new lands as long as they were devoid of, unknown to, or unclaimed by other Christians. The Doctrine of Discovery—still the basis for U.S. land claims, thanks to this case—itself depends on locating Indigenous origins outside full humanity as defined by the fifteenth-century Catholic Church and on conceptualizing Native peoples as temporary, migratory "occupants" (W. Echo-Hawk 55–86).

When President Jackson addressed Congress in 1830 to solicit support for his Indian Removal Act—which gave federal cover to what was already being done in the states and territories—he cited the long history of migration as an argument in favor of removal.

> Doubtless it will be painful to leave the graves of their fathers; but what do they more than our ancestors did or than our children are now doing? To better their condition in an unknown land our forefathers left all that was dear in earthly objects. Our children by thousands yearly leave the land of their birth to seek new homes in distant regions. Does Humanity weep at these painful separations from everything, animate and inanimate, with which the young heart has become entwined? Far from it. . . . And is it supposed that the wandering savage has a stronger attachment to his home than the settled, civilized Christian? Is it more afflicting to him to leave the graves of his fathers than it is to our brothers and children? (ix–x)

Jackson's rhetoric reflects an overwhelming belief that a "wandering savage" had no (or perhaps a less) "stronger attachment to his home" than anyone else then living in America.

An early version of Jackson's melting pot mythology eerily echoed in Barack Obama's 2014 words addressing changes to U.S. immigration policy: "My fellow Americans," he concluded, "we are and always will be a nation of immigrants. We were strangers once, too. And whether our forebears were strangers who crossed the Atlantic, or the Pacific, or the Rio Grande, we are here only because this country welcomed them in" (Obama).[19] From the fifteenth to the twenty-first century, the continued insistence that Native peoples crossed the waters to arrive in "this country" is symptomatic of daily devaluation of Indigenous lives that take place in larger, more visibly harmful examples: underfunded schools, housing, and health services; environmental racism and economic deprivation; crisis-level rates of missing and murdered women, girls, and Two-Spirit people; regular despoliation of sacred lands and violations of treaty rights. This political and discursive history about the current-day debates around Indigenous origins—and Native genomic testing, for that matter—is complex and it is urgent: since the question of Native origins was first asked by outsiders in the late fifteenth century, it has always been about life and land.

Given this context, why did the science writer Rutherford, in his assessment of human origins, mention—but quickly disregard—the threat to Indigenous sovereignty posed by refusing Indigenous origin stories? Because the very industry of tracing human origins upon which the "ancient DNA revolution" was launched—practices such as systematics, historical demography, statistics, geochronology, and archaeology—was constituted through hundreds of years of refusing Indigenous truths and humanity with the implicit purpose of asserting settler sovereignty.

At what point do we locate an origin for Indigenous Americans, those people from a place that was not even denominated as such until the sixteenth century? As bioarchaeologist Arion T. Mayes has explained, "Native Americans by definition did not exist until they were in the Americas" (136). Before colonialism and interactions with outsiders, there would have been no formal reason to articulate an attachment to Turtle Island, nor name a landed group identity, outside explanations that were kin- or custom-based. How does one abstractly describe a homeland—whether Tartary, Beringia, or Myaamionki—when it is part of one's very being, one's flesh an extension of the soil?

For at least five hundred years, despite vast technological changes, the debate has been monologic and repetitive: "This. No that. This. No."[20] Until Indigenous ontologies are taken into serious consideration by non-Natives— not just acknowledged and then dismissed—genomic origins stories will continue to depend on the refusal of Native worlds for the stabilization of the colonial episteme. The ancient DNA revolution affirms old questions based on impersonal abstractions, which in their interpretive priority assert settler superiority over Native life. Ancient American history, however, lives, in *the people*, in their stories, minds, and bodies. And as Little Turtle asked: Are there any proofs to the contrary?

Notes

1. For excellent recent overviews, see *SAA Archaeological Record*, vol. 19, nos. 1–3, Jan., Mar., and May 2019.
2. Oxford University Press, *OED Online*, s.v. "autochthon, n.," accessed Nov. 2020.
3. Although the specific "Tartars" in question had come from Beijing, the word was used loosely for much of Central and East Asia, especially Russian Siberia.

4. For definitions, see the Miami Tribe of Oklahoma's online *myaamiaatawaakani: Myaamia Dictionary*, myaamiadictionary.org.

5. The examples are too numerous to list and as varied as the tribal communities they come from. Anthropologists Erminie Wheeler-Voegelin and Remedios W. Moore provide a systematic accounting from a mid-twentieth-century folkloric approach, emblematic of the interest early anthropologists showed in origin narratives.

6. "They know nothing of their own history," wrote Cass in 1826, and "all those pretended traditions must have been mere fictions, probably invented to satisfy the inquiries of the white man" ("Indians" 59, 70).

7. This is in no way to imply that stories are fictional, merely that stories are constructed and articulated according to particular conventions and needs in a different way than other kinds of communication.

8. See, for example, Devlin; Sample, "Oldest Homo sapiens Bones Ever Found."

9. Researchers in 2017 identified the 540-million-year-old microscopic sea animal *Saccorhytus coronarius*, an early deuterostome, as the "oldest human ancestor" yet uncovered (Ghosh; Han et al.).

10. Although by no means consensus, the count of different *Homo* species (and/or subspecies) often includes *Homo neanderthalensis*, Denisovans, *Homo florensiensis*, *Homo habilis*, *Homo rhodesiensis*, *Homo heidelbergensis*, *Homo erectus*, *Homo naledi*, Red Deer Cave People, etcetera. *Homo luzonensis* earned their name in 2019 (Détroit et. al).

11. Genetic data matching Anzick-1's has been detected in samples from Belize, Chile, and Brazil, and geneticists are increasingly convinced that there was a major, post-LGM split resulting in "ancient human parallel lineages within North America" (Posth et al. 1189–91; Scheib et al.). He was finally reburied, almost fifty years after having been uncovered.

12. It also is believed to quash any further support for the "Solutrean hypothesis," which long proposed European influence for "Clovis complex" tools and therefore Atlantic (rather than Pacific) origins for America's Indigenous populations (Raff and Bolnick).

13. "We close by emphasizing the critical and dynamic role that Beringia played in several steps of our model: it was the homeland of Native Americans, and the initial setting for some of the most important evolutionary processes leading to at least an important part of their present-day biological and cultural diversity" (González-José et al. 175).

14. In an interview with Diné scholar Jennifer Nez Denetdale in 2004, Deloria explained: "What I'm saying is that fragments of knowledge of a far distant past are present in a lot of tribal traditions and the people themselves. . . . There are very intriguing things that tribal people remember, that don't make sense at the present time. But we've got to be willing to say that the earth was much different at another time. It wasn't the way we look at it now. The landscape testifies to that, there is evidence there. The mountains have come up and people have remembered it. The lakes have formed. I'm trying to develop little clusters of things that were probable and to get tribes to say, 'Hey, this relates to this'" (qtd. in Denetdale 135–36).

15. In English usage, "demography" is a nineteenth-century term (*OED Online*, s.v. "demography, n.," accessed Nov. 2020).

16. *OED Online*, s.v. "statistic, adj. and n.," accessed Nov. 2020.

17. Census taking was not accepted by all as an unmitigated good: for example, critics of the 1753 Census Bill in England feared becoming "the numbered vassals of indiscriminating power" (Buck 33). In the United States—which began its decennial census in 1790—"Indians" were not counted consistently until 1890. Although this would seem to contradict an argument in which census technologies were tied to settler colonial surveillance, it is not to imply that "Indians" were not counted, merely that they were not counted as part of the U.S. body politic until after the massive violence and policy changes of the 1870s and 1880s.

18. *Johnson v. M'Intosh*, 21 U.S. 543 (1823).

19. "There is an obvious danger in widening the chronological frame to the point that human action becomes structural, abstract and socially meaningless—even as the supposed lesson remains socially meaningful in the *now*. Over a 200,000-year-story—or even 50,000 years—we *could* in fact all be immigrants together; over a 500-year story, not so much. It is important not to confuse the two" (Deloria in this volume).

20. From Heid Erdrich's poem "Mitochondrial Eve," the lines of which serve as the chapter's epigraph.

References

Aldridge, Alfred Owen. "Franklin as Demographer." *Journal of Economic History*, vol. 9, no. 1, 1949, pp. 25–44.

Allentoft, Morton E., et al. "Population Genomics of Bronze Age Eurasia." *Nature*, vol. 522, no. 7555, 2015, pp. 167–72.

Bauman, Zygmunt. *Wasted Lives: Modernity and Its Outcasts*. Wiley, 2003.

Bortolini, Maria Cátira, et al. "Reconciling Pre-Columbian Settlement Hypotheses Requires Integrative, Multidisciplinary, and Model-Bound Approaches." *PNAS*, vol. 111, 2014, pp. E213–E214.

Braje, Todd, et al. "Finding the First Americans." *Science*, vol. 358, no. 6363, 2017, pp. 592–94.

Buck, Peter. "People Who Counted: Political Arithmetic in the Eighteenth Century." *Isis*, vol. 73, no. 1, 1982, pp. 28–45.

Buffon, Georges-Louis Leclerc. *L'Histoire naturelle, générale et particulière, avec la description du Cabinet du Roi*. Paris, 1749–1804. 36 vols.

Cajete, Gregory. *Native Science: Natural Laws of Independence*. Clear Light, 2000.

Callaway, Ewen. "Ancient Genomics Is Recasting the Story of the Americas' First Residents." *Nature*, vol. 563, no. 7731, 2018, pp. 303–4.

Cass, Lewis. "Indians of North America." *North American Review*, vol. 22, Jan. 1826, pp. 53–119.

Cass, Lewis. *Inquiries, Respecting the History, Traditions, Languages, Manners, Customs, Religion, &c. of the Indians, Living Within the United States*. Detroit, 1823.

Cruikshank, Julie. "Are Glaciers 'Good to Think With'? Recognising Indigenous Environmental Knowledge." *Anthropological Forum*, vol. 22, no. 3, 2012, pp. 239–50.

Curry, Andrew. "The First Europeans Weren't Who You Might Think." *National Geographic*, Aug. 2019.

Davenant, Charles. *Discourses on the Public Revenues, and on Trade*. London, 1698.

Deloria, Vine, Jr. "Indians, Archaeologists, and the Future." *American Antiquity*, vol. 57, no. 4, Oct. 1992, pp. 595–98.

Deloria, Vine, Jr. *Red Earth, White Lies: Native Americans and the Myth of Scientific Fact*. Scribner, 1995.

Denetdale, Jennifer Nez. "'Planting Seeds of Ideas and Raising Doubts About What We Believe': An Interview with Vine Deloria, Jr." *Journal of Social Archaeology*, vol. 42, no. 2, 2004, pp. 131–46.

Détroit, F., et al. "A New Species of *Homo* from the Late Pleistocene of the Philippines." *Nature*, vol. 568, no. 7751, 2019, pp. 181–86.

Devlin, Hannah. "Skull of Humankind's Oldest-Known Ancestor Discovered." *The Guardian*, 28 Aug. 2019.

Dillehay, Tom D., et al. "New Archaeological Evidence for an Early Human Presence at Monte Verde, Chile." *PLoS ONE*, vol. 10, no. 11, 2015.

Echo-Hawk, Roger C. "Ancient History in the New World: Integrating Oral Traditions and the Archaeological Record in Deep Time." *American Antiquity*, vol. 65, no. 2, 2000, pp. 267–90.

Echo-Hawk, Walter. *In the Courts of the Conqueror: The 10 Worst Indian Law Cases Ever Decided*. Fulcrum, 2012.

Erdrich, Heid. "Mitochondrial Eve." *Cell Traffic: New and Selected Poems*. University of Arizona Press, 2012, p. 8.

Farrell, Molly. *Counting Bodies: Population in Colonial American Writing*. Oxford University Press, 2016.

Franklin, Benjamin. "Observations Concerning the Increase of Mankind." 1755. *The Complete Works of Benjamin Franklin*, vol. 2, edited by John Bigelow, New York, 1887, pp. 223–34.

Froese, Duane, et al. "Timing of Bison Arrival in North America." *Proceedings of the National Academy of Sciences*, vol. 114, no. 13, Mar. 2017, pp. 3457–62.

Ghosh, Pallab. "Scientists Find 'Oldest Human Ancestor.'" *BBC News*, 30 Jan. 2017, bbc .com/news/science-environment-38800987.

Goebel, Ted, and Kelly E. Graf. "Beringian Archaeology and Ancient Genomics: A New Synthesis." *SAA Archaeological Record*, vol. 19, no. 3, May 2019, pp. 21–26.

González-José, Rolando, et al. "The Peopling of America: Craniofacial Shape Variation on a Continental Scale and Its Interpretation from an Interdisciplinary View." *American Journal of Physical Anthropology*, vol. 137, no. 2, 2008, pp. 175–87.

Graunt, John. *Natural and Political Observations Mentioned in a Following Index, and Made upon the Bills of Mortality*. London, 1662.

Han, Jian, et al. "Meiofaunal Deuterostomes from the Basal Cambrian of Shaanxi (China)." *Nature*, vol. 542, 2017, pp. 228–31.

Hoffecker, J. F., et al. "Beringia and the Global Dispersal of Modern Humans." *Evolutionary Anthropology*, vol. 25, no. 2, Mar./Apr. 2016, pp. 64–78.

Hofman, Courtney A., and Christina Warinner. "Ancient DNA 101: An Introductory Guide in the Era of High-Throughput Sequencing." *SAA Archaeological Record*, vol. 19, no. 1, Jan. 2019, pp. 18–25.

Hoppit, Julian. "Political Arithmetic in Eighteenth-Century England." *Economic History Review*, vol. 49, no. 3, 1996, pp. 516–40.

Houston, Alan Craig. *Benjamin Franklin and the Politics of Improvement*. Yale University Press, 2008.

Ironstrack, George. "Myaamionki Nakamooni ('Miami Land Song')." 2014. Reprinted in Mary Annette Pember, "How a University and a Tribe Are Teaming Up to Revive a Lost Language," *Yes!*, 9 May 2018, yesmagazine.org/peace-justice/how-a-university -and-a-tribe-began-mending-ties-and-revived-a-lost-language-20180509.

Jackson, Andrew. "Message of the President of the United States, to Both Houses of Congress. At the Commencement of the Second Session of the Twenty-first Congress. December 7, 1830." *Register of Debates, 21st Congress, 2nd Session*, Washington, D.C., 1831, pp. xi–x.

Jefferson, Thomas. *Notes on the State of Virginia*. London, 1787.

Lazaridis, Iosif, et al. "Ancient Human Genomes Suggest Three Ancestral Populations for Present-Day Europeans." *Nature*, vol. 513, no. 7518, 2014, pp. 409–13.

Linnaeus, Carl. *Systema Naturae*, vol. 1, 10th ed., Stockholm, 1758.

Llamas, B., et al. "Ancient Mitochondrial DNA Provides High-Resolution Time Scale of the Peopling of the Americas." *Science Advances*, vol. 2, no. 4, 2016.

Malthus, Thomas Robert. *An Essay on the Principle of Population*. London, 1798.

Mayes, Arion T. "These Bones Are Read: The Science and Politics of Ancient Native America." *American Indian Quarterly*, vol. 34, no. 2, 2010, pp. 131–56.

Moreno-Mayar, J. Víctor, et al. "Early Human Dispersals Within the Americas." *Science*, vol. 362, no. 6419, 2018, eaav2621.

Moreno-Mayar, J. Víctor, et al. "Terminal Pleistocene Alaskan Genome Reveals First Founding Population of Native Americans." *Nature*, vol. 553, no. 7687, 11 Jan. 2018, pp. 203–7.

Nelson, Diane M. *Who Counts: The Mathematics of Death and Life After Genocide*. Duke University Press, 2015.

Obama, Barack. "Remarks by the President in Address to the Nation on Immigration." 20 Nov. 2014. obamawhitehouse.archives.gov/the-press-office/2014/11/20/remarks -president-address-nation-immigration.

O'Rourke, Dennis H., and Jennifer Raff. "The Human Genetic History of the Americas: The Final Frontier." *Current Biology*, vol. 20, no. 4, pp. R202–R207.

Petty, William. *Political Arithmetick*. London, 1690.

Pinotti, Thomas, et al. "Y Chromosome Sequences Reveal a Short Beringian Standstill, Rapid Expansion, and Early Population Structure of Native American Founders." *Current Biology*, vol. 29, no. 1, Jan. 2019, pp. 149–57.

Posth, Cosimo, et al. "Reconstructing the Deep Population History of Central and South America." *Cell*, vol. 175, no. 5, 2018, pp. 1185–97.

Prucha, Francis Paul. *The Great Father: The United States Government and the American Indians*. University of Nebraska Press, 1984.

Raff, Jennifer. "What the Ancient DNA Discovery Tells Us About Native American Ancestry." *The Guardian*, 3 Jan. 2018.

Raff, Jennifer, and Deborah Bolnick. "Genetic Roots of the First Americans." *Nature*, vol. 506, no. 7487, 2014, pp. 162–63.

Raghavan, Maanasa, et al. "Genomic Evidence for the Pleistocene and Recent Population History of Native Americans." *Science*, vol. 349, no. 6250, 2015, aab3884.

Raghavan, Maanasa, et al. "Upper Palaeolithic Siberian Genome Reveals Dual Ancestry of Native Americans." *Nature*, vol. 505, no. 7481, 2 Jan. 2014, pp. 87–91.

Rasmussen, Morten, et al. "The Genome of a Late Pleistocene Human from a Clovis Burial Site in Western Montana." *Nature*, vol. 506, no. 7487, 13 Feb. 2014, pp. 225–29.

Reich, David. *Who We Are and How We Got Here: Ancient DNA and the New Science of the Human Past*. Oxford University Press, 2017.

Reich, David, et al. "Reconstructing Native American Population History." *Nature*, vol. 488, no. 7411, 2012, pp. 370–74.

Rosenthal, Caitlin. *Accounting for Slavery*. Harvard University Press, 2016.

Rutherford, Adam. *A Brief History of Everyone Who Ever Lived: The Stories in Our Genes*. Orion, 2016.

Sample, Ian. "Oldest Homo sapiens Bones Ever Found Shake Foundation of the Human Story." *The Guardian*, 7 June 2017.

Sample, Ian. "Piece of Skull Found in Greece 'Is Oldest Human Fossil Outside Africa.'" *The Guardian*, 10 July 2019.

Scheib, C. L., et al. "Ancient Human Parallel Lineages Within North America Contributed to a Coastal Expansion." *Science*, vol. 360, no. 6392, 2018, pp. 1024–27.

Skoglund, Pontus, and David Reich. "A Genomic View of the Peopling of the Americas." *Current Opinions in Genetic Development*, vol. 41, Dec. 2016, pp. 27–35.

Sutterfield, Joshua A. "aciipihkahki: iši kati mihtohseeniwiyankwi myaamionki / Roots of Place: Experiencing a Miami Landscape." MA thesis, Miami University, 2009.

Stiles, Ezra. *The United States Elevated to Glory and Honor*. New Haven, Conn., 1783.

TallBear, Kim. *Native American DNA: Tribal Belonging and the False Promise of Genetic Science*. University of Minnesota Press, 2013.

Vachula, Richard S., et al. "Evidence of Ice Age Humans in Eastern Beringia Suggests Early Migration to North America." *Quaternary Science Reviews*, vol. 205, Feb. 2019, pp. 35–44.

Volney, C[onstantin]-F[rançois de Chassebœuf, comte de]. *View of the Climate and Soil of the United States of America*. Philadelphia, 1804.

Wallace, Robert. *A Dissertation on the Numbers of Mankind in Antient and Modern Times*. Edinburgh, 1753.

Waters, Michael R. "Early Exploration and Settlement of North America During the Late Pleistocene." *SAA Archaeological Record*, vol. 19, no. 3, May 2019, pp. 34–39.

Watts, Vanessa. "Indigenous Place-Thought and Agency Among Humans and Non-Humans (First Woman and Sky Woman Go on a European World Tour!)." *Decolonization: Indigeneity, Education & Society*, vol. 2, no. 1, 2013, pp. 20–34.

Wheeler-Voegelin, Erminie, and Remedios W. Moore. "The Emergence Myth in Native
    North America." *Studies in Folklore*, vol. 9, 1957, pp. 66–91.
Williams, J. Thomas, and David B. Madsen. "The Upper Paleolithic of the Americas."
    PaleoAmerica: A Journal of Early Human Migration and Dispersal, vol. 6, no. 1, 2020,
    pp. 4–22.

3

Pym, *Mammoth Cave, and (Pre)histories of the U.S. Interior*

Melissa Gniadek

TOWARD THE BEGINNING OF MAT Johnson's *Pym: A Novel* (2011), Chris Jaynes finds himself at a meeting of the "Native American Ancestry Collective of Gary" (NAACG for short). This group of residents of Gary, Indiana, "looked like any gathering of black American folks" except for the fact that most of them were "outfitted in some form of indigenous attire" (Johnson 53). As it turns out, Jaynes's host Mahalia Mathis has brought him to a particularly special meeting: the group members are about to receive their DNA test results. A professor from the University of Chicago arrives, and before distributing individual results, he reveals that on average the members of the group have about "six percent Native blood among you, which is about the average for African Americans on the East Coast" (Johnson 55). While one woman has "thirty-two percent Indian," most of the DNA results tell other, unexpected stories (Johnson 56). Mathis, for example, is revealed to be "two percent Native. Twenty-three percent European. Seventy-five percent African," results that leave her lying unconscious on the linoleum floor of the Miller Beach Senior Center (Johnson 56). Here, Johnson provides a send-up of claims to indigeneity that have both cultural and financial motivations: "I'm going to send my baby to college on this evidence, just you watch," proclaims one group member in advance of the genetic reveal (Johnson 54). And Johnson critiques a simultaneous denial of African American ancestry.[1]

Johnson's satire of U.S. race and identity politics arrives at this scene not through a plotline driven by genetic testing companies and the corporatization of biological data but through the nineteenth-century text invoked in his novel's title: *The Narrative of Arthur Gordon Pym of Nantucket* (1838) by Edgar Allan Poe.[2] Jaynes has traveled to Indiana to meet Mathis after a late-night Googling session reveals her to be a descendent of Dirk Peters, the "hybrid" companion of Poe's fictional Pym. Jaynes, a Black professor of African American literature at a small liberal arts college, was denied tenure in part because he had failed to "purvey the minority perspective" that he had been hired to provide, instead teaching courses on "the intellectual source of racial Whiteness," which he locates in work like Poe's (Johnson 13, 8).[3] When fate brings Jaynes a manuscript written by Peters, his frustration over his career is channeled into a quest to discover the truth behind Poe's novel, a quest that leads him to assemble an all-Black crew to journey toward Antarctica in search of the infamous island of Black inhabitants that appears at the end of Poe's text (Johnson 38). Instead, he finds a community of white creatures who have the corpse-like, two-hundred-year-old Pym living among them. The narrative device of the occasionally catatonic, half-frozen Pym with his nineteenth-century notions about race allows for the explorers—and the readers—to reflect on racism in the present. But before this Antarctic journey, Jaynes visits the fateful NAACG meeting that prompts Mathis to later mail him a package containing Peters's skeleton, entrusting Jaynes with the task of finding someone "who can run that DNA test right" (Johnson 82, 83).

I begin with the Native American Ancestry Collective of Gary and the "box of bones" (Johnson 83) containing Peters's remains to highlight how questions of identity linked to ideas about deep pasts through geology and archaeology in Poe's 1838 novel travel through time and through a series of other fantastic texts. Poe's novel itself drew on numerous early nineteenth-century texts and theories, ranging from travel narratives to John Cleves Symmes Jr.'s hollow-Earth theory. Later authors, including Jules Verne, H. P. Lovecraft, and, most recently, Johnson, wrote texts inspired by Poe's *Pym*, taking up the invitation offered by its mysterious ending.[4] In this chapter, I turn not to the fantastic other worlds of Verne and Lovecraft but to the fantastic world of the U.S. interior, suggesting that a pamphlet about Kentucky's Mammoth Cave published in 1839, a year after Poe's *Pym*, provides an opportunity to reread *The Narrative of Arthur Gordon Pym* for its place in nineteenth-century conversations about deep time, race, and identity, conversations resurrected along with Peters's fictional remains and ideas about DNA testing in Johnson's 2011 novel. Situating the pamphlet "Wonderful Discovery! Being an Account of a Recent Exploration of the Celebrated Mammoth Cave" within the literary lineage that leads from Poe's 1838 novel to Johnson's recent reimagining highlights how Poe's text, though set in a fanciful, global space, engages questions of belonging, legibility, and succession in U.S. space, questions with tremendous currency in Poe's time as in our own. It reminds us that Poe's maritime novel reaches deep into America's terrestrial interiors in ways that highlight histories of race, indigeneity, and settler colonialism in U.S. literature.

∴

The story of a young man who goes to sea in pursuit of adventure, Poe's *Pym* has been read as an exploration of the limits of language and representation as well as an allegory of antebellum U.S. race relations.[5] Somewhat more recently, the novel has been read as a commentary on the production of colonial knowledge. Readings that fall into this final category make clear that *Pym*'s depiction of sea travel and exploration is not incidental to the themes of textual instability and the difficulty of knowing raised in its enigmatic scenes and fragmented form. In other words, the novel's themes of exploration and discovery ground the epistemological questions that it raises about language and representation in the experience of exploration, in the colonization of peoples and places, and in the histories built upon such endeavors, highlighting the violent and persistent uncertainty of colonial meaning making.[6] And though the novel engages histories of exploration and knowledge production in distant regions like the Pacific, its concerns are also linked to the histories of the continental United States, as evidenced by Pym reading Lewis and Clark's journals while trapped in the hold of the *Grampus*.

While the entire text engages the ideologies of colonial expansion and meaning making in cross-cultural encounters, these issues are condensed toward the end of the novel when the narrative reaches the island of Tsalal. This is, perhaps, because land rather than the sea provides a clear, familiar setting for colonial exploitation, depicted here largely through Pym's attitude toward the Tsalalians, who simultaneously suggest Pacific Islanders, Indigenous North Americans, and African peoples.[7] Pym finds himself in a land portrayed as explicitly foreign, with Black Tsalalians who are afraid of anything white, bizarre animals, and water that is "*not* colourless" nor "of any one uniform colour," all of which seems to point to the questions of racial difference that pervade this portion of the novel (Poe 171, 172). Making spatial the "denial of coevalness" that Johannes Fabian identifies as structuring Western encounters with the "Other," Pym frames each step further into the island as one away from any country "hitherto visited by civilized men" (Poe 171).[8] Every step is portrayed as one back in time. Pym reads the islanders as naïve savages, their land and resources easily secured by white men, easily brought into the "present" of a global economy. But he makes these assumptions erroneously.

Indeed, the perceived temporal distinction between the "civilized" mariners and the "savage" islanders is soon disrupted in one of the novel's most dramatic moments: the Tsalalians orchestrate a landslide that kills everyone who came ashore with Pym and Peters. This incident quite literally exposes and jumbles the colonial time-space within which Pym moves as well as the falsity of his assumptions about the utter otherness of the Tsalalians, who demonstrate more strategic wit than the Euro-American visitors had assumed. As the rock walls collapse due to Tsalalian ingenuity, so too do Euro-American colonial master narratives. Perceived distinctions between a "savage" past represented by the Tsalalians and a "civilized" global present crumble as the Tsalalians take control by setting a trap into which their visitors unwittingly walk.

Following the landslide, Pym scrambles to regain narrative control of his situation, immediately declaring that he and Peters are now "the only living white men upon the island," uniting the pair in opposition to the Tsalalians (Poe 185). When he is first introduced, Peters, "the son of an Indian squaw of the tribe of Upsarokas" and a "fur-trader" (Poe 87), is racialized in ways that suggest nineteenth-century stereotypes of blackness.[9] He is himself an "other," associated with both indigeneity and blackness. But this depiction shifts over the course of the novel until, following the landslide, Pym claims Peters as a fellow white man. Racial identity is here presented as relative; the novel's semantic sliding reveals the arbitrariness of racial classifications.

Pym's efforts to regain narrative control extend to the chasms that the two find themselves trapped in. Pym works to give order to his experience of cave exploration by measuring it with the precision of a geological study.

> Upon first descending into the chasm, that is to say, for a hundred feet downward from the summit of the hill, the sides of the abyss bore little resemblance to each other, and, apparently, had at no time been connected, the one surface being of the soapstone and the other of marl, granulated with some metallic matter. . . . Upon arriving within fifty feet of the bottom, a perfect regularity commenced. The sides were now entirely uniform in substance, in colour, and in lateral direction, the material being a very black and shining granite, and the distance between the two sides, at all points facing each other, exactly twenty yards. (Poe 193)

Pym seeks to rationalize his experience in the chasms as he diagrams, measures, and records, even as he and Peters quite literally move through a physical gap in time as they walk through the different geologic layers observed within the walls of the chasms. A series of figures giving the "general outlines" of the chasms appear in the text (Poe 194) (see figure 3.1).

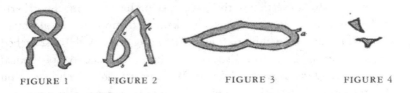

FIGURE 1   FIGURE 2   FIGURE 3   FIGURE 4

FIGURE 3.1. Pym's depictions of Tsalal's chasms.

These figures link Pym's efforts to map the chasms—his attempts to regain a sense of spatial and temporal control following the Tsalalian's actions—to other contemporary efforts to chart and understand geologic formations and the temporalities contained within them. Ideas about the times held within rock formations evoked through Pym's geologic descriptions would have been increasingly familiar to nineteenth-century readers. The association of geological features with a sense of deep time dates back at least to Nicolaus Steno's seventeenth-century realization that each layer of rock embodies a span of time in the past. This discovery revolutionized thinking about geologic timescales in a way that was just beginning to have widespread influence in the early nineteenth century through figures such as Charles Lyell, whose *Principles of Geology* (1830–33) institutionalized the discipline of geology.[10] Geology, as Virginia Zimmerman puts it, "burdened the nineteenth century with a sense of time that exceeded the limits of plot" (1). Biblical chronology was increasingly challenged as rocks and fossils told other stories with timeframes that reoriented ideas about the Earth's history.

New encounters with the Earth's pasts also brought about engagement with evidence of human pasts found within the landscape.[11] Such ideas enter Poe's novel when Pym and Peters find "indentures" on the wall of one of the chasms (see figure 3.2).

FIGURE 3.2. Pym's depiction of the chasm's "indentures."

With a very slight exertion of the imagination, the left, or most northerly of these indentures might have been taken for the intentional, although rude, representation of a human figure standing erect, with outstretched arm. The rest of them bore also some little resemblance to alphabetical characters, and Peters was willing, at all events, to adopt the idle opinion that they were really such. I convinced him of his error, finally, by directing his attention to the floor of the fissure, where, among the powder, we picked up, piece by piece, several large flakes of the marl, which had evidently been broken off by some convulsion from the surface where the indentures were found, and which had projecting points exactly fitting the indentures; thus proving them to have been the work of nature. (Poe 195)

Through this brief debate about whether the indentures on the chasm walls are "the work of nature" or "alphabetical characters" with representational meaning, Pym further demonstrates his need to assert control; his refusal to grant Tsalal the possibility of a human past or present with a written language signifies his refusal to reexamine his assumptions about the Tsalalians, even in the face of physical evidence. Embedded within the chasms, as the chasms are embedded within the landscape, the characters that may or may not be inscribed on the rock walls register the challenges of reading the pasts of place in relation to that place's inhabitants—pasts that might disrupt Pym's sense of self-possession. Yet Peters, himself a "hybrid," an embodiment of spatial histories that challenge Pym's Euro-American viewpoint, is willing to see other human histories inscribed within the land (Poe 93, 87).

Though the novel's "indentures" are sometimes linked to early nineteenth-century interest in Egyptology and Egyptian hieroglyphics, questions about evidence of human pasts had particular import in the New World context and in the U.S. context specifically as fascination with Indigenous "antiquities" in the late eighteenth and early nineteenth centuries became linked to efforts to forge a national identity.[12] From Thomas Jefferson's description of excavating a "barrow" in *Notes on the State of Virginia* (1787) through the founding of institutions such as the American Antiquarian Society (1812) and the Smithsonian Institution (1846), discovering, collecting, and cataloging evidence of the past occupation of North America became part of presenting the United States as culturally coeval with the major nations of Europe. Yet the colonial situation also required a narrative that denied a link between "prehistorical" Indigenous peoples and the present population. This was the case with myths about the Mound Builders, thought to have been a long-extinct civilization unrelated to contemporary Indigenous peoples: the remnants of pre-Columbian cities defined by large earthen mounds found throughout the Mississippi valley, such as Cahokia in present-day Illinois, were easier to explain as monuments of a displaced, bygone civilization. The mounds were clearly not "the work of nature," as Pym insists the chasms' indentures to be (Poe 195). But for Euro-American settlers to acknowledge them as the work of Indigenous peoples would have presented an obstacle to contemporary settler claims of belonging. Nonetheless, whether by studying or dismantling them to make space for fields and pastures, the mounds would be incorporated into the U.S. national narrative.[13]

Though he insists that the indentures in Tsalal's chasm walls are a natural phenomenon, Pym, like North America's settlers, is disorientated by the challenge they present to the narrative he needs to believe about the island and its past—a narrative in which security is obtained through his self-identification as "civilized" and as able to render the indentures harmless by capturing them in his notebook. Not long after this scene, Pym panics while climbing down the face of a precipice in a final attempt to escape the chasms, seemingly overwhelmed by the encounter with the indentures and the challenge they represent. Peters, whom Pym has labeled the only other white man on the island, catches him. The novel here obliquely links discourses of racial identity to emerging fields of study concerned with deep pasts, as contemporary geological and archaeological discoveries prompted Euro-American settlers to craft narratives that would curtail the cultural vertigo occasioned by encounters with those distant pasts, often by appropriating or denying the pasts of others.

Early archaeological encounters with the U.S. landscape have frequently been discussed in relation to the mounds and barrows mentioned here, and these were certainly primary sites of encounter with the human pasts of the continent. But as *The Narrative of Arthur Gordon Pym* suggests, the inverse topography of caves, caverns, and subterranean spaces could also bring about encounters with physical evidence of deep human spatial pasts. These too were sites where encounters with the past shaped ideas about relationships and identities in the present. This was certainly the case with Mammoth Cave.

∴

Today, Kentucky's Mammoth Cave is the largest known cave system in the world. About 350 miles of passageways have been explored. Hundreds more may exist. Now a national park as well as a UNESCO World Heritage Site and an International Biosphere Reserve, the cave is one of the oldest tourist attractions in North America; guided tours have been offered since at least 1816. Euro-American settlers knew about Mammoth Cave for years before it became a tourist attraction, however. The cave was one of many in central

Kentucky mined for saltpeter (an ingredient in gunpowder) during the eighteenth and early nineteenth centuries. If you take a historical tour of the cave
today, you are likely to be told that saltpeter mining in Mammoth Cave—
mining accomplished through enslaved labor—intensified during the War
of 1812 as foreign supplies of gunpowder were cut off.[14] According to oral
tradition, the cave was part of changing dynamics on the surface of the land,
providing a resource that fueled Euro-American settlement and shaped the
young nation. The histories of Mammoth Cave and the texts that circulated
about it help us understand *Pym*'s subterranean topographies not only as contemporary settings for adventure and geological discovery but also as sites
that exemplify how the settler colonial imaginaries that govern engagement
with U.S. interiors deal in deep times.

Mammoth Cave became better known outside Kentucky in 1816 when
Nahum Ward of Massachusetts published a three-installment description of
the cave in Worcester's *Massachusetts Spy*. The *Spy* was started by Isaiah Thomas,
who had founded the American Antiquarian Society in 1812; the publication of Ward's article linked exploration of Mammoth Cave to Thomas and
his project of preserving America's antiquities. Ward's article was reprinted
throughout the United States and later appeared in newspapers in England as
well. It describes his 1815 trip into the cave and general observations about his
surroundings in terms not unlike those of Poe's later fictional descriptions of
chasm exploration: "The walls of the cavern are perpendicular in every passage
that I traversed. The arches are regular in every part, and have bid defiance
even to earthquakes," Ward writes (8 May 1816, p. 3). He gives approximate
measurements for various passages and chambers and notes that he sketched a
plan of the cave. He also acknowledges that he was accompanied by guides but
does not specify that they were undoubtedly the enslaved African American
men who were the real experts on the cave. The article ends as Ward finds the
"mummy" that he already knew to be in the cave. These human remains had
been discovered years earlier in another nearby cave and placed in Mammoth
Cave "for preservation" (Ward, 29 May 1816, p. 4). One of the owners of
the cave gave Ward the mummy, which he carried first to Ohio and then to
Massachusetts, where the remains were exhibited and eventually, after some
controversy, given to the American Antiquarian Society. In 1876 the remains
were transferred to the Smithsonian Institution, where they are still held.[15]
In later years, much more would be learned about millennia-long histories
of Indigenous exploration of and use of Mammoth Cave and other nearby
subterranean spaces.[16] In the early nineteenth century, however, finds like the
"mummy" fueled a popular cultural imaginary that saw the cave as a sublime
space containing pasts that might be reframed and exhibited in the present.

Following the publicity brought by Ward's article and the "mummy," as well as improvements in travel that made getting to Mammoth Cave slightly easier, tourism increased. But travel was still arduous, and publications such as the 1839 pamphlet "Wonderful Discovery! Being an Account of a Recent Exploration of the Celebrated Mammoth Cave," published in New York, brought attention to a site that most Americans would never visit in person, one that combined contemporary interest in geographic and geological discoveries with interest in antiquities and the distant pasts of the American continent.

Framed as a letter to an unnamed "professor in one of the eastern colleges" from "Montgomery E. Letcher, Esq.," "Wonderful Discovery!" quickly shifts into the form of a journal, purporting to be a copy of Letcher's daily record of an expedition into Mammoth Cave. This detail conjures Poe's novel, published the year before, which also slips in and out of the journal format. Letcher's letter begins with mention not of Poe or *Pym*, however, but of John Cleve Symmes Jr., whose hollow-Earth theory also influenced Poe. In 1818 Symmes declared that the Earth was hollow and that openings at each pole allowed access to the interior. He advertised his idea in a newspaper circular.[17] An 1820 novel, *Symzonia*, published under the pseudonym "Captain Adam Seaborn" and sometimes incorrectly attributed to Symmes, harnessed Symmes's theory as it described an expedition to an inner world. "Wonderful Discovery!" draws on both Symmes's theory and *Symzonia*, as Letcher's introductory letter proclaims: "The earth is hollow and inhabited, and the world must now rank him [Symmes] with Columbus and Galileo" (3). The narrative goes on to describe the expedition into Mammoth Cave, which consisted of Letcher, a Dr. Rowan, Professor Simmons, and "eight able bodied negroes" from Letcher's plantation to carry provisions and tools (4).

The basic plot of "Wonderful Discovery!" follows that of *Symzonia* as it describes a trip to an internal world populated by people who speak a foreign language, who have unfamiliar customs (including flying on large birds in "Wonderful Discovery!" and flying in ships in *Symzonia*), and who, in the case of "Wonderful Discovery!," are explicitly white. Unlike *Symzonia*, however, which pays a great deal of attention to the culture of the "Internals" and their governmental structures as a way to critique the external world, the main thrust of "Wonderful Discovery!" is not the portrayal of a utopian civilization used to critique the United States. Instead it describes the process of settlement inside the Earth in ways that replicate ideas about settlement often imposed on external spaces. In the process, "Wonderful Discovery!" engages with the recently published *Pym*. For example, descriptions of the trip into the cave echo aspects of Poe's chasms. In describing an early portion of the journey, Letcher writes:

The descent was slight but perceptible, a fine hard earthen bottom, for the first mile we penetrated, save here and there a few scattered lime stones, that in the course of time had fallen from the roof, the heighth [sic] of the passage averaged about twenty feet, but the width varied greatly; sometimes six feet, then it would extend to nearly fifty, here a rock would jut out in a most fantastic form, resembling a wild human figure, or perhaps some non-descript monster. (6)

Indeed, like Poe's *Pym*, "Wonderful Discovery!," fanciful as it is, contains scientific-sounding geologic descriptions that reflect awareness of the Earth's deep history. "The rock within this space was a kind of porphyritic stone mixed with granite and a species of ore resembling iron, and the whole had evidently been acted upon by fire as it presented that moltern [sic] appearance peculiar to metallic substances, cooled in a half dissolved state," Letcher writes at one point (10). "The archway above us was filled with numerous fissures, and it seemed as if at some former period internal fire had cracked and split open the whole passage," his reading of the Earth continues (11). His delight in making sense of the geological structures is supplemented by observations about animal and human pasts.

We found numerous bones of some enormous animal, together with tusks, resembling those of the mammoth in the museum at Philadelphia. . . . The bones were very numerous, and from the height of the entrance, the animals when living never could have entered. It was evident therefore that they had been placed here by the hands of man. . . . Not a great distance further, one of the negroes struck something with his foot which sounded like metal, and on picking it up we found it be [sic] the iron head of a spear, very much corroded, shaped like those of the ancient Romans. (Letcher 12)

Here, ancient animals are contemporaneous with ancient humans, who are themselves compared, through their remains and their tools, to the familiar ancient civilization of Rome. This all seems part of a distant past, but for Letcher this discovery is "proof . . . that the end of our journey was near" and that they are about to emerge into an interior world populated by living beings who seem out of time yet who are also clearly contemporaneous with the explorers (12).

This fact of contemporaneity is emphasized through the narrative's attention to clock time. Letcher's journal entries record dates, but they often also specify the precise time of events ("half past 10, A. M.," or "at 2, P. M.," etcetera) (5). In this way, his diary keeps track of "external" time in the space of the caves, viewing the strange internal world as coexistent with the outer one. And as the travelers explore the internal world, they also see sights that remind them of the external world: "We passed a herd of wild buffaloes who on our near approach started off at full speed and were soon out of sight, their appearance, and indeed, the whole scene, reminded us of one of our rich western prairies" (Letcher 15). This comparison, like those in many travel and exploration narratives, explains the unfamiliar in terms of the familiar; moreover, buffalo and prairies explicitly link the interior space to aboveground territorial expansion and settlement. Though the external world is described as the "old world" (15) in opposition to the "new" internal one—conjuring the geographic and temporal distinction used to separate Europe from the Americas—there persists a sense that these worlds exist simultaneously and that they are undergoing similar changes. Letcher describes flying over the landscape on one of the ostrichlike birds that the inhabitants of the internal world use for travel. Over the course of this ride, his view moves from fields and meadows to the compact space of a village so that the time of the journey becomes a vision of a linear trajectory of settlement, devoid of its accompanying violence. Fields become villages, and as Letcher lands in those villages, he discovers manufacturers and shops. He sees a mercantile, capitalist world similar to that above ground, an impression made most explicit not in a description of commerce but in Letcher's encounter with a funeral procession. Witnessing the funeral, "I forgot that I was in a different country from my own," Letcher writes, "for in the grave all distinction of country ceases, and I thought only of the dead as a brother" (23). Letcher here claims kinship with peoples at once contemporaneous with and physically remote from the world around the cave in Kentucky that brought the explorers to the internal world. This expression of human brotherhood is conspicuous in an era when amateur archaeologists, from Jefferson to those exploring Mammoth Cave, used the human remains of other cultures as evidence to both give U.S. space a deep history by appropriating those remains into a Western time-space and to distinguish U.S. imperial ambitions from those of other communities, past and present.

Despite the familiar story of physical settlement and the suggestion of communion in death, however, Letcher's account also offers constant reminders of difference that echo details within Poe's *Narrative of Arthur Gordon Pym*. For example, as in *Pym*, descriptions of hieroglyphics seem intended to link the living internal population to a past that reinforces their otherness. And in his description of his ride over the landscape, Letcher mentions a stream reminiscent of *Pym*'s segregated water: "a stream liquid and distinct as a river of molten gold,—meandering in the distance; the effect of a different light sheeted it with silver, and then perhaps in the extreme range of the eye, it lost itself in a ribbon of delicate blue" (19).

While the racial discourse of "Wonderful Discovery!" is less complex than that of Poe's *Pym*, African American labor is as central to the expedition as Peters's assistance is to Pym's experience. In the nineteenth century, enslaved labor was central to encounters with Mammoth Cave. Details about the enslaved laborers who may have mined saltpeter are scarce, but more is known about the labor involved in the tours that brought visitors underground. The only way to explore Mammoth Cave was on a guided tour, and most of the cave guides who led small groups of men and women on lengthy, lard-oil-lamp-lit treks through twisting passageways and across underground rivers were African American men enslaved or leased by the men who owned the cave itself. The eight men who accompany the explorers in "Wonderful Discovery!" are presented as racist stereotypes; they are sources of labor who also provide comic relief and occasional entertainment. Whereas Peters can be seen to challenge such stereotypes, the eight men in "Wonderful Discovery!" seem semantically fixed. They do, however, evoke actual histories of Mammoth Cave that point back to Peters and Pym.

The most well known of Mammoth Cave's enslaved guides was Stephen Bishop. Bishop was brought to work in the cave in 1838 after his enslaver purchased the property. He guided visitors through the cave until shortly before his death in 1857. Bishop essentially authored the modern cave, exploring miles of passageways and producing detailed maps of the caverns (see figure 3.3). Present-day Mammoth Cave tour guides regale visitors with stories about Bishop's cave exploration and his own lively tours. Indeed, Bishop himself became a feature of the cave—someone visitors might read about and then expect to see when they arrived at the cave. And he helped turn the cave itself into a kind of text, allowing visitors to write their names on walls already marked in places by evidence of much-earlier Indigenous presence in the form of occasional torch marks or scraped gypsum crust, if one knew how to recognize those marks (see figures 3.4 and 3.5).[18]

∵

While texts such as "Wonderful Discovery!" might seem to be racist fantasies of colonial control played out in fanciful realms, placing this text and the histories of Mammoth Cave that it engages in the literary lineage that leads from *Symzonia*, to *The Narrative of Arthur Gordon Pym of Nantucket*, to Mat Johnson's *Pym* highlights how these texts raise questions about legibility and succession

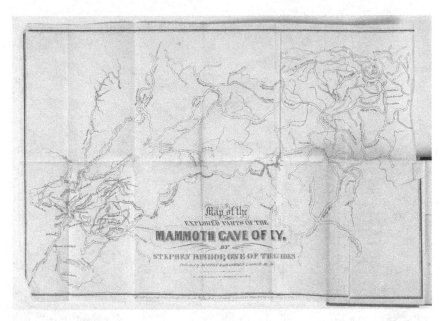

FIGURE 3.3. "Map of the Explored Parts of the Mammoth Cave of KY, by Stephen Bishop, One of the Guides." From Alexander Clark Bullitt, *Rambles in the Mammoth Cave, During the Year 1844* (Louisville, Ky.: Morton & Griswold, 1845). Courtesy of American Antiquarian Society.

in U.S. space. Although arguably less explicitly concerned with the challenges to knowledge of place posed by evidence of deep pasts than is Poe's *Pym*, "Wonderful Discovery!" too articulates questions about relationships between peoples across times, using the physical space of Mammoth Cave and nascent geologic and archaeological ideas as a (rather literal) entry point for more fantastic speculations. Those fantastic speculations in turn recall histories of Mammoth Cave and the texts that it produced: not only "Wonderful Discovery!" but also the map made by an enslaved African American tour guide and names burned onto the walls by nineteenth-century travelers. These texts, too, serve as reminders of how enslaved labor was conscripted into crafting the narratives of deep pasts that would seek to legitimize but also challenge settler claims to territory. To recognize Stephen Bishop's role in excavating and narrating the pasts of the cave, and the role of other African American guides and laborers in turning the cave into a profitable endeavor through tours and mining, is imperative in any attempt to retrieve the histories of race

FIGURE 3.4. Stephen Bishop's signature (written backward) inside Mammoth Cave. National Park Service photo by Rick Toomey.

FIGURE 3.5. Nineteenth-century smoke signatures in Mammoth Cave. National Park Service photo by Rick Toomey.

hidden between the lines of the histories of proto-archaeology that Mammoth Cave exposes.[19] We should not overemphasize the options available to Bishop and other guides since they were constrained by the structures of slavery, but neither should we deny the ways in which Bishop and other guides actively maneuvered through and around those structures and actually left more than a slight trace in the unofficial record of early American archaeology. In this sense, we might think about Bishop as a historical analogue for Dirk Peters, companion, guide, and also, notably, the character who returns to the United States at the end of Poe's *Pym*.

Thinking about these particular texts together requires us to rethink the stories that we tell about the construction of deep pasts and their relation to the present in U.S. space in ways that keep different narratives about race, labor, and indigeneity present. Resurrected in Mat Johnson's 2011 novel, Peters's fictional remains conjure his fictional nineteenth-century body, which itself negotiates and seeks to make legible the pasts of place inscribed into Tsalal's chasms. In Johnson's *Pym*, Peters's remains become a physical reminder not only of histories of slavery and African American labor but also of anxieties about identity and succession. Peters's descendent Mahalia Mathis's ideas about her own genetic makeup point not only to contemporary concerns but also to historical entanglements involving land, race, indigeneity, and the stories told about them that have been part of the legacy of Poe's *Pym* from the beginning. Though it is not usually read in these terms, *The Narrative of Arthur Gordon Pym of Nantucket* is part of a broader conversation about early nineteenth-century geology, archaeology, and narratives about the deep past constructed in attempts to legitimate the settler colonial present in the U.S. interior.

Notes

1. For how "information gleaned from DNA is used to establish social inclusion or exclusion, mediate social justice claims, or resolve sociohistorical and political controversies," see Nelson 19–20. See also Wailoo et al.

2. Two installments of the first part of the novel appeared in the *Southern Literary Messenger* in 1837.

3. The novel immediately links this search for the "source of racial Whiteness" to Toni Morrison's arguments about the Africanist presence essential in forming American literature in her 1992 study *Playing in the Dark: Whiteness and the Literary Imagination*.

4. Lovecraft's *At the Mountains of Madness* (1936), with its mysterious ancient civilization and its mural-covered caverns, is a notable part of the tradition leading from Poe's novel to Johnson's novel. Even earlier, Verne's 1897 *Le sphinx des glaces* (translated into English as *An Antarctic Mystery*) was a relatively direct sequel to *The Narrative of Arthur Gordon Pym*. In 1899 Charles Romeyn Dake published *A Strange Discovery*, in

which a doctor recounts the story that his patient, Dirk Peters, told him about his mysterious Antarctic journey.

5. The island on which Pym lands toward the end of the novel is, famously, full of Black inhabitants who have a taboo against anything white.

6. For such readings, see Gitelman; Paul Lyons 54–66; and, especially, Dana Nelson 90–108. These readings are complicated by those that see *Pym* as "the most racist novel written by a major American writer" (Weaver 58).

7. See Paul Lyons 58 for a discussion of Tsalalians in the Oceanic context. See Weaver (especially 56) for a discussion of the Tsalalians as enslaved Africans but also as indigenes.

8. Fabian defines the "denial of coevalness" as "a persistent and systematic tendency to place the referent(s) of anthropology in a Time other than the present of the producer of anthropological discourse" (31, emphasis omitted).

9. Peters, Pym comments, "was one of the most purely ferocious-looking men I ever beheld. He was short in stature—not more than four feet eight inches high—but his limbs were of the most Herculean mould. His hands, especially, were so enormously thick and broad as hardly to retain a human shape. His arms, as well as legs, were *bowed* in the most singular manner, and appeared to possess no flexibility whatever. His head was equally deformed, being of immense size, with an indentation on the crown (like that on the head of most negroes) and entirely bald" (Poe 87). This racist depiction follows immediately from the passage about Peters's parentage.

10. On Steno, see Cutler. On the rise of geology and conceptions of the scale of time, see Albritton; Allen 146–85; Gould.

11. For reflections on the developing field of geology and its influence on nascent practices of archaeology, see Barnhart 235.

12. On Egypt in nineteenth-century American and European culture, see Dobson and Tonks; Irwin; Trafton.

13. For a contemporary publication that makes clear how ideas about America's pasts were being deployed, see *Archæologia Americana* (1820), the first volume of the *Transactions and Collections of the American Antiquarian Society*. For a recent account of the Mound Builder myth and some of the cultural production surrounding it, see Hay 113–42.

14. For histories of Mammoth Cave, see Algeo; Sears 31–48. For a focus on histories of race and slavery in Mammoth Cave, see Joy Lyons; West. Peter West notably discusses how cave tourism negotiated tensions between Black knowledge and authority and "conventions of white domination" in ways particularly relevant to my argument here.

15. For a recent history of the development of nineteenth-century American archaeology that puts the "Kentucky mummy" at its center, see Snead. For an account that focuses on the Ward family and their role in appropriating Indigenous pasts, see Kertész. See also Barnhart 348–50 for discussion of treatment of human remains and early nineteenth-century ideas about American antiquities. Fantastic speculations about these remains and their significance can be found in various online conspiracy theory forums to this day, indicating the persistence of narratives that deny Indigenous histories.

16. For a concise, recent survey of archaeological research on Mammoth Cave, see Crothers.

17. See Symmes.

18. For information on Bishop, see Joy Lyons; West.

19. For a discussion of a visual representation of Black labor in the context of a barrow excavation, see Chaney's analysis of John J. Egan's *Panorama of the Monumental Grandeur of the Mississippi Valley* (118).

References

Albritton, Claude C. *The Abyss of Time: Changing Conceptions of the Earth's Antiquity After the Sixteenth Century*. 1980. Dover, 2002.

Algeo, Katie. "Mammoth Cave and the Making of Place." *Southeastern Geographer*, vol. 44, no. 1, 2004, pp. 27–47.

Allen, Thomas M. *A Republic in Time: Temporality and Social Imagination in Nineteenth-Century America*. University of North Carolina Press, 2008.

American Antiquarian Society. *Archæologia Americana: Transactions and Collections of the American Antiquarian Society*, vol. 1, Worcester, Mass., 1820.

Barnhart, Terry. *American Antiquities: Revisiting the Origins of American Archæology*. University of Nebraska Press, 2015.

Chaney, Michael A. *Fugitive Vision: Slave Image and Black Identity in Antebellum Narrative*. Indiana University Press, 2008.

Crothers, George M. "The Prehistoric Archaeology of Mammoth Cave." *Mammoth Cave: A Human and Natural History*, edited by Horton H. Hobbs III et al., Springer International, 2017, pp. 29–38.

Cutler, Alan. *The Seashell on the Mountaintop: How Nicolaus Steno Solved an Ancient Mystery and Created a Science of the Earth*. Plume, 2003.

Dake, Charles Romeyn. *A Strange Discovery*. New York, 1899.

Dobson, Eleanor, and Nichola Tonks. "Introduction: Ancient Egypt in Nineteenth-Century Culture." *Nineteenth-Century Contexts: An Interdisciplinary Journal*, vol. 40, no. 4, 2018, pp. 311–15.

Fabian, Johannes. *Time and the Other: How Anthropology Makes Its Object*. Columbia University Press, 1983.

Gitelman, Lisa. "Arthur Gordon Pym and the Novel Narrative of Edgar Allan Poe." *Nineteenth Century Literature* 47, no. 3, Dec. 1992, pp. 349–61.

Gould, Stephen Jay. *Time's Arrow, Time's Cycle: Myth and Metaphor in the Discovery of Geological Time*. Harvard University Press, 1987.

Hay, John. *Postapocalyptic Fantasies in Antebellum American Literature*. Cambridge University Press, 2017.

Irwin, John T. *American Hieroglyphics: The Symbol of the Egyptian Hieroglyphics in the American Renaissance*. Yale University Press, 1980.

Jefferson, Thomas. *Notes on the State of Virginia*. 1787. Penguin, 1999.

Johnson, Mat. *Pym: A Novel*. Spiegel & Grau, 2011.

Kertész, Judy. "History, Memory, and the Appropriation of the American Indian Past: A Family Affair." *New England Collectors and Collections*, edited by Peter Benes, Dublin Seminar for New England Folklife, Boston University, 2006, pp. 199–207.

Letcher, Montgomery E. (pseudonym). "Wonderful Discovery! Being an Account of a Recent Exploration of the Celebrated Mammoth Cave." New York, 1839.

Lovecraft, H. P. *At the Mountains of Madness*. First serialized in *Astounding Stories*, Feb., Mar., Apr. 1936.

Lyell, Charles. *Principles of Geology*. London, 1830–33. 3 vols.

Lyons, Joy Medley. *Making Their Mark: The Signature of Slavery at Mammoth Cave*. Eastern National Park and Monument Association, 2006.

Lyons, Paul. *American Pacificism: Oceania in the U.S. Imagination*. Routledge, 2012.

Morrison, Toni. *Playing in the Dark: Whiteness and the Literary Imagination*. Harvard University Press, 1992.

Nelson, Alondra. *The Social Life of DNA: Race, Reparations, and Reconciliation After the Genome*. Beacon, 2016.

Nelson, Dana D. *The Word in Black and White: Reading "Race" in American Literature, 1638–1867*. Oxford University Press, 1992.

Poe, Edgar Allan. *The Narrative of Arthur Gordon Pym*. 1838. *Collected Writings of Edgar Allan Poe*, vol. 1, *The Imaginary Voyages*, edited by Burton R. Pollin, Twayne, 1981.

Seaborn, Adam (pseudonym). *Symzonia: A Voyage of Discovery*. 1820. Scholars' Facsimiles & Reprints, 1965.

Sears, John F. *Sacred Places: American Tourist Attractions in the Nineteenth Century*. Oxford University Press, 1989.

Snead, James E. *Relic Hunters: Archaeology and the Public in Nineteenth-Century America*. Oxford University Press, 2018.

Symmes, John Cleves. "Light Gives Light, to Light Discover—Ad Infinitum.'" St. Louis [Missouri Territory], 10 Apr. 1818.

Trafton, Scott. *Egypt Land: Race and Nineteenth-Century American Egyptomania*. Duke University Press, 2004.

Verne, Jules. *Le sphinx des glaces*. Paris, 1897.

Wailoo, Keith, et. al. *Genetics and the Unsettled Past: The Collision of DNA, Race, and History*. Rutgers University Press, 2012.

Ward, Nahum. "Mammoth Cave." *Thomas's Massachusetts Spy, or Worcester Gazette*, 8 May 1816, p. 3; 15 May 1816, p. 2; 29 May 1816, p. 4.

Weaver, Jace. "Mr. Poe's Indians: *The Narrative of Arthur Gordon Pym of Nantucket* and Edgar Allan Poe as a Southern Writer." *Native South*, vol. 5, 2012, pp. 38–60.

West, Peter. "Trying the Dark: Mammoth Cave and the Racial Imagination, 1839–1869." *Southern Spaces*, 9 Feb. 2010. southernspaces.org/2010/trying-dark-mammoth-cave -and-racial-imagination-1839%E2%80%931869.

Zimmerman, Virginia. *Excavating Victorians*. State University of New York Press, 2008.

4

Witnessing Catastrophe

CORRELATIONS BETWEEN CATASTROPHIC PALEOENVIRONMEN-
TAL EVENTS AND FIRST NATIONS' ORAL TRADITIONS IN
NORTH AMERICA'S PACIFIC NORTHWEST

Rick Budhwa

WESTERN RESEARCHERS AND INDIGENOUS PEOPLES often disagree about interpretation of the past (Nicholas and Markey). Whereas academics employ written history, archaeology, and geology to document the past, Indigenous peoples pass down their knowledge orally. Oral traditions record, among other things, groups' epistemologies and environmental observations, and are as accepted by Indigenous peoples as science is among Westerners (Biolsi and Zimmerman). However, many Indigenous communities have had their pasts denied to them. Academics, particularly archaeologists, have reconstructed Indigenous histories, despite often lacking cultural knowledge or failing to involve them in the process (Klassen et al.). In order to grasp a less ethnocentric and more complete perspective of North America's past, this chapter contends, archaeologists must consult Indigenous sources—especially oral traditions (see also Budhwa, "An Alternate Model").

Archaeologists' primary concern about studying oral traditions is historical accuracy (Nicholas and Markey 288–90). Rather than outright rejecting oral traditions, they should be deeply analyzed alongside archaeological data. Only then can oral traditions provide plausible interpretations. Alan McMillan, for example, examined Nuu-chah-nulth stories referencing orcas to elucidate how these animals influenced their social organization and rituals. The current chapter—a revised synthesis of my "Witnessing Catastrophe" (2002)—contrasts oral traditions referencing catastrophic paleoenvironmental events with archaeological/geological evidence.

Epistemological Differences

Indigenous and Western cultures endorse different epistemologies. Many Westerners hold the view that science explains all, and knowledge is objective and impersonal. In contrast, among Indigenous societies, the perspective that spirituality permeates all aspects of life, and knowledge is personal and owned, is common (Barnhardt and Kawagley 14–16). Such variations are salient when reviewing oral traditions; for example, the Western understanding of linear time is inconsistent with the cyclical, multilayered nature of time in oral traditions (Crowell and Howell 19). Indigenous societies also conceptualize "places" in manners tethered to cultural knowledge, which often conflicts with how Westerners perceive place (Budhwa and McCreary 199–200).

Though these worldviews may clash, holistic interpretations of the past require multiple inquiry lines (Nicholas and Markey 301–2). As this chapter shows, correlations exist between scientifically verifiable events and oral traditions, making it appropriate to employ oral traditions when studying Indigenous prehistory. While "prehistory" implies a "lost time" before Western historical documentation, Indigenous North Americans reliably recorded local happenings for millennia before European ships arrived on their shores. What colonial culture regards as "prehistory" is in fact covered by cultural narratives and therefore, I suggest, "historical."

Research Objective

Catastrophic events—instantaneous phenomena that affect many people and/ or leave significant evidence (e.g., earthquakes, landslides, tsunamis, volcanic eruptions)—are well represented from both geological/archaeological and Indigenous perspectives. This study compares Indigenous accounts of paleoenvironmental catastrophes in North America's Pacific Northwest (PNW) with the scientific record. Three cases are presented: Mount Mazama's eruption in southern Oregon, 7,000 before the present (BP), the Bonneville/Cascade landslide in Washington, 900–350 BP, and the megathrust earthquake/tsunami that originated off the PNW's coast 300 BP. These events were selected because they: (a) were the greatest of their kind in the PNW during the Holocene (12,000 BP–present), (b) had significant environmental impacts, and (c) were geologically distinct. The Pacific Northwest (see figure 4.1) was chosen as the study area because catastrophic events frequently occurred here throughout the Holocene (Baker). As PNW Indigenous occupation dates to at least 14,000 BP (McLaren et al., "Prerogatives" 176), some oral traditions

FIGURE 4.1. Study area.

likely describe catastrophes. To identify pertinent stories, the oral traditions belonging to modern Indigenous groups likely to have ancestors living near an event when it happened were searched.

Geological/archaeological evidence for catastrophic paleoenvironmental events was compared with apparently related oral traditions, via qualitative tables. Similarities, differences, and/or patterning were explored. Due to this medium's multilayered nature, oral traditions were closely read to elucidate surface and deeper meanings. As products of human cultures, cultural biases are inherent to oral traditions. Additional biases can arise as traditions are shared and interpreted within and across cultures over time as well as when cultures converge and become influenced by one another (e.g., the cultural

influence of early European settlers on PNW Indigenous peoples and vice
versa). A further layer of biases may emerge when interpreting oral traditions,
particularly from a non-Indigenous perspective. Story meaning (e.g., social
purpose) is not fixed: when recorded in writing, meaning becomes static;
without the performance that traditionally accompanies the telling, the original storyteller's intentions are potentially obscured (Cruikshank; Vansina).
Translations of oral traditions to English or other languages are frequently
inexact. Further, space and time are differentially conceptualized in Indigenous and Western societies: while Indigenous conceptions of time tend to be
cyclical, Western conceptions tend to be teleological-linear; while the Western sense of place usually rests on a Lockean notion of property, Indigenous
epistemologies include place in a complex mnemonic structure—attributing
events to particular places rather than to dates in a calendar. These factors
must be considered when studying oral traditions.

Though PNW Indigenous stories are well documented, relatively little
research has integrated oral tradition–based understandings of catastrophic
events. McLaren and colleagues recently associated Heiltsuk stories mention-
ing floods in British Columbia with archaeological/geological indicators of
sea-level rises 15,000 BP. Aron L. Crowell and Wayne K. Howell correlated
Tlingit oral traditions in Alaska with geological/archaeological data to illuminate the Little Ice Age's human consequences. Loren R. Baker, Ruth S. Ludwin
et al., and Coll Thrush and Ludwin also explored connections between PNW
Indigenous stories and earthquakes and/or tsunamis. This chapter links oral
traditions to similar events but in greater detail and more holistically.

Humans have inhabited the PNW for more than 14,000 years (McLaren
et al., "Prerogatives" 176). Although most Indigenous groups' locations at
European contact are undoubtedly different from those in the past, some
places do have long histories of occupation: take, for example, the 9,000- to
10,000-year-old Namu site in British Columbia (McLaren et al., "Prerogatives" 156), and the 11,000- to 14,000-year-old villages on Calvert and
Hunter Islands (McLaren et al., "Prerogatives" 164, 175; McLaren et al., "A
Post-glacial Sea Level" 155–59). Yet we cannot be certain these are current
occupants' direct ancestors (see figure 4.2). Though some argue sites were continuously occupied (McLaren et al., "Prerogatives" 181), culture styles only
became recognizable within the last 4,000–5,000 years. Further, all PNW
Indigenous peoples were devastated by European colonization and diseases.
Many oral traditions were surely lost.

All societies use oral tradition—the oldest form of knowledge transmis-
sion/retention—but the medium is especially important to Indigenous North
Americans. In the Delgamuukw case, Canada's Supreme Court ruled in 1997

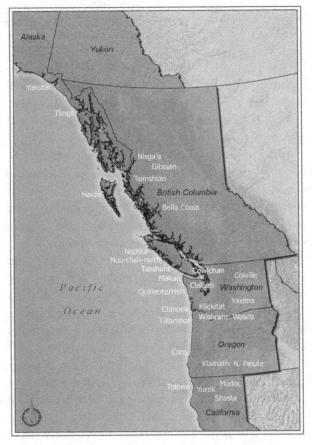

FIGURE 4.2. Study area with Indigenous groups' locations.

that a Gitksan account of a scientifically verifiable paleoenvironmental event constituted sufficient evidence to grant Aboriginal title (Borrows 538–40). Stories are integral to Indigenous constructions of reality, outlining individuals' places in their worlds and social systems (Cruikshank). Jan Vansina defines oral traditions as "verbal messages . . . reported statements from the past beyond the present generation" (19). Oral tradition thus refers to both unwritten information from the past and its preservation process. As cultures' worldviews become manifest in their stories (Cruikshank), oral tradition reveals knowledge about their societies' sociocultural life, their imaginative placement within the nonhuman environment, and stories' structural characteristics.

Oral traditions contain data that may not be exclusive to the past. Researchers studying a story's meaning must determine the extent to which components from the distant past have been influenced by elements from the more recent past, and vice versa. Scholars must deal with issues of metaphor and symbolism as well (Vansina 86). If one studies a narrative in isolation without knowledge of a group's language, use of metaphor and symbolism, and other stories, meanings beyond the surface of the story may remain obscure. Interpreters of oral traditions should also recognize that they typically describe group experiences (Vansina 19). These accounts belong to a group and are often reshaped to emphasize meanings or associations to other stories (Cruikshank 40–41; Vansina 19, 24).

Studying oral traditions alongside scientific data on catastrophic events could provide new information on archaeology and paleoenvironmental events. In a Tlingit story, a woman secluded at menarche calls upon a glacier for companionship, causing its advancement (Swann 151). Archaeologists investigating how glaciers affected precontact PNW peoples could use its descriptions of glacial movements and earth shaking to substantiate and challenge ice-flow theories or generate hypotheses. If archaeologists can elucidate how specific catastrophic events are represented in a group's stories, perhaps they could use others to identify unknown events (Hanks 178–79).

Catastrophic events are frequently connected—for example, an earthquake causing a landslide that displaces water and triggers a tsunami—a sequence apparent in geological/archaeological records (Plafker). If similar event sequencing presents in an oral tradition, it is more probable that a comparable event transpired. The larger the magnitude of an event, the greater is the likelihood that it is recorded in stories, and the more elaborate its treatment may be in the oral tradition. Though assessing oral traditions' historical and descriptive accuracy is difficult, corroborating verifiable spatial aspects with geological/archaeological evidence can affirm historical accuracy in a Western/scientific perspective.

Mount Mazama's Climactic Eruption

Indigenous groups near volcanoes often attributed their power to the supernatural (Swanson). Volcanoes continue to affect people across the globe. The 2018 Fuego Volcano eruption in Guatemala killed hundreds and displaced thousands ("Thousands Flee"). In the PNW, a massive eruption occurred 7,000 BP, when Mazama exploded in south Oregon.

FIGURE 4.3. Volcanoes near Mazama. The Klamath, Modoc, and Northern Paiute historically lived in the marsh areas near Mazama (Howe).

The eruption of the 3,700-meter-high Mount Mazama drastically altered the surrounding environment (Harris 111–25). Pyroclastic flows devastated land up to 64 kilometers away. Ejected pumice and ash extended 30 kilometers above Mazama, coating 2.6 million square kilometers of land (Williams and Goles). While huge volumes of magma were expelled, Mazama's support weakened, and the magma chamber's roof—the mountain's upper portion— collapsed, creating a caldera. Over centuries, precipitation filled the caldera, creating Crater Lake (800 meters deep).

Many volcanoes erupted near Mazama during the Holocene, depicted in figure 4.3. Only two, however, formed calderas: Newberry (which erupted shortly after Mazama, ca. 6,700 BP) and Mazama (Sherrod et al. 3).

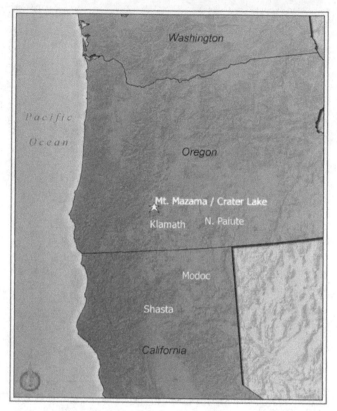

FIGURE 4.4. Mazama and Indigenous groups' historic locations.

Archaeological finds in Oregon dating to 13,000 BP indicate human in-
habitation prior to Mazama's eruption, though sites (e.g., rock shelters) were
small and infrequently occupied (Howe 1–12). Between 7,000 and 2,000 BP,
human presence in the Great Basin increased (Jennings 113–19). Sites (e.g.,
pithouses) were small but frequently inhabited (see figure 4.4).

A search for Modoc and Paiute stories explicitly relating to the eruption
of Mount Mazama proved fruitless.[1] One Klamath story appearing to refer to
that eruption has been included in Ella Clark's collection *Indian Legends of the
Pacific Northwest* published in 1953 (53–55). A comparative analysis of that
story and the geological/archaeological reconstruction of Mazama's eruption
(Harris 111–25; Homuth; Williams and Goles) has led to the following possible correlations.

Table 4.1. Descriptive Comparison: "The Origin of Crater Lake"

	Native oral account	Geological account
Pre event	A long time ago, so long that you cannot count it, the white man ran wild in the woods and my people lived in rock-built houses. Sometimes the Chief of the Below World came up from his home inside the earth and stood on the mountaintop— the high mountain that used to be. At that time there was no lake. Instead, there was an opening that led to the lower world. Through it the Chief of the Below World passed from his home to the outside world.	Evidence of human occupation in caves and rock shelters prior to Mazama's eruption 7,000 BP Mazama was 3,700 meters high. There were no significant water bodies on Mazama. The only activity within 30,000 years prior to the climactic eruption was a few preclimactic eruptions/ lava flows.
During event	When he came up from his lodge below, his tall form towered above the snow-capped peaks. His head touched the stars around the lodge of the Chief of the Above World, the all-powerful chief. In a voice like thunder, he swore that he would have revenge on the people of Loha, that he would destroy them with the Curse of Fire. Raging and thundering, he rushed up through the opening and stood upon the top of this mountain. Slowly the mighty form of that chief descended from the sky and stood on top of Mount Shasta. From their mountaintops the two chiefs began a furious battle. In a short time all the spirits of earth and sky took part. Mountains shook and crumbled. Red-hot rocks as large as the hills hurtled through the skies. Burning ashes fell like rain. The Chief of the Below World spewed fire from his mouth. Like an ocean of flame it devoured the forests on the mountains and in the valleys. On and on the Curse of Fire swept until it reached the homes of the people. Fleeing in terror before it, the people found refuge in the waters of Klamath Lake. The Chief of the Above World heard the voices of the medicine men and spoke to the people from the top of Mount Shasta. "Your wise men have spoken the truth. You have not listened to my voice, though I have spoken again and again. Now you are being punished. Your land is being laid waste." Once more the mountains shook. Once more the earth trembled. This time the Chief of the Below World was driven into his home and the top of the mountain fell upon him. When the morning sun rose, the high mountain was gone. The mountain which the Chief of the Below World had called his own no longer towered near Mount Shasta.	The eruption began with an expulsion of pyroclastic materials, covering an immense area (2,600,000 square kilometers). This stage likely lasted a few days. The second stage consisted of magma "boiling over" from Mazama's interior. This expulsion was not as high/vertical as the preceding phase. Given the moisture in the ash cloud, thunder/lightning likely occurred. The nearby Mount Shasta (4,317 meters high) erupted every 600–800 years. Mazama's eruption would have shaken the region. Ashfall covered the area. Lava covered the volcano's flanks, flowing into valleys. People's homes were likely situated near Klamath Lake. Klamath Lake is the closest place to escape lava. Implies knowledge of Shasta's eruptions, frequent in the Holocene. Most of the land flanking Mazama was covered with pyroclastic flows/lava/ash. After pyroclastic materials were expelled, a void was created, and the mountain collapsed, forming a caldera.

Post event   For many years, rain fell in torrents and filled the   It would have taken 250–500 years to fill
                  great hole that was made when the mountain fell   the crater with precipitation to present-
                  upon the Chief of the Below World. The Curse   day levels. There has not been another
                  of Fire was lifted. Peace and quiet covered the   significant eruption since 7,000 BP.
                  earth. Never again did the Chief of the Below
                  World come up from his home. Never again did
                  his voice frighten the people.

Post event   Now you understand why my people never visit   Little archaeological data have been found
adaptation   the lake. Down through the ages we have heard   at Crater Lake, and this small amount of
                  this story. From father to son has come the warn-   evidence is attributed to hunting expedi-
                  ing, "Look not upon the place, for it means death   tions, not habitation.
                  or everlasting sorrow."

The geological/archaeological account and the Klamath story regarding Mazama's pre-eruption environment appear consistent. Preclimactic eruption, Mazama was volcanically active but lacked a lake. Nearby peoples lived in pithouses and caves (Howe 1–12).

Mazama's climactic eruption had three stages: expulsion of pumice/ash, magma chamber emptying, and collapse of the upper mountain (Harris 111–25; Homuth). The Klamath story also yields three stages. The first is when a "tall form" came out of the mountain and "stood" on top. A distinction is made between the form and its weapon ("Curse of Fire"). Volcanic eruptions are frequently described in oral traditions as immediately erupting fire and power (Cashman and Cronin 408). The standing of a non-fire-like figure upon the mountaintop may be interpreted as a Plinian eruption preceding the magma/fire event.

The second stage is when the "Chief of the Above World . . . descended from the sky and stood on top of Mount Shasta," the start of a "furious battle" with the "Chief of the Below World." A typical description of volcanic eruptions follows: "Mountains shook and crumbled. Red-hot rocks as large as the hills hurtled through the skies." The "ocean of flame" represents magma flowing down the mountain, initiating fires. Thunder/lightning and rainfall likely succeeded the ash cloud, due to its entrapment of moisture. For comparison, during two months following Mount St. Helens's 1980 CE eruption, ten thousand earthquakes were recorded nearby (Mullineaux 24). Thus thunder/lightning, rain, and earthquakes were probably present during Mazama's eruption, correlating with the statement "all the spirits of earth and sky took part."

The third stage consists of the magma chamber and upper mountain collapsing, forming a caldera. Calderas are rare, yet the story states, "The Chief of the Below World was driven into his home, and the top of the mountain fell upon him." Other correlations exist between geological reconstructions and oral tradition, including people seeking refuge in Klamath Lake, rainwater filling Crater Lake, and Mazama's subsequent tranquility. Further, Crater Lake today is beautiful and peaceful—yet media dating to 1886 report that Indigenous persons refused to travel to it (Winthrop). Few artifacts have been found around the crater (Brown), suggesting limited hunting or ceremonies. It was clearly a feared place.

Thunder/lightning, earthquakes, nearby eruptions, and the filling of Crater Lake all occurred during and after Mazama's climactic eruption and may have been incorporated into the story over time. Thunder/lightning could have resulted from ash clouds. Nearby volcanoes (Shasta and Newberry) erupted after the mega-eruption of Mazama (Harris 109–16; Sherrod et al. 3). If Natives were present during Mazama's eruption and remained in the area for generations, they could have witnessed Crater Lake's filling. Though persistence of human life in the direct vicinity of the crater during and after the eruption is unlikely, people probably climbed up to Crater Lake afterward and observed the gradual filling of the caldera with water.

Additional evidence that the Klamath account describes Mazama and not Newberry (the only other nearby volcano whose eruption formed a caldera) is that Newberry experienced multiple eruptions over millennia (Sherrod et al. 1). Each event's magnitude was not comparable to Crater Lake's formation. It is less likely the Klamath would have recorded lesser events.

Though other stories depict eruptions, the antiquity and correlation strength with the scientific record make this Klamath account unique. In 1883 Mount Krakatoa erupted in Indonesia, producing a caldera. Before, the science underlying eruptions and caldera formations was unclear (Homuth); yet Natives understood this rare event sequence well before geologists. The ancestors of the Klamath—however they called themselves—must have witnessed the event.

The Bonneville/Cascade Landslide

Landslides, such as the 2017 Mocoa Slide in Colombia that killed more than three hundred people (Cheng et al.), are other catastrophic events. A significant slide in paleoenvironmental Oregon/Washington is the Bonneville/Cascade landslide. The date of the Bonneville/Cascade landslide was traditionally 1100 CE (Harris 209–14); however, others have argued it occurred five hundred years later (O'Connor et al.). The slide buried an immense area, damming the Columbia River and producing a massive backwater lake. The river eventually broke the dam, reshaping the Columbia Gorge and likely leading to Indigenous oral traditions about the "Bridge of the Gods."

Limited data suggest human occupation in the Columbia Gorge area spans more than twelve thousand years (Sobel et al. 28). Precontact Native cultures varied along the Columbia, though all were riverine and subsisted off salmon (Sobel et al. 30–33). On the lower Columbia, groups lived in plank houses. On the middle/upper river, they moved frequently in small groups. As the slide occurred just before European contact, many peoples were likely living in their historic locations. Anthropological/archaeological evidence suggests the Klickitat, Wishram, Yakima, Wasco, and Colville inhabited the area during the landslide (see figure 4.5). Archaeological evidence of villages and seasonal camps was destroyed by the slide, the lake's filling, and/or its emptying.

FIGURE 4.5. Map of the Bonneville/Cascade landslide and nearby peoples.

Geological/archaeological data demonstrate that four closely spaced slides detached from the Columbia River Gorge, blocking the river and forming a large backwater. Given the gorge's instability (Harris 209–14), a large earthquake was not needed to trigger the landslide. It is impossible to accurately determine the backwater's volume and how much land was displaced. Estimates have the bridge as high as 100 meters and several meters wide (Harris 209–14). If correct, the backwater could have been 150 kilometers long. To produce such a large lake, the bridge likely lasted several years. The backwater eventually overflowed the dam, leaving only heavy rocks that formed the Cascade Rapids and bent the river southward.

Volcanic tremors and/or earthquakes could have triggered the landslide. Mounts Hood, Adams, and St. Helens erupted around the time the landslide happened (Mullineaux 21–23). Given the region's geology, thousands of contemporaneous earthquakes also could have transpired nearby (McMillan and Hutchinson 85). For example, large earthquakes occurred around 300 and 1000 BP (McMillan and Hutchinson 84). Regardless, between 1100 and 1600 CE, the water broke through and swept toward the ocean (Harris 209–14; O'Connor et al. 97), affecting—likely killing—many people.

Numerous Indigenous legends reference the Bridge of the Gods (e.g., Clark 20–23, 91–95). Many are well documented, as are early Europeans' accounts of the landslide's aftermath, which noted drowned trees upstream (Lawrence and Lawrence). The Klickitat account, the most detailed (Clark 20–23), is contrasted with the geological account (Harris 209–14; O'Connor et al.).

Table 4.2. Descriptive Comparison: "The Bridge of the Gods"

	Native oral account	Geological account
Pre event	Long ago, when the world was young, all people were happy. The Great Spirit, whose home is in the sun, gave them all they needed. No one was hungry or cold. But after a while, two brothers quarrelled over the land. The older one wanted most of it, and the younger one wanted most of it. The Great Spirit decided to stop the quarrel. One night while the brothers were asleep he took them to a new land, to a country with high mountains. Between the mountains flowed a big river.	No correlation. Environmental description: the Columbia River flows between Mounts Hood and Adams.

During event	Then the Great Spirit built a bridge over the big river. To each brother he said, "I have built a bridge over the river, so that you and your people may visit those on the other side. It will be a sign of peace between you. As long as you and your people are good and friendly with each other, this bridge . . . will remain." It was a broad bridge, wide enough for many people and many ponies to walk across at one time. For many snows the people were at peace and crossed the river for friendly visits. . . . Wyeast [Mount Hood] and Klickitat [Mount Adams] grew jealous of each other and soon began to quarrel. They became so angry that they fought. Their people also took up the quarrel, so that there was much fighting on both sides of the river. Many warriors were killed. This time the Great Spirit was angered by the wickedness of the people. He broke down the Bridge of the Gods, the sign of peace between the two tribes, and its rocks fell into the river. They continued to quarrel over Loo-wit even after they were mountain peaks. They caused sheets of flame to burst forth, and they hurled hot rocks at each other. Not thrown far enough, many fell into the river and blocked it.	Implies an instantaneous event, performed by the Great Spirit. The bridge was a series of landslides in the Columbia Gorge at what is now the Cascade Rapids. Estimates have the bridge as high as 100 meters. The resulting lake could have been 150 kilometers long. There is evidence for drowned trees upstream. To produce such a lake, the bridge could have lasted several years. Mount Hood erupted between 400 and 600 CE and again between 1400 and 1800 CE. Mount Adams had eruptive episodes between 100 and 800 CE and around 500 CE. Mount St. Helens had several eruptions—1200, 1480, and 1800 CE—with lesser episodes in between. The dam broke via earthquake, volcanic eruption, or backwater overflow. Some rocks were too large for the current to carry and formed the Cascades. General descriptions of lahar, lava, and/or tephra ejection. It is unlikely expulsed volcanic materials would have been sufficiently substantial to block the river.
Post event	That is why the Columbia is very narrow and the water very swift.	The Cascade Rapids were formed after the dam collapsed. The larger boulders remained.
Post-event adaptation	No description.	When the river resumed flowing into the Pacific, its course was diverted 1 kilometer southward.

The Klickitat story correlates with geological/archaeological evidence. The Great Spirit "built" a bridge over the river. When angered, it "broke" the bridge, and rocks fell into the river. This implies instantaneous occurrences. The bridge's creation and, if it was destroyed by a seismic activity, destruction would indeed have been geologically instantaneous. If backwater overflow destroyed the bridge, this also could have been rapid.

The storyteller, Lulu Crandall (Clark 20), states the bridge was wide enough for people and horses to cross simultaneously. Stephen L. Harris

(209–14) estimates the dam could have been one hundred meters high. To block the Columbia, it must have been quite thick. The story also indicates the bridge lasted several "snows," likely meaning winters. To drown and kill forests upstream, the river must have been dammed for multiple years.

Slides generally reoccur in similar locations, and there have been other landslides in the area of the Bonneville/Cascade event (Sobel et al. 25–27). Some may argue Natives inferred a slide happened by observing the debris instead of witnessing an event, or that the story was an amalgam of previous events. Though both are possible, details from the most recent Bonneville/Cascade landslide are present in this story; so even if it incorporates others, it still contains historical information tied to this event.

A massive flood swept through the Columbia Valley between 1400 and 1480 CE, which Jim E. O'Connor et al. propose was caused by the Bridge of the Gods' collapse (9). If we accept O'Connor et al., the bridge was likely breeched 500–600 BP due to regional volcanic or seismic activity. Mount St. Helens's 500 BP eruption, for example, would have produced tremors throughout the Columbia Gorge. This accords with descriptions of the mountains producing "sheets of fire" and "hurling hot rocks." Perhaps, then, the "ground shaking" signifies volcanic rather than seismic activity. If this is the case, all environmental activity described in this story may have contemporaneously transpired.

The Cascadia Subduction Zone Megathrust Earthquake/Tsunami

Earthquakes can trigger tsunamis, with earthquake magnitude directly affecting tsunami height and damage (Satake et al.). The 2004 Indian Ocean Tsunami—in which a magnitude 9 earthquake induced multiple tsunamis—killed more than 225,000 people in East/Southeast Asia (Lay et al.). A notable PNW example is the 1700 CE earthquake/tsunami that shook the Cascadia Subduction Zone.

Tsunamis are caused by water displacement via landslides, earthquakes, and/or volcanic eruptions. They can travel thousands of kilometers at more than 700 kilometers per hour, because as water depth increases, so does tsunami speed (Satake et al.). Tsunamis can reach hundreds of meters inland, causing erosion and destroying structures and vegetation. As they give little warning, their effects can be deadly.

The Cascadia Subduction Zone (CSZ) is where four continental plates violently interface in the Pacific Ocean west of the PNW (Atwater et al.

371–73). At the CSZ, the North American plate slides over the Juan de Fuca plate, which usually moves 2–5 centimeters per year (Hyndman). If it is blocked, significant pressure builds. When released, megathrust earthquakes (≥9 magnitude) can occur.

In the Pacific Northwest, earthquakes produced tsunamis in 1946 and 1949 (Thrush and Ludwin 1–2). Sedimentological characteristics of Vancouver Island's west coast signify earlier paleoearthquakes/tsunamis transpired (Benson et al.)—such as the 1700 CE earthquake/tsunami. Evidence for land/water displacement in the PNW is scant; most older shoreline deposits are underwater or buried (Plafker 917). Scientific evidence of the 1700 tsunami has been recently identified. It was generated by one CSZ megathrust earthquake, or a rapid series of lesser earthquakes, rupturing the CSZ (Atwater et al.).

Within written PNW history, megathrust earthquakes have never been documented. The following geoarchaeological evidence indicates that one occurred around 1700 CE:

(a) buried tidal marshes implying sudden land subsidence,
(b) changes in tree-ring growth showing root drowning,
(c) sand layers on top of tidal marshes (moved by the tsunami),
(d) landslide layers on the deep seafloor (caused by seismic shaking),
(e) dated tsunami evidence from local and distant (Japanese) sources. (Ludwin et al.; Satake et al.)

Archaeological data indicate several villages on Washington's and Vancouver Island's coasts were abandoned during the late Holocene (McMillan and Hutchinson), likely because of earthquakes/tsunamis. Evidence (e.g., drowned vegetation, waterlogged matting) indicates the most recent CSZ subsidence occurred three hundred years ago (Hyndman; Ludwin et al.; McMillan and Hutchinson).

The megathrust earthquake's range is unknown. I thus surveyed the stories of groups well documented in the historical record: the Haida, Nuu-chah-nulth, Cowichan, Makah, Klallam, Tseshaht, Quileute, Chinook, Tillamook, Tolowa, and Yurok (see figure 4.6). Oral traditions recording both tsunamis and earthquakes are rare. This seems rather peculiar, as they are geologically related, and other complex event sequences are preserved (e.g., Mazama).

The story best describing a tsunami, the Nuu-chah-nulth's "The Tsunami at Pachena Bay," recorded by Chief Louie in 1964 (Arima et al. 230), is compared with the geological account (Atwater et al.; Benson et al.; Hyndman; Satake et al.).

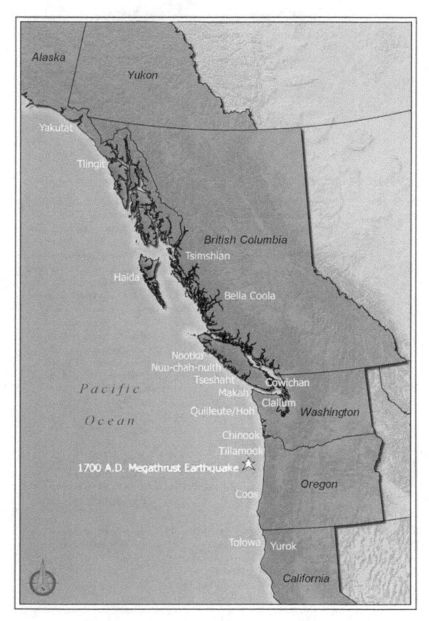

FIGURE 4.6. 1700 CE megathrust earthquake and local native groups.

Table 4.3. Descriptive Comparison: "The Tsunami at Pachena Bay"

	Native oral account	Geological account
Pre event	It is said that they were a big band. Their village site was Loht'a. I think they numbered over a hundred persons. There is now no one left alive due to what this land has done. They had practically no way or time to try to save themselves. I think that it was at nighttime the land shook. It was a sandy beach, it is said its name was "Place-on-Rocky-Shore-for-Spearing."	Late Holocene villages existed along Vancouver Island's west coast. Villages could have sustained more than 100 people. Refers to past earthquakes/tsunamis and their effects on Natives. Implies the earthquake occurred rapidly at night, aspects verified by geoarchaeological/historical evidence. A rocky shore with a sandy beach is an apt description of Vancouver Island's west coast, where this group was located.
During event	It was floating, it is said consisting only of sand, a house right up against a hill out of the woods, its name "Place-of-Many-Tyee-Salmon." They had no time to get hold of canoes, no time to wake. They sank at once, were all drowned; none survived. It is said that no one ever knew what happened. I think a big wave smashed into the beach. The Pachena Bay people were lost. Their food was whale meat. Nothing was known about what happened and what became of them. But they who lived at "House-Up-Against-Hill," the wave did not reach because they were on high ground. Right against a cliff were the houses on high ground at "Coldwater Pool." Because of that, they came out alive. They did not drift out to sea with the others.	Perhaps describes a hunting/fishing house/camp at a higher elevation, near an area with salmon. "Floating" may refer to sand liquefaction that earthquakes can cause. Therefore, the house could "float," then sink into the sand. The tsunami's speed, ferocity, and time are stressed. As it is mentioned within the same context as an earthquake, the tsunami was likely induced by an earthquake. The tsunami was large enough to drown a village. A CSZ earthquake would cause a tsunami, likely extending far inland. Such a wave would cause materials, debris, and people to drift into the ocean.
Post event	Everything drifted away; everything was gone. To the Chiefs of old this land was very great in their sight because they ate the whale that drifted on the shores of their land, also drift sea lion and everything that drifted onto their land.	With tsunamis, marine animals' carcasses commonly wash ashore.
Post-event adaptation	None	

Correlations appear between this oral tradition and the geological/archaeological record about the same type of tsunami event. Other Indigenous stories also seem to mention earthquake-induced tsunamis (Baker 26–39; Ludwin et al.; Thrush and Ludwin 5–6). Although none are explicitly related to the 1700 CE earthquake/tsunami, this, being the largest and most recent one, seems the most likely choice (Baker 57). The event's geological sequence, however, is not sufficiently distinct to distinguish it from others.

The 1700 earthquake/tsunami was undoubtedly significant enough to enter oral traditions. Indigenous populations would have been affected by shoreline subsidence—for example, abrupt changes in shoreline elevation likely impacted coastal people's marine resources (McMillan and Hutchinson 81).

Given the 1700 earthquake/tsunami's recency, one would expect many detailed accounts—but this is not so. Because this event happened just before European contact, perhaps colonization and introduced epidemics somehow impaired its establishment in oral tradition. It is possible that these factors devastated Indigenous populations more than prior catastrophic events and there were simply not a sufficient number of individuals telling and sharing any associated stories to ensure they would be passed down and remembered. Older events may have transpired during periods of greater overall population stability (even if a group that may have initially recorded an event had been decimated), meaning there were likely ample storytellers to transmit/preserve information. This may explain the inclusion of complex information about older events (e.g., Mazama) but not this more recent event.

Conclusion

This chapter has examined whether scientifically verifiable catastrophic paleoenvironmental events are represented in PNW oral traditions, whether it is possible to determine if a specific event is represented in a story, and how oral traditions compare to scientific data. The cases here demonstrate that similarities exist between the different epistemic languages of Indigenous traditions and Western scientific knowledge.

Recognizing how different information manifests is necessary to comprehend oral traditions' meanings. Event sequencing and uniqueness are paramount in determining whether a tradition depicts a specific event versus a class of events. Scholars interpreting oral traditions must also be familiar with the societies from which they originate. Without comprehensive cultural knowledge, it is difficult to distinguish between stories with and without historical basis.

Interestingly, this research did not find a correlation between historical accuracy and catastrophe dates. The correlations between the Mazama account (leading back to 7,000 BP) and the scientific record seem stronger than the much more recent Bonneville/Cascade landslide (900–350 BP) and the 1700 CE earthquake/tsunami accounts. Mazama's eruption was the most unique (and oldest) event discussed, and its distinct event sequence more easily allowed for correlations between Indigenous and scientific accounts. In stories, environmental information likely achieves a state of permanence (fusing with historically unrelated moral content), allowing its transmission without much change over millennia. Perhaps due to the cultural rupture caused by epidemics, information associated with the 1700 earthquake/tsunami was unable to achieve a state of permanence, potentially explaining why the older stories seem to have stronger correlations with scientific evidence than the more recent ones.

Research on representations of paleoenvironmental events in oral traditions is beneficial for both scholars and Indigenous communities. Such studies can broaden understanding of prehistoric North America, demonstrate a peoples' long-term occupation (for land claims), and improve responses to catastrophic events by illuminating Indigenous survival strategies.

Further research is needed for academics to interpret oral traditions by using the techniques of oral history studies. It is insufficient to rely on interpretations based on superficial content or apparent meaning, as information may be hidden in the latent content or symbolism. The aim of such research should be to develop rich interpretations of the past inclusive of all epistemic approaches. This is essentially the goal of archaeology—though it is often overlooked.

Note

1. See the chapter by Gesa Mackenthun in this volume.

References

Arima, E. Y., et al. *Between Ports Alberni and Renfrew: Notes on West Coast Peoples.* Canadian Museum of Civilization, 1991.

Atwater, Brian, et al. "Radiocarbon Evidence for Extensive Plate-Boundary Rupture About 300 Years Ago at the Cascadia Subduction Zone." *Nature*, vol. 378, no. 23, 1995, pp. 371–78.

Baker, Loren R. "Cascadia Earthquake and Tsunami Events as Reflected in Aboriginal Oral Tradition." MES thesis, Evergreen State University, 2011.

Barnhardt, Ray, and Angayuqaq Oscar Kawagley. "Indigenous Knowledge Systems and Alaska Native Ways of Knowing." *Anthropology & Education Quarterly*, vol. 36, no. 1, 2005, pp. 8–23.

Benson, B. E., et al. "Tsunami Deposits Beneath Tidal Marshes on Northwestern Vancouver Island, British Columbia." *Quaternary Research*, vol. 48, no. 2, 1997, pp. 192–204.

Biolsi, Thomas, and Larry J. Zimmerman. "Power of the Spoken Word: Native Oral Traditions in American Indian History." *Rethinking American Indian History*, edited by Donald Fixico, University of New Mexico Press, 1997, pp. 101–16.

Borrows, John. "Sovereignty's Alchemy: An Analysis of *Delgamuukw v. British Columbia*." *Osgoode Hall Law Journal*, vol. 37, no. 3, Fall 1999, pp. 537–96.

Brown, Richard. "Indian Relics on Mount Mazama." *Nature Notes* (Crater Lake National Park), vol. 18, 1952, pp. 16–17.

Budhwa, Rick. "An Alternate Model for First Nations Involvement in Resource Management Archaeology." *Canadian Journal of Archaeology*, vol. 29, no. 1, 2005, pp. 20–45.

Budhwa, Rick. "Witnessing Catastrophe: Correlations Between Catastrophic Paleoenvironmental Events and First Nations' Oral Traditions in North America's Pacific Northwest." MA thesis, Simon Fraser University, 2002.

Budhwa, Rick, and Tyler McCreary. "Reconciling Cultural Resource Management with Indigenous Geographies: The Importance of Connecting Research with People and Place." *A Deeper Sense of Place: Stories and Journeys of Indigenous Collaboration*, edited by Jay T. Johnson and Soren C. Larson, Oregon State University Press, 2013, pp. 195–214.

Cashman, Katharine V., and Shane J. Cronin. "Welcoming a Monster to the World: Myths, Oral Tradition, and Modern Societal Response to Volcanic Disasters." *Journal of Volcanology and Geothermal Research*, vol. 176, no. 3, 2008, pp. 407–18.

Cheng, Deqiang, et al. "The Characteristics of the Mocoa Compound Disaster Event, Colombia." *Landslides*, vol. 15, no. 6, June 2018, pp. 1223–32.

Clark, Ella Elizabeth. *Indian Legends of the Pacific Northwest*. University of California Press, 1953.

Crowell, Aron L., and Wayne K. Howell. "Time, Oral Tradition, and Archaeology at Xakwnoowú, a Little Ice Age Fort in Southeastern Alaska." *American Antiquity*, vol. 78, no. 1, Jan. 2013, pp. 3–23.

Cruikshank, Julie. *The Social Life of Stories*. University of Nebraska Press, 1998.

Hanks, Christopher C. "Ancient Knowledge of Ancient Sites: Tracing Dene Identity from the Late Pleistocene and Holocene." *At a Crossroads: Archaeology and First Peoples in Canada*, edited by George Nicholas and Thomas Andrews, Archaeology Press, 1997, pp. 178–89.

Harris, Stephen L. *Agents of Chaos: Earthquakes, Volcanoes, and Other Natural Disasters*. Mountain Press, 1990.

Homuth, Earl. "Crater Lake." *Nature Notes*, vol. 1, no. 2, Aug. 1928, pp. 4–6.

Howe, Carrol B. *Ancient Tribes of the Klamath Country*. Binfords and Mort, 1968.

Hyndman, Roy D. "Giant Earthquakes of the Pacific Northwest." *Scientific American*, vol. 273, no. 6, Dec. 1995, pp. 68–75.

Jennings, Jesse. "Prehistory: Introduction." *Handbook of North American Indians: The Great Basin*, vol. 11, edited by Warren L. D'Azevedo and William C. Sturtevant, Smithsonian Institution, 1986, pp. 113–19.

Klassen, Michael A., et al. "First Nations, Forestry, and the Transformation of Archaeological Practice in British Columbia, Canada." *Heritage Management*, vol. 2, no. 2, Fall 2009, pp. 199–238.

Lawrence, Donald B., and Elizabeth G. Lawrence. "Bridge of the Gods Legend, Its Origin, History and Dating." *Mazama*, vol. 40, no. 13, 1958, pp. 33–41.

Lay, Thorne, et al. "The Great Sumatra-Andaman Earthquake of 26 December 2004." *Science*, vol. 308, no. 5725, 20 May 2005, pp. 1127–33.

Ludwin, Ruth S., et al. "Folklore and Earthquakes: Native American Oral Traditions from Cascadia Compared with Written Traditions from Japan." *Myth and Geology*, edited by L. Piccardi and W. B. Masse, Geological Society Special Publications, 2007, pp. 67–94.

McLaren, Duncan, et al. "A Post-glacial Sea Level Hinge on the Central Pacific Coast of Canada." *Quaternary Science Reviews*, vol. 97, 2014, pp. 148–69.

McLaren, Duncan, et al. "Prerogatives, Sea Level, and the Strength of Persistent Places: Archaeological Evidence for Long-term Occupation of the Central Coast of British Columbia." *BC Studies: The British Columbian Quarterly*, no. 187, 2015, pp. 155–91.

McMillan, Alan D. "Non-Human Whalers in Nuu-chah-nulth Art and Ritual: Reappraising Orca in Archaeological Context." *Cambridge Archaeological Journal*, vol. 29, no. 2, 2018, pp. 1–18.

McMillan, Alan D., and Ian Hutchinson. "Archaeological Evidence for Village Abandonment Associated with Late Holocene Earthquakes at the Northern Cascadia Subduction Zone." *Quaternary Research*, vol. 48, no. 1, July 1997, pp. 79–87.

Mullineaux, D. R. "Summary of Pre-1980 Tephra-fall Deposits Erupted from Mount St. Helens, Washington State, U.S.A." *Bulletin of Volcanology*, vol. 48, Feb. 1986, pp. 17–26.

Nicholas, George, and Nola Markey. "Traditional Knowledge, Archaeological Evidence, and Other Ways of Knowing." *Material Evidence: Learning from Archaeological Practice*, edited by Robert Chapman and Alison Wylie, Routledge, 2015, pp. 287–307.

O'Connor, Jim E., et al. "An Exceptionally Large Columbia River Flood Between 500 and 600 Years Ago; Breaching of the Bridge-of-the-Gods Landslide?" *Geological Society of America*, Program with Abstracts, vol. 28, no. 7, 1996, pp. 97–113.

Plafker, George. "Alaskan Earthquake of 1964 and Chilean Earthquake of 1960: Implications for Arc Tectonics." *Journal of Geophysical Research*, vol. 77, no. 5, 1972, pp. 901–25.

Satake, Kenji, et al. "Time and Size of a Giant Earthquake in Cascadia Inferred from Japanese Tsunami Records of January 1700." *Nature*, vol. 379, no. 18, 1996, pp. 246–49.

Sherrod, David, et al. *Volcanic Hazards at Newberry Volcano, Oregon Report # 97–0513*. Open File Report, U.S. Geological Survey, Virginia, 1997.

Sobel, Elizabeth A., et al. "Environment and Archaeology of the Lower Columbia." *Chinookan Peoples of the Lower Columbia*, edited by Robert T. Boyd et al., University of Washington Press, 2013, pp. 23–41.

Swann, Brian. *Coming to Light: Contemporary Translations of the Native Literatures of North America*. Random House, 1994.

Swanson, Donald A. "Hawaiian Oral Tradition Describes 400 Years of Volcanic Activity at Kīlauea." *Journal of Volcanology and Geothermal Research*, vol. 176, no. 3, 2008, pp. 427–31.

"Thousands Flee as Guatemala's Fuego Volcano Erupts." *BBC News*, 19 Nov. 2018, bbc .com/news/world-latin-america-46261168.

Thrush, Coll, and Ruth S. Ludwin. "Finding Fault: Indigenous Seismology, Colonial Science, and the Rediscovery of Earthquakes and Tsunamis in Cascadia." *American Indian Culture and Research Journal*, vol. 31, no. 4, 2007, pp. 1–24.

Vansina, Jan. *Oral Tradition as History*. University of Wisconsin Press, 1985.

Williams, Howel, and G. Goles. "Volume of the Mazama Ash Fall and the Origin of the Crater Lake Caldera: Andesite Conference Guidebook." *Oregon Department of Geology and Mineral Industries Bulletin*, vol. 62, 1968, pp. 37–41.

Winthrop, Robert. "Crater Lake in Indian Tradition: Sacred Landscape and Cultural Survival." *Nature Notes*, vol. 28, 1997, pp. 18–47.

5

"A Fearful Hope"

EXTINCTION, TERMINATION, RUINATION, AND THE COLONIAL POLITICS OF AMERICAN ANTIQUITY

Gesa Mackenthun

"EXTINCTION" HAS RETURNED AS A new buzzword currently related to the incredible loss of biodiversity (2.9 billion fewer birds are taking wing in North America today than in 1970; see Zimmer). The idea is loudly evoked by public actions of civil disobedience directed against an economic system that allows, and is even built on, such loss. In his speech at the United Nations on 18 September 2018, as in many speeches before and since, UN Secretary-General António Guterres urged the world's leaders to take action.

According to the World Meteorological Organization, the past two decades included 18 of the warmest years since 1850, when records began. . . . Extreme heatwaves, wildfires, storms and floods are leaving a trail of death and devastation. What makes all of this even more disturbing is that we were warned. Scientists have been telling us for decades. Over and over again. Far too many leaders have refused to listen. Far too few have acted with the vision the science demands. We see the results. Oceans are becoming more acidic, threatening the foundation of the food chains that sustain life. Corals are dying in vast amounts, further depleting vital fisheries. And, on land, the high level of carbon dioxide in the atmosphere is making rice crops less nutritious, threatening well-being and food security for billions of people. As climate change intensifies, we will find it harder to feed ourselves. Extinction rates will spike as vital habitats decline. More and more people will be forced to migrate from their homes as the land they depend on becomes less able to support them. . . . Nothing less than our future and the fate of humankind depends on how we rise to the climate challenge.

More than 97 percent of the scientific experts share Guterres's description of the condition of the Earth; they agree that inaction will lead to an exponential increase of the destructive phenomena. A plaque in the Hall of Biodiversity at the American Museum of Natural History (AMNH) reads: "Right now we are in the midst of the Sixth Extinction, this time caused solely by humanity's transformation of the ecological landscape" (qtd. in Kolbert 267).

Extinction Stories Big and Deep

Extinction has become one of the major concerns of our days as the depletion of nonhuman species regularly causes headlines. It has also become part of *cultural discourses* with varying political agendas. Mark Barrow traces the historical genealogy of the modern discourse on human-initiated species extinction, while Ursula Heise points out the important cultural work performed by narratives of ecological decline and extinction that bring about public awareness of the precariousness of the ecological system and the enormous loss of nonhuman life as a result of the industrialization of agriculture, global warming, waste disposal, and other causes. Extinction in environmentalist discourse, she writes, while largely reflecting a correct scientific assessment of the global predicament, has also mined powerful literary and aesthetic narrative modes such as the elegy, the tragic, the sublime, the picturesque, the pastoral, and the apocalyptic (Heise 7). Fictional and nonfictional narratives about species extinction and biodiversity decline, Barrow and Heise argue, and reflect cultural needs, from nostalgia for a life in "natural" plenitude to ethical concerns about interspecies responsibility. Neither Barrow nor Heise focus on the *colonial* uses of extinction discourse. In historical-anthropological thinking, extinction became a topic of debate at the turn of the nineteenth century, significantly caused by the romantic discovery of Mediterranean and non-European ancient cultures and of fossil remains of extinct species. While the romantic ruin came to symbolize the philosophical insight, expressed by historians like Edward Gibbon and artists like Thomas Cole, that human civilizations are wont to decline from states of seeming perfection into savagery and even nonexistence (as in Cole's last painting in his *Course of Empire* cycle), patched-together skeletons of mastodons and other fossils traveled around the Atlantic world as reminders of the transience of both human and nonhuman life on earth. The scientific discoveries of Lyell and Darwin opened up a whole new time horizon within which it now became possible to think about the long-term succession, and extinction, of species and human cultures.

While the world is facing ecological collapse, "Big History" has become a big topic, as Philip J. Deloria's chapter in this volume shows. In his immensely popular book *Sapiens: A Brief History of Mankind* (2011), Yuval Noah Harari explains world history to the common reader as well as the economic elite at international summits at Davos. Reducing the research from various fields of history to a deterministic-biological narrative, Harari argues that the human species consists of imperial predators who will eventually destroy life on the planet as we know it but ultimately—fortunately—replace it with artificial intelligence (see esp. chapter 4). Like the plaque in the AMNH placing responsibility for ecological deprivation on "humanity's transformation of the ecological landscape," Harari's generalizations on the human species are, strictly speaking, incorrect. It is difficult, for example, to subsume human activities under the general rubric of natural processes; such reification downplays the sociological aspect of choice in human decision-making—one of the key elements of Enlightenment liberalism. Just as important, it is not *humanity* that has dramatically transformed the ecological landscape, causing havoc to the planet. Countering the omnipresent anthropocentric argument that humans *in general* produced the ecological crisis, anthropologist Elizabeth Povinelli reminds us that "*humans* did not create this problem. Rather, a specific mode of human society did, and even there, specific classes and races and regions of humans." The antagonism, then, is not between humans and nonhumans but "between various forms of human life-worlds and their different effects on the given world" (Povinelli 12). The thinking deployed in *Sapiens* rests on a fiction of totality that, as Elizabeth DeLoughrey writes, "necessarily obscure[s] the differences across Anthropos" (15). It is one of the dangers and disadvantages of "Big History" that it levels the distinctions between colonizers and colonized, Global North and Global South—that is, between the perpetrators of modernity's ecological disasters and those who are the first to bear the brunt of them.

Inspired by present predictions of impending ecological doom, this chapter presents a few thoughts on re-viewing the powerful colonial trope of "extinction"—as well as the related tropes "termination" and "ruination"—in an attempt to find out what our knowledge of the colonial and archaeological-geological past is able to teach us in preparing for the challenges of the future. More particularly, it seems important to find alternatives for the "terminal narrative" of extinction that is part and parcel of colonial modernity. After all, history also offers us an abundance of experiences that may generate hope and that should, therefore, deserve to be narrated and acted upon.

What, I wonder, is the cultural work produced by the tropes of extinction, termination, and ruination? How do they perform within colonialist discursive settings established in the nineteenth century, and what potential, if any, do they hold for a *relational* epistemology that tries to think beyond the confines of coloniality?[1] Considering initial assessments of the invention and construction of "extinct," "prehistorical" populations in America and of the institutionalized form of extinction discourse in the U.S. government's Termination Policy—which was initiated in 1953 and repealed in 1988, and proactively produced cultural extinction—the chapter focuses on a "prehistorical" natural catastrophe: an ancient volcanic eruption that led to the formation of today's Crater Lake. My contention is that the presence of that event in the Indigenous cultural archive shows this knowledge to belong to the *historical* period because it is part of a collective *story*. The recording of that geological cataclysm and its aftermath, I argue, presents a case of *ruination*, a term that in my reading indicates a more sustainable response to the fatalism inherent in "extinction" and "termination."

Terminal Narratives

"Terminal narrative" is Michael V. Wilcox's term for "historical accounts of demographic collapse, missionization, military conquest, and acculturation [that] have long dominated contact period studies and colonial archaeologies—particularly as they are reflected in explanatory models of disease-based population crashes." Each account, Wilcox contends, "has contributed to an enduring (and ironic) mythology of the perpetually vanishing primitive, and affirmed a sense of disunity, rupture, and alienation between contemporary Indigenous peoples and the material remains of their ancestors" (151). Old World pathogens, Wilcox writes, were rhetorically used in historiography as "a politically neutral agent of colonial destruction, helping to emphasize a conceptual break between a prehistoric landscape inhabited by Native peoples and a historical landscape in which Indigenous peoples are gradually reduced and marginalized" (152). Apart from the fact that the original encounter in the Americas led to severe loss among the Indigenous populations, this was not the ultimate cause of the diminishment of survivors during colonial times.[2] But, instrumentalized, that original catastrophe came to form a powerful narrative of epidemic extinction. The "central agent of destruction" (Wilcox 151) was thus connected to a "natural" agent. "Disease" replaced, in the historical narrative, the "slow violence" of economic and ecological degradation (Nixon), of colonial dispossession and genocidal war.

The "disunity, rupture, and alienation between contemporary Indigenous peoples and the material remains of their ancestors" that Wilcox mentions has been at the heart of colonial mythology from its beginnings, showing signs of a *terminal creed* (Vizenor).[3] The idea of a rupture between contemporary Indigenous populations and their ancestors' material works grew over many decades. Colonial commentators of the late eighteenth and early nineteenth centuries were of the opinion that America had been more or less continuously settled before the arrival of the Europeans. In Query XI of his *Notes on the State of Virginia* (1787), Thomas Jefferson, for example, assumes, on the basis of comparative linguistics, that Native Americans must have had a long history in America because their languages had become radically different from one another—a process that takes a long time, "perhaps not less than many people give to the age of the earth" (102).[4] He therefore regrets "that we have *suffered so many of the Indian tribes already to extinguish*, without our having previously collected and deposited in the records of literature, the general rudiments at least of the languages they spoke" (101, emphasis added). Jefferson's transitive "to extinguish"—implying that their demise was either a natural process or of the Indians' own making—is remarkable in such a linguistically aware writer. Mid-nineteenth-century commentators on the "prehistory" of Native American societies such as Henry Brackenridge and the adventurer-archaeologist John Lloyd Stephens still were of the opinion that the builders of the so-called ruins they saw in the American West and in the U.S. interest zones in Mesoamerica were the work of a culture that had disappeared relatively recently. In a letter to Jefferson in 1813, Brackenridge surmised that the builders of Cahokia might have fallen prey to an epidemic "immediately before we became acquainted with them" (qtd. in Kennedy 184). Stephens, writing on Yucatán in 1841, proposes that the cities whose structures he laid bare might have been continuously inhabited even after the period of the Spanish conquest. He judges by the comparatively fast growth of the tropical trees and shrubs that, although the cities were completely overgrown when he discovered them, they must have been inhabited until only a few generations ago (1: 168–69). They were, he thought, the remains of a bygone "race" whose "degraded" remnant still "lingers round" the sites of former splendor (2: 298). "The first generation of American statesmen-archaeologists," Roger G. Kennedy writes,

> did not require exotic peoples to explain the monumental architecture they found in the Mississippi watershed. . . . [They] simply assumed that the people they found in the valley had been preceded by other Indians who had known more effulgent circumstances—"a more populous people" but not a different one. (236)

Corresponding on the issue half-jokingly in 1813, Thomas Jefferson and John Adams were still relaxed about the matter of ancient American cultures. The "question of Indian origin," writes Jefferson on 27 May 1813, "like many others pushed to a certain height, must recieve [*sic*] the same answer, 'Ignoro.'" On 11 June, Adams replied that to him the question amounted to "non curo," adding:

> I Should as soon Suppose that the Prodigal Son, in a frolic with one of his Girls made a trip to America in one of Mother Careys Eggshels, and left the fruits of their Amours here: as believe any of the grave hypotheses, and Solemn reasonings of Philosophers or Divines upon the Subject of the peopling of America.

In the nineteenth century, speculations about ancient transatlantic colonizations and the violent displacement of a former, foreign-born population intensified with the Mound Builder myth, which "persisted in the face of an awesome burden of evidence to the contrary" (Dippie 17–18). With the Indian removal policy, the story of an ancient extermination conducted by contemporary Indians intensified together with the prognosis of the "modern" Indians' own impending extinction. This narrative of successive Indigenous extinctions formed a powerful component of the discourse on continental expansion. Following earlier hypotheses of Benjamin Barton and others about transatlantic diffusion (see Mucher, chapter 4), Josiah Priest in 1830 offered a whole list of non-Indian Mound Builders, adding Romans, Greeks, and Chinese to Barton's Vikings, whom Barton assumed to be the ancestors of the Mexican Toltecs (Kennedy 236–37). Giving the Toltecs "an infusion of Viking blood," writes Kennedy, "makes them almost Normans, who, as everyone knew, were first cousins to the Anglo-Saxons" (236). Writing from a position close to the frontier at the height of the Indian Wars in 1873, Chicago archaeologist John Wells Foster concluded from his investigations of the Mississippi mounds that a "broad chasm is to be spanned before we can link the Mound-builders to the North American Indians. They are essentially different in their form of government, their habits, and their daily pursuits" (347). While the Mound Builders were a complex agricultural society, Foster regarded modern Indians, who he encountered himself, as completely lacking any "Arcadian virtues, sung by the poets, as characteristic of primitive society." Foster rather agreed with Cotton Mather that they were "the veriest ruins of mankind to be found on the face of the earth" (348). "To suppose that such a race threw up . . . symmetrical mounds," Foster wrote elsewhere, was "preposterous" (qtd. in Kennedy 238). It is rather to be assumed, according to Foster, that the peaceful Mound Builders "were expelled from the Mississippi Valley by a fierce and barbarous race, and that they found refuge in the more genial climate of Central America," where they perfected their civilizational skills (Foster 351).

The terminal creed of a rupture existing between present-day Indians and the builders of the earth and stone structures in the West and South, then, coincided with diffusionist theories of ancient European settlement of America in the context of frontier warfare.[5] On this fertile ground, late nineteenth-century social Darwinism predicted the demise of Native Americans considered culturally "unfit" to adapt to modernity. The narrative of the inevitability of Native American extinction became a powerful tool in the redistribution of real estate, especially after the "closing of the frontier." The General Allotment Act (1887) and the termination policy, which abrogated tribal status and abolished the land title of more than one hundred tribes, practiced cultural extinction as an instrument of assimilation. Termination interpreted extinction not in a biological Darwinian sense but sociologically. The "termination," conducted by the hegemonic power, effectively meant social death (to use Orlando Patterson's term). The policy of extinction-by-termination was officially ended in the 1988, but its effects last today.

The latest chapter of the Native American extinction narrative consists of holding historical and "prehistorical" forms of Indigenous "savagery" responsible for the extinction of nonhuman species. This extinction narrative emerged in the late 1960s, as the Red Power movement for self-determination gained speed, and continues today as Indigenous groups frequently take the lead on civil actions for environmental protection. Its older form, the Pleistocene Overkill hypothesis, monocausally locates responsibility for the demise of "prehistorical" megafauna with the ancestors of present-day Native Americans intruding from Asia and causing a voracious and bloody "Blitzkrieg" extinction. The story's more recent variant translates that historical "crime" to the quasi extinction of the American bison—which has long been shown to be the work of white hunters operating within a global industrial economy in need of buffalo leather (Mackenthun, "Bisoncide"). Such anthropocentric colonial myths function to diminish the moral authority of Native Americans as protectors of the nonhuman world and ultimately serve the interests of the fossil fuel industry. They are diametrically opposed by Indigenous story traditions that give abundant evidence of a "multispecies" epistemology incongruent with the bisoncide story.

Ruined Mountain

The Klamath and Modoc tribes were subject to Termination. The Klamath inhabit an area in Southern Oregon and share their territory and storyworld (and today their tribal representation) with the Modoc and Yahooskin. They entered into colonial relations in the 1850s, with most of the Klamath moving to reservations while some members of the Modoc offered desperate resistance in the Modoc War (1872–73) but were defeated and deported to the Indian Territory in Oklahoma. Despite the territorial losses caused by war and the Allotment Act, the Klamath and Modoc did relatively well in the early twentieth century because they specialized in lumber production. Their economic independence was crushed, however, when the tribes were subjected to the termination policy that led to the loss of all tribal lands and "legal extinction" (Fixico, chapter 4), while non-Indian companies bought up their land and lumber mills. After the revocation of termination, the tribes continue to struggle for economic independence, political recognition, the return of tribal lands, and restoration from social ruination (Fixico, chapter 4; Lewis).

Ann Laura Stoler explores such political implications of the terms *ruin* and *ruination* in her book *Imperial Debris* (2013). Inspired by Walter Benjamin, Stoler invites us to read ruins as "petrified life," as "traces that mark the fragility of power and the force of destruction." Ruins, in her view, are to be seen as "sites that condense alternative senses of history," always attended by processes of "ruination as an ongoing corrosive process that weighs on the future" (9). The continuing construction of Native American and First Nations societies as "prehistorical" or at least as not properly "settled," whose past is condensed in dead human and architectural remains, is part of such a "corrosive" narrative, especially as the characterization of Indigenous cultures as relics of empire is counterproductive to efforts by both Indigenous and non-Indigenous groups to keep the ruinous consequences of the modern extraction economy off their lands. Relying on the dictionary definition of *ruination*, Stoler's analysis attends to ruination as "more than a process that sloughs off debris as a by-product" of empire, more precisely as a *"political project* that lays waste to certain peoples, relations, and things. . . . To focus on ruins is to broach the protracted quality of decimation in people's lives, to track the production of new exposures and enduring damage" (11).

While Stoler thinks of "ruination" as the deadly work of empire whose aesthetic discourse posits ruins as a romantic reminder of ancient national glory, one of her sources for the term, Caribbean writer Michelle Cliff, has used the concept in a rather different way in her novel *No Telephone to Heaven* (1987). Referring to the process by which natural growth reclaims land formerly under colonial cultivation, "ruination" indicates a nonterminal process of destruction followed by ecological restoration. Used in this sense, ruination can be seen as an ecological synonym of "resilience"—and a foundation of Klamath and Modoc society.[6] Their stories contain traces of cataclysmic memories—most prominently the eruption and successive collapse of Mount Mazama, or Gi'was yaina, as the Klamath call the place of the ancient catastrophe. The U.S. place-name is Crater Lake; it is at the center of one of the earliest U.S. National Parks.

The Klamath and Modoc inhabit a volcanic area, part of the Cascadian range to which Mount St. Helens also belongs. Geologists have dated the event leading to the formation of Crater Lake to about 7,700 years ago (Harris; Williams). Archaeologists excavating a rock shelter eighty miles from Fort Rock found sandals underneath the ash layer related to Mount Mazama, which indicates the antiquity of human habitation in the area. The notation of the collapse of Gi'was in the Klamath and Modoc story archive adds epistemic continuity to the cultural continuity marked by the sandals (see the chapter by Rick Budhwa in this volume).

The oldest stories, collected in the nineteenth century by the Swiss American linguist Albert Gatschet and the American journalist and translator Jeremiah Curtin, lack direct reference to a volcanic outbreak. They instead relate the event in the form of an existential battle between two powerful beings: Kmu'kamsh, the geological creator of the world—also called Skel or Old Marten—and the Lemeish (or Lewa), one or several (usually five) Thunder beings who inhabited the place called Gi'was (Gatschet II: 49). Furnished with a magical cap that he had formerly stolen from the North Wind (the ruler of today's Yamsay Mountain), Old Marten / Kmu'kamsh, accompanied by his younger brother Weasel (Tcûskai), enters the lodge of the Five Thunders at Gi'was and freezes their home so that they cannot enter. When he finally takes the cap off, they deviously invite him for a feast on human flesh in order to overwhelm him once he is asleep. In another version (Curtin, *Myths* 113), the feast is accompanied by a wrestling contest won by the witty Old Marten (Skel). He manages to beat the Thunders at their own game, binding their hair together and then setting their lodge on fire. At the climax of the story, Kmu'kamsh the creator god stands on top of the burning mountain, popping open the hot hearts of the Thunders as they fly up into the sky (Gatschet I: 111–14; Curtin, *Myths* 80). The cultural archive contains further stories about fire mountains and lakes of pitch that are usually produced by Kmu'kamsh to punish other mythological characters. These versions, summarized here for the sake of clarity, were collected directly from Klamath and Modoc survivors—one of them a Modoc elder named Ko-a-lak'-ak-a ("Hard Working Woman"), evidently an expert storyteller whom Curtin had encountered during her exile in the Indian Territory.[7] In his posthumously published *Memoirs*, Curtin writes that Ko-a-lak'-ak-a had in her mind all the lore her people possessed a hundred years ago. She was the daughter and granddaughter of a chief and when a child her grandfather taught her the wisdom of the Modocs. She had a wonderful memory. Though she was no longer young and her health was poor, she was willing to give me the myths and beliefs of her tribe. She had more stories in her head than I dreamed it [was] possible for any one to learn and keep without aid of books. (331)

Ko-a-lak'-ak-a's "willingness" to share her knowledge must be viewed in the context of the desperate condition in which Curtin found the survivors of the Modoc resistance. In fact, her generosity can be read as an act of *hiring* the white man in order to preserve her knowledge, most of which would probably have been lost without both her and Curtin's dedication to recordkeeping.[8] She made a precise estimation of her people's situation and of the character of the strange man who traveled the country, who listened to stories and spent whole weeks learning the language from her (reportedly she spoke no English [Curtin, *Memoirs* 332]). Ethnography conveniently regards people like Ko-a-lak'-ak-a as "informants" or "interlocutors," but it would be more correct to view her as a historical *agent*, placing her knowledge in the hands of someone who she hoped would deal with it in a responsible manner.

Neither Gatschet nor Curtin knew of the ancient volcanic events at Gi'was when they collected the stories; Gatschet in fact interprets the story of the destruction of the Thunders in meteorological terms. Only in 1896, after a geological expedition led by Silas Diller, did it become clear that Crater Lake was the site of a former mountain (called Mount Mazama by the colonists), which collapsed due to a volcanic eruption. After this year, renditions of the Kmu'kamsh story integrate that geological knowledge into their plot and imagery, along with other Euro-American elements.

The most widely circulated version is based on an unpublished manuscript written by Civil War veteran and Oregon settler William Colvig, who collected the story from a Klamath chief, Lalek, in the 1860s but only wrote it down in its final version in 1921. Colvig's version "romances" the story by presenting Skel and Lao (the Thunder figure) as competitors for the affection of a human woman. Skel is the "Chief of the Above World" standing atop Mount Shasta; Lao, lord of the "Below World," stands atop "the high mountain that used to be." At the culmination of their battle,

mountains shook and crumbled. Red-hot rocks as large as the hills hurtled through the skies. Burning ashes fell like rain. The Chief of the Below World spewed fire from his mouth. Like an ocean of flame it devoured the forests on the mountains and in the valleys. On and on the Curse of Fire swept until it reached the homes of the people. Fleeing in terror before it, the people found refuge in the waters of Klamath Lake. (Clark 54)

In this extreme crisis, two medicine men sacrifice themselves to rescue the people and walk into the mouth of the volcano, the "entrance of the Below World" (55). The "Chief of the Below World was driven into his home, and the top of the mountain fell upon him. When the morning sun rose, the high mountain was gone" (55).

More recently, the Klamath storyteller Barbara Alatorre gave her own rendition of the story. Again, the two chiefs compete for the favors of a human woman, Loha. The "bad" chief, here called Monadalkni, sends an emissary, Skooks, to demand her hand.

As Skooks' hideous crimson red eyes gaped at the maiden, the Ma'Klaks [Klamath] of the village watched her other suitors disappear in a flash of orange light. Loha raced to her father's tule lodge crying out, "No, I don't want to live in a mountain!" The Klamath chief quickly called elders and medicine men to council in his lodge. They decided that Loha must be whisked away to their Modoc brothers to the south.

Skooks returned the next night demanding Loha's whereabouts, but no one in the tribe would speak. When Monadalkni learned of the maiden's disappearance, he shook with violent anger and threatened fiery vengeance on Loha's people. Monadalkni began running back and forth in the passageways beneath Moy-yaina [Gi'was/Mazama], throwing lightning bolts and causing the mountain to explode with such force that molten lava rained like hot pitch upon the People of the Lakes. Giant fireballs shot out of the mountain as it erupted in deafening booms—five times in succession! Women and children took refuge in Klamath Lake, crying and calling out for the Great Spirit to save them.

Monadalkni ran to the top of the mountain and faced Gmo'Kamc. They fought enraged, silhouetted against the red glow illuminating the rumbling Cascades. (Alatorre)

Kmu'kamsh, standing on top of Mount Shasta (the volcano dominating Modoc country to which the maiden had been brought), forces the bad chief into the mountain and causes the mountain to crash. Medicine men then pray for rain to fill the crater, "creating the lake called Gii-was. Cradled in the bosom of Tum-sum-ne (Klamath/Modoc for 'the big mountain with top cut off'), Gii-was became a holy place the Ma'Klaks kept secret for more than

7,000 years, until one day in 1852 when a white man accidentally discovered it. In 1902, Gii-was became Crater Lake National Park" (Alatorre).

Alatorre's version contains elements from both the Colvig version and that found in Gatschet and Curtin. It activates the metaphorical repertoire of gothic romance and introduces an additional character for more effect—Skooks with his "hideous crimson red eyes." Alatorre also includes the element of the transcultural sacredness of the place—as a place of fasting and vision seeking, and a natural heritage site.[9]

Surprisingly, there is a general consent that the story is 7,700 years old. The Kmu'kamsh-Gi'was story complex, connecting the destruction of the Thunders and an active fire mountain with the place where there is now Crater Lake, is strong cultural evidence for a long-term collective memory whose preservation was only possible because a culturally continuous population had resided in that area for many millennia: an almost "uncanny" example in sedentariness, unmatched by any European "tribe," as Vine Deloria Jr. remarks (167). Ruth S. Ludwin and Coll Thrush, Julie Cruikshank, Rick Budhwa (in this volume), and others have convincingly argued that Indigenous stories do remember cataclysmic geological events.[10] Owing to an extremely rare concurrence of seismic activity and longevity of inhabitance, the stories related to Gi'was arguably represent the oldest evidence of the cultural effects of a volcanic eruption on a group of humans in world history. Even in the Hegelian sense, then, the knowledge transmitted by the Klamath and Modoc belongs to the realm of *history*, not "prehistory"—a history remembered for more than seven thousand years.

There are not many cases of a comparable literary coverage of dateable volcanic eruptions and their traumatizing effects before 1883 (Mount Krakatoa). Pliny's account of the eruption of Mount Vesuvius in 79 CE comes to mind, or the more complex poetic coverage of the effects of the eruption and collapse of Tambora, Java, in 1815, which caused crop failures, starvation, and disease throughout the world and left its cultural imprint on Lord Byron's poem "Darkness." Amazingly, the poem includes a volcanic eruption, though Byron knew nothing about the cause of the climate catastrophe. He imagines the volcano as a source of light, warmth, and "fearful hope" for the people suffering from the "year without a summer."[11] The second aesthetic documentation of the effects of the Tambora eruption is, of course, Mary Shelley's sunless universe of *Frankenstein*, written, like Byron's poem, in 1816 at Lake Geneva—a place severely struck by the disaster (Wood, chapter 3). The Klamath oral tradition to which the Gi'was stories belong can be seen as a comparable cultural work, created to close the wound around a historical trauma—if not a spiritual trauma at the incomprehensible actions of the creator Kmu'kamsh, who, like the Christian God, is both creator and destroyer of the world inhabited by his human and nonhuman sons and daughters. The Indigenous multispecies universe offers an intellectual alternative to the anthropocentric perspective we have become so used to.

Ruination and the Work of Companion Species

The word *Gi'was* deserves more attention in this context, because, as Gatschet's dictionary reveals, the Klamath name of Crater Lake has more than one meaning.[12] In addition to referring to Crater Lake (Gĩ'wash É-ush) as well as "Crater Mountain"—which Gatschet assumes to refer to Mount Scott just east of Crater Lake (II: 49)—"Gi'wash," although with a different pronunciation of the *g* sound, is also the name applied to a *"blueish-gray squirrel, of the size of the marten: Sciurus Douglassii"* (Gatschet II: 49, 245).[13] Apart from the possibility that a minor language shift may have occurred over seven thousand years of language history, the pine squirrel Gi'was, contrary to its name, behaves in ways worthy of Old Marten and his younger brother Weasel. Like the pine marten, one of the embodiments of Kmu'kamsh, the pine squirrel—"of the size of the marten"—seasonally changes the color of its fur. Both obviously live in pine trees; the squirrel keeps its food stores in holes high up in the trees.[14] In *The Mountains of California* (1894), John Muir renders a delightful account of this animal, regarding it as one of the most impressive creatures of the Western mountain area. He emphasizes its transformative powers and its great impact on seed distribution, which makes the pine squirrel appear like the "master forester" of the pine forest. The squirrel even assists in the regrowth of the forest after fire seasons by hiding and burying pine seeds.

Gi'was, then, is both a place and an animal figure that represents natural restoration and resilience. The Klamath and Modoc, who observed the squirrel's contribution to biotope health, made a note of this in their stories—a case of traditional ecological (or Indigenous) knowledge (TEK).[15] In a lesser-known and probably more recent Modoc story ("Wus Wants to Marry a Butterfly," included in Curtin, *Myths* 214–18), a squirrel is the older teacher of the story's protagonist, Wus (Fox), who would like to marry the beautiful butterflies. Djaudjau, the Flying Squirrel, instructs the wayward Wus to first receive a solid spiritual education before thinking of sex with butterflies. Djaudjau takes Wus to many sacred lakes for the purpose of spiritual cleansing. When Wus finally meets the butterflies, they reject him, which makes Wus angry. On his way home, he meets a mysterious couple in a house who feed and entertain him and dissuade him from further persecuting his amorous aim. Their name is Guíwas. Wus subsequently moves away from the mountain, but the squirrel Djaudjau announces that he himself will stay: "'I am named for the mountains and I will never leave them.'" The story ends with "Old Djaudjau . . . hunting on those mountains yet. People who travel on high mountains often hear him calling his own name. Wus and his mother went to Klamath Lake, and people say that they live there now" (Curtin, *Myths* 218).

These narratives, I contend, remember a catastrophe (or several) that has left a damaged Earth in Klamath/Modoc country. Yet they do not express terminal creeds but speak of recovery and resilience. They make precise observations of how the natural world rebuilds itself after a cataclysmic conflagration, and they articulate a "multispecies" episteme that Indigenous people were able to retain *despite* quasi destruction by the colonial clash. We are now relearning this episteme through the deconstruction of the nature-culture split of rationalism, aided by a reinvigoration of Indigenous ontologies (De-Loughrey 30–31). It is an episteme that values the contribution of various animals to the making and remaking of the world.

A recent picture book for children, the collaboration of a scientist and an artist, tells a quite similar story. In *Gopher to the Rescue! A Volcano Recovery Story* (2012), Terry Catasús Jennings and Laurie O'Keefe explain the restoration of an area after a volcanic eruption (their example is Mount St. Helens in 1980) by focusing on the activity of animals, especially the gopher, who helps replenish the Earth by hoarding bulbs, nuts, and seeds in his subterranean burrow. What connects the gopher story with the Klamath and Modoc traditions is that they avoid the plot of terminal narratives and instead embed catastrophic events in a redemptive plot of rebuilding and natural resilience. They do this by representing nonhumans as companion species engaged in collective worldmaking—in "ruinating" the land by replanting it and filling it with new life.[16] "Ruination," after all, has an ambivalent meaning in Cliff's usage (and in that of her source, Barry Floyd), referring to the process by which land formerly used for agriculture has lapsed back into "bush."[17] The Jamaican forest of Cliff's novel obliterates the graves of the colonial landowners: "A wild design of color" encloses the garden and grave of the protagonist's grandmother. A "flame-of-the-forest," which, when in bloom, resembles a volcanic cloud, "sparked the disorder, as the heavy jasmine scented the ruination" (8). In spite of the morphological similarity of the signifiers "ruin" and "ruination," the evoked referents could hardly be more different: one employed by the colonial repertoire for nostalgically dwelling on the catastrophic passing of empires; the other emphasizing the cyclical restorative force of nature.

The ruination narratives of the Klamath and Modoc, of Jennings, O'Keefe, and Cliff concur with Heise's urge to move beyond tragic and terminal narratives and toward stories responsive to the imperative of multispecies cosmopolitan justice (6, 244). Klamath and Modoc stories, full of transspecies worldmaking, effectively share in the kind of nonanthropocentric philosophy Heise calls for. They thrive in spite of termination, just as the tribes will hopefully continue to recover from that recent traumatic period in their long, collective history.

Coda

Ancient stories, like those remembering the cataclysmic events at Gi'was, can teach listeners about the dangers of Evil Gamblers, the destruction they produce, and the methods of outwitting them at their own game: Lao and the Thunders are manifestations of this evil principle common to many Indigenous mythologies.[18] The stories of Evil Gamblers are indeed terminal narratives, preceded and preparative of terminal actions, as history has made all too clear. Western discourse abounds with more or less violent narratives about the past and apocalyptic visions of the future, but it has been virtually unable to produce nonapocalyptic future visions. Imperial plots are very old—not to say petrified and "prehistoric"—but mostly devoid of peaceful worldmaking intelligence. Indigenous multispecies stories belong to a different episteme. They follow the rule of orally transmitted knowledge that, while recording landmark events from different moments in the collective past, are primarily dedicated to preserving the Earth for being inhabited by seven future generations. Therefore, in addition to "singing" the deeds of ancient heroes, poets, and artisans, let's replace terminal narratives of extinction with stories of ruination, resilience, and hope—let us sing the stories of martens, squirrels, pine trees, and gophers! Knowledge of transcultural archives can help imagine such narratives and such futures.[19]

Notes

1. "Relationalist epistemology" is inspired by the work of Arturo Escobar, who pushes the critique of the coloniality of modernity, conducted by Walter Mignolo, Aníbal Quijano, and others (see Mignolo and Escobar; Mignolo and Walsh), into integrating non-Western, Indigenous, and grassroots worldviews that "escape the division of nature and culture" and effect an ethical empowerment of nonhuman agents, including "mountains, water, soil, the forest" (Escobar 397).

2. A recent archaeological study controversially suggests that 95 percent of the continent's inhabitants—about fifty-six million people—vanished during the first few decades of the colonial encounter. The study claims that that population cataclysm (the "Great Dying," as it is sometimes called) may have led to a severe decline in atmospheric CO_2 and thus to a global temperature drop during the Little Ice Age due to the plummeting of agricultural and horticultural activity (Koch et al.). The study of course hinges on the assumption that a mass extinction of this dimension—the database for which is rather fragmentary—did actually occur.

3. "Terminal creed" is Vizenor's term for static, total belief systems that he identifies with Western culture. The cannibal figure Evil Gambler is associated with terminal creeds (147).

4. Jefferson assumes the languages of America to be "of greater antiquity than those of Asia" (*Notes on Virginia* 102).

5. As Annette Kolodny's chapter in this volume shows, the rupture theory of displacement continued into twentieth-century academic discourse.

6. Indigenous residents of the Klamath River region narrating the process of healing from the perspective of the tribes affected by Termination Policy demonstrate their communities' power of resilience (Lara-Cooper and Lara), while scientists working in water and resource management discuss conflicting aspects of resilience occurring between Indigenous and non-Indigenous residents of the Upper and Lower Klamath River (the formerly "terminated" Klamath Tribes, Northern Californian tribes like the Yurok, Karok, and Tolowa). They analyze the complexity of legal and ecological conflicts with regard to river governance in the era of global climate change and rising aridity in the Pacific Northwest, arguing that resilience depends on a cooperative approach to the common challenge (Chaffin et al.).

7. For a full discussion, see Mackenthun, *Embattled Excavations*, chapter 4.

8. Curtin and Gatschet went about their work with an almost immeasurable dedication—Curtin learning the languages of various Pacific tribes and Gatschet patiently constructing his two-volume set of Klamath language and cultural knowledge. Their activities, and the knowledge they helped preserve, forms an important counterpoint to the genocidal policy of their time—in spite of the fact that both were conducted within the pervasive extinction discourse.

9. Obviously the establishment of such "sacred" natural places by colonial society was complicit with the project of Indian dispossession, just as early naturalists preferred to enjoy the "wilderness" without Native people in it (Spence).

10. Jan Vansina, expert on oral traditions around the world, lists calamities as conducive of long-term memory and dates one oral tradition from Polynesia to sixty generations (175–76).

11. Byron imagines the people burning their homes and palaces in order to have light in the complete darkness: "And men were gather'd round their blazing homes / To look once more into each other's face; / Happy were those who dwelt within the eye / Of the volcanos, and their mountain-torch: / A fearful hope was all the world contain'd;

/ Forests were set on fire—but hour by hour / They fell and faded—and the crackling trunks / Extinguish'd with a crash—and all was black" (412).

12. The meaning of "léwa" is "to play" (e.g., a ballgame) (Gatschet II: 189). Lewa/Lao is an evil gambler.

13. The present-day Klamath dictionary also distinguishes between the two terms, having "giiwas" for Crater Lake and "gi?was" for the pine squirrel. "Klamath Tribes Language Project," klamathtribes.org/language/vocabulary, accessed 23 Nov. 2020.

14. See "Pine Squirrel," Wikipedia, en.wikipedia.org/wiki/Pine_squirrel, accessed 23 Nov. 2020; "Douglas Squirrel," Wikipedia, en.wikipedia.org/wiki/Douglas_squirrel, accessed 23 Nov. 2020.

15. In other stories (which received a masterful structuralist analysis from Claude Lévi-Strauss), a squirrel is a plot-decisive character—as a wife of Kmu'kamsh's son Aishish, whom Kmu'kamsh seduces and abducts.

16. "Companion species" is Donna Haraway's term (chapter 1).

17. "An impressive variety of herbaceous shrubs and woody types of vegetation appears in succession, becoming thicker and taller over the years until 'high ruinate' forest may emerge" (Floyd qtd. in Cliff 1; Stoler 19–20).

18. The figure of the Evil Gambler is prominent in modern literature by Native American writers such as Leslie Marmon Silko and Gerald Vizenor. The motif of cannibalism appears in the second story relating to Gi'was—of Lewa/Lao killing and dismembering Kmu'kamsh/Skel, playing a ballgame with his head and then intending to feed him to his children inhabiting Gi'was lake. Skel's animal friends put him back together; Skel kills and dismembers Lewa and feeds him to his own children. Lewa's head, shunned by his children, becomes the volcanic cone now called Wizard Island (Clark 56–58; Gatschet II: 189).

19. I thank the Klamath, Modoc, and Yahooskin Tribes for their permission to use their tribal stories. I also thank Tim Colvig, Oakland, California, for allowing me to use the Crater Lake story manuscript of his ancestor Judge William Colvig.

References

Adams, John. "John Adams to Thomas Jefferson, 11 June 1813." *Founders Online*, National Archives, founders.archives.gov/documents/Jefferson/03–06–02–0171.

Alatorre, Barbara. "'How Crater Lake Came to Be: A Klamath Indian Legend Special for the Herald and News." Crater Lake Institute, *Herald and News*, 25 Feb. 2002, craterlakeinstitute.com/crater-lake-new-archives/2002–2/2002–02–6/?hilite=%27Alatorre%27.

Barrow, Mark V. *Nature's Ghosts: Confronting Extinction from the Age of Jefferson to the Age of Ecology*. University of Chicago Press, 2009.

Byron, George Gordon Lord. "Darkness." 1816. *Selected Poems*, Penguin, 2006, pp. 412–15.

Chaffin, Brian, et al. "Resilience, Adaptation, and Transformation in the Klamath River Basin Socio-Ecological System." *Idaho Law Review*, vol. 51, 2014, pp. 157–93.

Clark, Ella Elizabeth. *Indian Legends of the Pacific Northwest*. University of California Press, 1953.

Cliff, Michelle. *No Telephone to Heaven*. Vintage, 1987.

Colvig, William. "The Legend of Crater Lake." 1921. Unpublished manuscript. Private archive, Tim Colvig.

Cruikshank, Julie. *Do Glaciers Listen? Local Knowledge, Colonial Encounters, and Social Imagination*. University of British Columbia Press, 2005.

Curtin, Jeremiah. *Memoirs of Jeremiah Curtin*, edited by Joseph Schafer, State Historical Society of Wisconsin, 1940.

Curtin, Jeremiah. *Myths of the Modocs*. Boston, 1912.

Deloria, Vine, Jr. *Red Earth, White Lies: Native Americans and the Myth of Scientific Fact*. Scribner, 1995.

DeLoughrey, Elizabeth. *Allegories of the Anthropocene*. Duke University Press, 2019.

Dippie, Brian D. *The Vanishing American: White Attitudes and U.S. Indian Policy*. Wesleyan University Press, 1982.

Escobar, Arturo. "Afterword." *Globalization and the Decolonial Option*, edited by Walter D. Mignolo and Arturo Escobar, Routledge, 2010, pp. 369–401.

Fixico, Donald L. *The Invasion of Indian Country in the Twentieth Century: American Capitalism and Tribal Natural Resources*. 2nd ed., University Press of Colorado, 2012.

Floyd, Barry. *Jamaica: An Island Microcosm*. St. Martin's Press, 1979.

Foster, John Wells. *Pre-Historic Races of the United States of America*. Chicago, 1873.

Gatschet, Albert S. *The Klamath Indians of Southwestern Oregon*. Washington, D.C., 1890. 2 vols.

Harari, Yuval Noah. *Sapiens: A Brief History of Mankind*. Vintage, 2011.

Haraway, Donna J. *Staying with the Trouble: Making Kin in the Chthulucene*. Duke University Press, 2016.

Harris, Stephen J. *Fire Mountains of the West: The Cascade and Momo Lake Volcanoes*. Mountain Press, 1988.

Heise, Ursula. *Imagining Extinction: The Cultural Meanings of Endangered Species*. University of Chicago Press, 2016.

Jefferson, Thomas. *Notes on the State of Virginia*. London, 1787.

Jefferson, Thomas. "Thomas Jefferson to John Adams, 27 May 1813." *Founders Online*, National Archives, founders.archives.gov/documents/Jefferson/03-06-02-0138.

Jennings, Terry Catasús, and Laurie O'Keefe. *Gopher to the Rescue! A Volcano Recovery Story*. Arbordale, 2012.

Kennedy, Roger G. *Hidden Cities: The Discovery and Loss of Ancient North American Civilization*. Penguin, 1994.

Koch, Alexander, et al. "Earth System Impacts of the European Arrival and Great Dying in the Americas After 1492." *Quarternary Science Reviews*, vol. 207, 1 Mar. 2019, pp. 13–36.

Kolbert, Elizabeth. *The Sixth Extinction: An Unnatural History*. Picador, 2014.

Lara-Cooper, Kishan, and Walter S. Lara Sr. *Ka'm-t'em: A Journey Toward Healing*. Great Oak Press, 2019.

Lévi-Strauss, Claude. *The Naked Man*. Vol. 4 of *Introduction to a Science of Mythology*. 1971. Translated by John and Doreen Weightman, Harper and Row, 1981.

Lewis, David G. "Klamath Termination: Water, Timber and Sovereign Rights." *Ethnohistory Research*, 17 July 2015, ndnhistoryresearch.com/2015/07/17/klamath-termination/.

Ludwin, Ruth S., and Coll Thrush. "Finding Fault: Indigenous Seismology, Colonial Science, and the Rediscovery of Earthquakes and Tsunamis in Cascadia." *American Indian Culture and Research Journal*, vol. 31, no. 4, 2007, pp. 1–24.

Mackenthun, Gesa. "Bisoncide and Neo-Savagism: The Myth of the Unecological Indian." *America After Nature*, edited by Catrin Gersdorf, Winter, 2016, pp. 163–98.

Mackenthun, Gesa. *Embattled Excavations: Colonial and Transcultural Constructions of the American Deep Past*. Forthcoming.

Mignolo, Walter, and Arturo Escobar, eds. *Globalization and the Decolonial Option*. Routledge, 2009.

Mignolo, Walter, and Catherine E. Walsh. *On Decoloniality: Concepts, Analytics, Praxis*. Duke University Press, 2018.

Mucher, Christen. *Before American History*. University of Virginia Press, forthcoming.

Muir, John. "The Douglas Squirrel." *The Mountains of California*, New York, 1894, pp. 226–43.

Nixon, Rob. *Slow Violence and the Environmentalism of the Poor*. Harvard University Press, 2011.

Patterson, Orlando. *Slavery and Social Death*. Harvard University Press, 1982.

Povinelli, Elizabeth. *Geontologies: A Requiem to Late Liberalism*. Duke University Press, 2016.

Quijano, Aníbal. "Coloniality of Power, Eurocentrism, and Latin America." *Globalization and the Decolonial Option*, edited by Walter Mignolo and Arturo Escobar, Routledge, 2009, pp. 181–224.

Spence, Mark David. *Dispossessing the Wilderness: Indian Removal and the Making of the National Parks*. Oxford University Press, 1999.

Stephens, John Lloyd. *Incidents of Travel in Yucatan*. 1843. Dover, 1963. 2 vols.

Stoler, Ann Laura. *Imperial Debris: On Ruins and Ruination*. Duke University Press, 2013.

Vansina, Jan. *Oral Tradition as History*. University of Wisconsin Press, 1985.

Vizenor. Gerald. *Narrative Chance: Postmodern Discourse on Native American Indian Literatures*. University of Oklahoma Press, 1989.

Wilcox, Michael V. "Indigenous Archaeology and the Pueblo Revolt of 1680: Social Mobility and Boundary Maintenance in Colonial Contexts." *Rethinking Colonial Pasts Through Archaeology*, edited by Neal Ferris et al., Oxford University Press, 2014, pp. 150–72.

Williams, Howel. *The Ancient Volcanoes of Oregon*. University of Oregon, 1948.

Wood, Gillen D'Arcy. *Tambora: The Eruption That Changed the World*. Princeton University Press, 2014.

Zimmer, Carl. "Birds Are Vanishing from North America." *New York Times*, 19 Sep. 2019.

6

Myth Making and Unmaking

INDIGENOUS SACRED SITES, SETTLER COLONIAL MOBILITY, AND
ONTOLOGICAL OPPRESSION

Keith Thor Carlson with Naxaxalhts'i
(Sonny McHalsie)

Setting the Scene

IN 1858 FRENCH SOCIETY BECAME transfixed with a small natural
cave in the Pyrenees, not because it contained valuable minerals or because
humans had earlier invested their labor in the site to somehow render it special. Rather, it was valued because people believed the accounts of a young
Occitan girl who claimed to have been visited there by an apparition of the
Virgin Mary. Over the following decades, millions of the faithful made pilgrimages to Lourdes in the belief that they could receive from the site mirac-
ulous healing and insights. Lourdes, few would have felt the need to argue,
was, and is, deeply deserving of preservation (Evans; Jansen and Notermans).
At the same time, across the English Channel, Sir John Lubbock was working
through academic and parliamentary circles arguing that the British government had an obligation to preserve for posterity what today would be called
cultural heritage resources. In Lubbock's opinion, this obligation transcended
the rights of the private and corporate property owners who controlled the
land where such sites existed, regardless of the owner's own economic vision
or aspirations (Sax).[1] In Canada, meanwhile, Governor General Lord Dufferin
was the most high-profile public figure calling for historical sites such as the
original fortifications of Quebec City to be preserved from urban development
(Todhunter).

Whereas nineteenth-century British, European, and Canadian societies
were awakening to the merits of preserving both tangible and intangible
heritage sites that were linked to their own histories and spiritualities, they

were unconcerned over settler actions destroying Indigenous tangible and intangible heritage sites throughout their global empires. In the wake of the 1858 Fraser River gold rush in Britain's newly proclaimed colony of British Columbia, for example, Royal Engineers were using explosives to build road, steamboat, and railway transportation routes along the Fraser River, blasting away many of the sacred transformer sites that the Stó:lō Coast Salish understood to have been created by Xe:Xá:ls (the myth-age transformer siblings).

Xe:Xá:ls were understood by the Stó:lō as having changed the previously chaotic world into its current permanent and predictable form. Certain large stones, from the Stó:lō perspective, were ancestors who had been transformed by Xe:Xá:ls and whose spirits remained sentient. Moreover, these boulders and rock formations were mnemonic features that properly trained Indigenous people could read like words in a book in order to recall ancient stories explaining the origins of tribal leaders and providing moral and philosophical lessons to the living (Carlson, "Orality About Literacy"). These sites were central not only to Stó:lō heritage but to Stó:lō community health, for in the right circumstances, the sentient spirits in the landscape could share memories with people and in so doing invest new historical understandings and knowledge into human society. Such knowledge helped people chart courses into the future.

For the purpose of this chapter, the important fact is not that the settler colonists who arrived in Stó:lō territory were incapable of coming to know and value Indigenous lands in terms beyond those that could either be aesthetically appreciated or commercially quantified. Rather, settler colonialism required its practitioners to be ontologically blind to values that would have disrupted or challenged the colonial incumbency to displace Indigenous people from their lands and resources (Spivak 90–91). And indeed, while the miners and then farmers who arrived in Stó:lō territory in the wake of the gold rush were driven by capitalist economic aspirations, they were also motivated and animated by a series of their own mythical and philosophical narratives and understandings—key among them the American concept of Manifest Destiny and its Canadian counterpart, Dominion. Thus, whereas British/European and settler heritage sites that reflected deep history and mysterious intangible meaning were being recognized in Europe and North America as worthy of societal protection in the face of rapid private and corporate developments, no such considerations were extended to Indigenous sacred spaces and historical places. Under settler logic, such consideration could not exist lest settler colonialism itself be compromised.

Settler Colonial Myths, Sacredness, and
Movement over the Land

Scholarship led by Patrick Wolfe and more recently given theoretical sophistication by Lorenzo Veracini has established North American settler colonialism as a structure of ongoing domination that operates in a host of complicated ways to separate Indigenous peoples from their traditional lands (see also Barker and Battell). But to an extent that has not yet been fully explored, settler colonialism has been built upon an intellectual foundation that defined Britain, Europe, and North American settler spaces not merely as sites of economic and political power and modernity but as geographies that were made knowable through history and religion—that is, in ways that went beyond Western aesthetics and that were other than purely mercantile and economic.

In the mid-nineteenth century, settler society had conveniently determined that North American Indigenous people resembled what they believed their own European ancestors had been like at some point in the distant past. But, from the westward-looking perspective of colonists and settlers, unlike their own ancestors, the continent's Indigenous people had become trapped in a state where the passage of history was not marked by pivotal moments of documented (let alone documentable) temporal change, and where superstition and spirituality had failed to be challenged by the light of rational science and/or legitimated and given shape by organized religion.[2] During the era when concepts such as "extinction" and "evolution" had not yet been fully defined but were nonetheless shaping and giving form to settler colonial public discourse and government policy, colonists' understandings of Indigenous people as *ni foi, ni roi, ni loi* and as being mere *occupants* of a *terra nullius* rather than *citizens* of a *homeland* had profound implications (A. Pratt; Richardson).

It is no coincidence that by the mid-nineteenth century, Indigenous people had become a minority in settler colonial states. North American Indigenous peoples' susceptibility to infectious Eurasian crowd diseases such as smallpox, measles, and influenza meant that not only did Indigenous people quickly find themselves in a militarily compromised position vis-à-vis early colonists and settlers but that colonists could come to increasingly rationalize their policies aimed at dispossessing Indigenous people of their lands through the myth that Indigenous people were a dying or vanishing race. The Stó:lō had been hit by a devastating smallpox epidemic in 1782 that killed between 60 percent and 90 percent of their population (Carlson, "Numbers Game"). A series of subsequent outbreaks of diseases previously unknown to the Stó:lō such as tuberculosis and venereal diseases, coupled with alcoholism and the

periodic return of smallpox, mumps, and measles over the coming generations, had left the Stó:lō, like other Indigenous communities, a demographic
shadow of their former self (Boyd, chapter 2; Carlson, *Power of Place* 91–111;
C. Harris, "Voices of Disaster" 591). If Indigenous people were dying out,
settler colonial rhetoric ran, there would soon come a time when they would
no longer require land. As historian Brian D. Dippie has demonstrated, Indian policy in North America emerged accordingly.

Thus, a key differentiation between classic extraction colonialism (as occurred under the British and French in India and Indochina and under the
Japanese in Korea) and settler colonialism in North America is that over time,
settler colonial societies develop a habitus that multigenerational residence
bestows territorial and democratic rights of self-determination. In their view,
the settlers' territorial and political dissociation from the former mother country endows them with allodial rights to the land they now inhabit.

Rhetorically, the principles of Western democracy hold that citizens within
a defined political region have a right to self-determination. A closely related
Western principle was, and remains, that citizens have a right to mobility.
Indeed, settler colonial nations in particular sustain themselves through the
coupling of the logic of democracy and the pragmatics of mobility. To create
North American settler colonial states, early immigrants from Britain and
Europe (and then later Asia and elsewhere) necessarily secured for themselves
the right to relocate. In Canada, mobility rights are constitutionally protected
in Section 6 of the Canadian Charter of Rights. In the United States, similar
mobility rights derive from the Constitution's Privileges and Immunities
clause. Thus, while the colonial process is rhetorically about settlement, in
practice it is about mobility.

Once established, settler colonies embraced a philosophy that regarded
ongoing and sustained immigration as not only positive but necessary. Along
the lower reaches of the Fraser River in 1857, there were fewer than one hundred non-Indigenous residents, most of whom worked for the Hudson's Bay
Company. But over the course of four short months in the spring of 1858,
more than thirty thousand mostly American miners flooded into the region
searching for gold—a population influx that to this day remains the largest in
British Columbia's history. While racism curbed certain historical expressions
of immigration (e.g., settlers of British descent in British Columbia sought at
various times to restrict Chinese, Eastern European, South Asian, and African
immigration), it also worked to accelerate immigration from racially and
culturally "desirable" countries. Following the 1858 gold rush, the British
government pursued an aggressive policy aimed at attracting loyal British

farmers to British Columbia to displace the American miners, whom they hoped would be transient (C. Harris, *Resettlement*).

Over time, settler colonialism worked to promote a culture bent on assimilating less racially valued immigrants into the dominant settler body politic. Immigration increased demand for Indigenous territory, causing both land and commodity prices to rise, which further entrenched settlers' ideas of Indigenous peoples' lifeways as a barrier to settler progress and modernity. In Stó:lō territory, Britain created the crown colony of British Columbia in 1858 as a direct response to the arrival of the American gold miners. British Columbia merged with the adjacent colony of Vancouver Island in 1867 and was integrated into the Canadian Dominion in 1871. At each stage, Indigenous people were disenfranchised and uninformed about, let alone involved with, the negotiations. Throughout, settler society consolidated its identity as a permanent community of citizens.

Settler colonies, therefore, are ideologically disposed to facilitate the displacement of Indigenous people from their ancestral lands by declaring, somewhat paradoxically, that mobility is essential to progress and economic growth. Corporations and laborers relocate to be near the resources they commodify and extract, and then relocate again when the resources (such as minerals and trees) have been depleted. Along the Fraser River, the thirty thousand miners who had arrived in the spring of 1858 had by 1862 largely moved on to other gold fields farther into British Columbia's interior. Stó:lō resources and transformer sites were impacted by the initial influx of miners and then even more significantly by the creation of transportation infrastructure designed to facilitate the movement of people not only *into* their territory (as in the case of loyal British farmers) but *through* it (in the case of miners).

As a consequence, while relocative mobility has been prized by settler colonists, it has necessarily been viewed with ambivalence and apprehension by Indigenous people such as the Stó:lō who are "Indigenous" precisely because of the historically deep and intimate relationship they have with the lands of their ancestors. Whereas the term *Aboriginal* simply means the original or first people, the word *Indigenous* refers to people who originated in a particular place. The difference is subtle but important. To be the "Aboriginal first people" in a place does not necessarily equate with having originated there, and indeed some settler nationalists have consistently argued that Aboriginal people in North America are simply the descendants of an earlier wave of pre-Columbian immigrants, and as such their rights are not fundamentally different from subsequent settler colonial immigrants who came later. Assimilation policies, in this light, have been regarded by successive generations of settlers as justifiable because they equate Native populations with other ethnic minorities who arrived as part of subsequent migrations. Regarded from this perspective, the assimilation of Indigenous people is, and was, just as justifiable and desirable to the dominant British Canadian settlers as the assimilation of early Irish and Ukrainian immigrants in Montreal and in the Canadian prairies.

"Indigenous," by way of contrast, explicitly defines people as having emerged from, within, and upon a particular land and waterscape. It positions them as autochthonous. This definition sits more comfortably with Stó:lō and other Indigenous people's own historical understandings of themselves as revealed through their epic oral narratives explaining the creation of the world and the establishment of their communities. In Canada, this distinction has been powerfully illustrated by Indigenous knowledge keepers who, confronted by settler government spokespersons asserting the right to regulate and control Indigenous lands by virtue of legislation, have posed the simple and powerful question, "If this is your land, where are your stories?" (Chamberlin). As Stó:lō historian and contributor to this chapter Naxaxalhts'i (aka Sonny McHalsie) regularly explains to settler colonists who participate in the culture tours he offers, "archaeologists have found evidence that we've been here for 9,000 years; our Elders share stories that show that we have always been here."

What this means, in one sense, is that Indigenous people struggle within settler colonial societies in large part because they cannot fully engage mobility the way settler Canadians do. Consider, for example, how the *potential* of relocating that every Canadian has enjoyed (and has seen as an opportunity) has meant that, as individuals, settler Canadians have been absolved from having to concern themselves with the long-term vitality and viability of their local environments. Indigenous people, by way of contrast, can never afford such an itinerant attitude. Settler colonists tend to move into a location, deplete its resources, and even destroy its local economy and ecosystems (as first the gold miners, then the builders of the roads and railroads, then the forestry loggers, and more recently farmers did in Stó:lō territory), secure in the knowledge that they can relocate without compromising either their Canadian citizenship or their Canadian identity.

This is not to imply that settlers do not, and have not, grown attached to and fond of local environs, or that environmental sustainability is not a growing and important concern for many Canadians. Rather, it is to insist that such attachments are by definition profoundly different than those carried by Indigenous people such as the Stó:lō who are guided by the concept of *tómiyeqw*. Tómiyeqw translates as both great-great-great-great-grandparent and great-great-great-great-grandchild. Tómiyeqw culturally obliges Stó:lō people to consider the health of a region seven generations into the future, and to do so in a manner that would be intelligible and acceptable to people who had lived seven generations earlier. Thus to Indigenous people, "*where* they are is *who* they are" (Wolfe 388). To settlers, by way of contrast, *who* Indigenous people are is too often *what* they are—and, in settler eyes, what they have most often been is an obstacle to accessing land as well as reminders of their own transient settler identity.

Mobility and migration are, therefore, at the heart of the perpetual process of colonial resettlement, or rather colonial *re*settlement practice. Every domestic shift in settler populations from one region of a settler colonial state to another signals for Indigenous people either increased competition for resources within a populating area or a struggle to deal with the lands transformed by the depletion of resources in a depopulating area. The impact of the historical efforts to disconnect Indigenous people from their ancestral territory is inherently more than the sum of economic losses associated with exploitable land and resources.

In the United States, the centrality of settler mobility can be traced back to the still potent myth of "Manifest Destiny" and its tarnished scholarly counterpart, the "Frontier Thesis." Manifest Destiny is the belief that God intended for Anglo-Protestant Americans to dominate the entire continent (O'Sullivan 430; J. Pratt 795–98). The Frontier Thesis was expounded by historian Frederick Jackson Turner in 1893. Turner posited that American history is best understood as a series of waves of westward settler expansion. On each successive frontier, Americans encountered and conquered a wilderness that included Indigenous people. It was this process of conquest and domestication that created the quintessential American character—muscular, manly, and democratic. The domestication of the wilderness and the relocation of its "wild" inhabitants to reservations and the subsequent reaping of their lands was, to Turner, also the result of divine providence.

Certain academics and public intellectuals have at various times argued that the Frontier Thesis also explains Canadian history (the most prominent of these being University of British Columbia historian Walter Sage in the 1930s). Indeed, the biblically inspired name chosen by Canada's founders, "Dominion of Canada," literally embodies the idea that the Canadian settler state assumed God's "dominion also from sea to sea, and from the river unto the ends of the earth" (*King James Bible*, Psalm 72:8). To this were added the Roman understanding of sovereignty and absolute ownership of a territory.

Thus, while the United States and Canada asserted sovereignty over vast territories, they reduced the Indigenous people to the role of mere occupants and wards of the colonial governments. Sustained through the hegemony of *translatio imperii* (the medieval concept that defined history as a geographical east-west movement of empire and knowledge), Manifest Destiny and Dominion were, and remain, political myths that are impossible to measure, prove, or disprove; they rest on acceptance through belief. In North America, these mythical constructs of settler colonialism routinely serve to dismiss Indigenous mythical ways of knowing about the land and the deep past.

Settler Colonialism's Ontological Challenge to Indigenous Ways of Knowing

Central to the Stó:lō Coast Salish Indigenous community's efforts to self-identify are the ancient stories that explain the origins and transformation of an earlier chaotic myth-age world into the largely stable and predictable one Stó:lō people recognize today. In the Stó:lō language, these narratives are called sxwoxwiyá:m and they principally describe the actions of the transformer siblings, Xe:Xá:ls. Sometimes the transformations discussed in sxwoxwiyá:m were consensual; sometimes not. Sometimes the transformations were morally guided by a desire to reward or punish; sometimes not.

Sxwoxwiyá:m provide the Coast Salish peoples with a raison d'être. One especially detailed early recording of a sxwoxwiyá:m was shared by Chief George Chehalis (from the Sts'ailes First Nation) with anthropologist Franz Boas in 1884 (92–101). Chief Chehalis's sxwoxwiyá:m articulated an ontology that was incompatible with the early miners' and settlers' understanding of Indigenous spaces as a *terra nullius* as well as with the stark contrast the newcomers drew between an earthy physical realm and an heavenly spiritual one. Though the European immigrants were familiar with the notion of specific sites that had spiritual value, from their perspective, they had left these sites behind in Europe.

Over the past three decades, both authors of this chapter have had the privilege of working closely with Coast Salish knowledge keepers who have shared accounts of ancient transformations. They have explained that Xe:Xá:ls transformed a variety of people into plants, animals, and stones that continue to exist today. They have further elucidated the ways in which these original people's sentient life force (shxweli) continues to exist within transformer stones, plants, and animals. As such, the Stó:lō recognize ongoing kin ties between themselves and the environment (Carlson, "Orality About Literacy;" Carlson, *Power of Place*, chapter 3; McHalsie). Tribal founders were among the most prominent characters in the sxwoxwiyá:m of Xe:Xá:ls. For example, Xe-:Xá:ls transformed the ancestor of the Leq'á:mel tribe into a sturgeon, and as a result, to this day members of the Leq'á:mel First Nations regard sturgeons to be their relatives (their ancestor's spirit still resides in all sturgeon). Likewise, Xe:Xá:ls transformed the ancestor of the Matsqui tribe into a beaver, the ancestor of the Yale tribe into a mountain goat, and the ancestor of the Chehalis tribe into an otter, and so on all along the lower Fraser River.

Not everyone whom the Xe:Xá:ls siblings transformed was the founder of a tribal community, however. A great elk hunter was transformed into a stone that can be seen in the Fraser River near the town of Yale to this day, as was a great seal hunter who was turned into a rock located on a lower stretch of the Harrison River. A dangerous hag with a toothed vagina was likewise transformed into stone at another site along the edge of the Harrison River.

Through transformations, Xe:Xá:ls created a distinctly local Indigenous landscape that remains today populated with attentive and potentially responsive rocks, creatures, plants, and animals. Associated with each transformer figure is a narrative and spiritual energy that intersects, cuts across, and informs other transformer stories in complicated ways. Geographically fixed transformer stones, for example, are associated with particular places and likewise associate certain people with those particular places. Both the Elk and the Seal Hunter stones, Elder Matilda Gutierrez has explained, need to be visited in situ for their anchored stories to be properly and fully appreciated. Elder Rosaleen George, meanwhile, has explicated the ways in which the tribal origin transformer stories associated with various animals and plants that are found throughout the broader region serve to remind people from all Stó:lō tribes that seasonal visits and familial interconnections are fundamental to the health of Stó:lō interpersonal relations as well as the ways Stó:lō people relate to space. A living beaver, regardless of where it is located throughout the broader Stó:lō territory, can serve as a mnemonic to people of all Stó:lō tribes of the origin story of the Matsqui tribe and how that animal once embarked on an epic journey to bring back fire to the Stó:lō people so they would have light to see by and heat to cook with. Such tribal origin stories simultaneously tie one group of Stó:lō people to a particular subregion of the broader Stó:lō landscape (e.g., the Matsqui to their core territory in the central Fraser Valley) while emphasizing ancient tribal cooperation, interconnectedness, and shared authority. Many of the transformer stories, therefore, serve to reinforce the economic and ceremonial interconnectivity that inspired anthropologist Wayne Suttles to describe "the whole Coast Salish region as a kind of social continuum" (15). The story of the mother mountain, Lhílheqey, is an especially well-known such narrative that fosters a sense of unity among members of all Stó:lō tribes, if for no other reason than that on clear days, Lhílheqey can be seen from almost anywhere in Stó:lō territory. But beyond this, elders from different generations, such as Dan Milo and Andy Commodore, have each independently situated Lhílheqey within a transformer narrative that depicts her as having been placed in that prominent position by Xe:Xá:ls for the explicit purpose of watching over the Stó:lō people and the annually returning salmon of the Fraser River. Lhílheqey the mother mountain therefore serves as an attentive caring mother of all Stó:lō people and their salmon relatives. Her presence and her visibility remain constant sources of comfort.

The systematic and nonconsultative destruction and/or structural compromising of specific transformer stones by settler colonists thus has had profound impacts on Coast Salish people's sense of self and of place. Damaging and destroying transformer sites is not only seen by Stó:lō people as harming the ancestors (something they regard as inherently dangerous to all the living) but is also interpreted as compromising the delicate balance between the forces contributing to social and economic cohesion among and between Stó:lō tribal communities (Carlson, *Power of Place* 37–78).

In the wake of the 1858 Fraser River gold rush, a host of transformer sites were demolished to facilitate the extraction of precious metal or to make way for industrial transportation corridors. In the sxwoxwiyá:m of the Elk Hunter (Tewit), we learn that he was accompanied by his hunting dog (Sqwemay) when they were both transformed by Xe:Xá:ls into large stones located in, and protruding from, the waters of the Fraser River. The hunter and the elk stones are still there today. Before her death a decade ago, Elder Matilda Gutierrez explained that this cluster of large rocks constituted a special place that knowledge keepers of the past referred to when they taught children that Xe:Xá:ls was real, and that belief in the legitimacy of the stories was an important way of honoring their ancestors. The Hunting Dog stone, however, was blasted by engineers in 1860 to make steamboat navigation safer. As such, the overall integrity of the story is now compromised by Sqwemay's absence.

A separate transformer stone with its own story was also blasted a few years later near the junction of the Harrison and Fraser Rivers to make way for steamboats. So too was the "chamber pot" that Xe:Xá:ls had made blown to pieces by an early British farmer to turn meadows and scrublands into agricultural fields. Railway expansion in the mid-twentieth century similarly caused the Skwōwech (sturgeon) stone to be buried in riprap, rendering it no longer visible or visitable. Axétel (Canada Goose) was another transformer stone that early settlers obliterated with dynamite more than a century ago to make room for fields of hops to supply Canada's beer industry. Kwiyaxtel, a man whom Xe:Xá:ls changed into stone after he challenged their authority, was blasted with dynamite during railroad construction in 1913. Sqayexi ya (the Mink) and his Sx'eles (penis) likewise were stones formerly located near the settler town of Chilliwack until they too were demolished to make way for the railroad. Stó:lō people were never consulted prior to any of these destructive acts, nor were they ever compensated (if compensation for such action is indeed even possible).

The large smooth transformer stone located near where Harrison Lake flows into the Harrison River is described in a sxwoxwiyá:m as having formerly been a whale that followed the salmon and seals up the Fraser River system more than eighty kilometers from the ocean and into fresh water. Knowledge keepers emphasize that the whale spirit in this stone, and its story, were used by elders of an earlier generation to emphasize to youth the importance of being brave and sufficiently bold to venture beyond the places that one knows to be safe and familiar in order to try new things, to be tenacious in the pursuit of one's goal, to be innovative in the face of tradition, and to recognize the importance of ecological diversity in a Coast Salish world where certain food resources are only available at certain times within any particular tribal homeland, etcetera. Today the whale stone is inaccessible to Stó:lō people due to a settler having built his house on top of it. Elders carry stories of many more sites that have been destroyed or alienated throughout the region.

Finding, documenting, and preserving the memory of these and other sites has become the passion and life mission of Naxaxalhts'i (Sonny McHalsie). In 1983, when first working for his community as an archaeology assistant, he helped document fourteen separate destroyed transformer sites (Mohs). Since then, he has worked with additional elders and knowledge keepers to identify nearly double that many. As an employee of the Stó:lō Research and Resource Management Centre, part of Naxaxalhts'i's job involves communicating information with settler Canadians about Stó:lō culture. During guided tours of his ancestral homeland, Naxaxalhts'i shares accounts of the importance of the remaining transformer sites and the depth of the cultural and spiritual loss associated with those that have been alienated. He explains, for example, how in the year 2000, officials for the Canadian Pacific Railroad (CPR) determined that a rock outcropping on a mountain high above the railway posed a hazard, and so without consulting Stó:lō officials, they destroyed it. The sxwoxwiyá:m about the once massive mountain-top rock explained that it was a pointing index finger known as Mometes that had been put there by Xe:Xá:ls to remind Stó:lō people to "be good" and to heed the teachings of their elders. Its destruction erased a chapter from the Stó:lō people's epic account of how the world came to be and how people are to behave. In sharing stories of ancient creation and transformation alongside descriptions of the past and present threats posed to transformer sites, Naxaxalhts'i is making clear that settler colonialism needs to be understood as a structure of ongoing oppression and not merely as past historical events and occurrences.

Science, Courts, and Sacredness

While the destruction of these transformer stones was and remains profoundly distressing to Stó:lō people, it is important to bear in mind that the early colonists responsible for initiating their physical destruction were largely ignorant of the cultural harm and spiritual violence that their actions were causing to Indigenous peoples and ontologies. To my knowledge, none of these early settlers purposefully and maliciously set out to destroy a Stó:lō transformer site simply because it was a transformer site. But of course neither did the settlers make any efforts to learn how and why these sites were important to the Stó:lō people in order to facilitate their preservation. The appropriation, exploitation, and ultimate obliteration of these sacred landscape features was, in other words, functional to the settler colonial strategy of displacement and not necessarily intentional.

In these early years, when settler colonialism was finding its footing and entrenching itself, the alienation of transformer sites was a by-product of a pervasive, and convenient, ignorance of Indigenous ways of valuing land and its features. By the twentieth century, however, voices of Indigenous protest, coupled with published anthropological scholarship, made it increasingly difficult for settler society to sustain any claim to being unaware of the ontological implications of their actions. Any continuing dismissal of Indigenous ways of knowing as irrelevant vis-à-vis settler land rights points toward a recognition that to respect officially Indigenous ways of being and ways of knowing would fundamentally threaten the logic of the settler colonial episteme. In this way, the critique of Indigenous mythology and spirituality implicit in the alleged objective and unprejudiced scientific discourse of settler ideology indicates the untrammeled hegemony of that ideology.

Just over thirty years ago, when expanding global trade motivated the Canadian National Railroad (CNR) to try to "twin-track" its railway through the delicate Fraser canyon ecosystem and spiritual landscape, the Stó:lō and other Indigenous communities had the capacity to mobilize themselves in ways that had simply not been possible when the original road and rail corridors were pushed through in the nineteenth and early twentieth centuries. Drawing on archaeological and environmental evidence, they made abundantly clear to the railroad corporation and to the federal and provincial governments that they opposed the expansion due to the way it would impact and destroy fishing habitat, ancient settlement sites, *and* their sacred transformer sites. Through video documentaries and widespread media campaigns, Indigenous people along the Fraser River corridor tried to educate settlers about their lands and their worldviews (Coqualeetza). These efforts, however, failed to resonate with either the corporation or the federal and provincial governments. It was only after Indigenous people filed a court injunction that a halt was brought to the railway expansion project. Significantly, the part of the plea that the courts found compelling was not that relating to Indigenous sacred sites but rather that pertaining to environmental impacts. To this day, the Stó:lō and their Indigenous neighbors rest uneasy, worrying that at some point, with ever-increasing demands for rail cargo in and out of Canada's port of Vancouver, the proposed expansion project may proceed again. Indeed, Indigenous interests in protecting specific lands have only secured traction in settler colonial legal and political institutions when they could be linked to ecological or environmental issues that find support within ecologically minded groups of settler Canadian society.[3]

Such battles are ongoing. At the time of the writing of this text, the Stó:lō and other Indigenous people are clashing with settler society over the proposed creation of a $7.6 billion pipeline through their territory to carry bitumen oil more than 1,500 kilometers from the province of Alberta to the port of Vancouver. It is important to note that not all Stó:lō people and communities are necessarily opposed to the creation of a pipeline, though most certainly are (Rabson); and of course, not all of Canadian settler society necessarily supports the pipeline development, though many who are employed in the oil industry and in construction certainly do.

During the federal government's National Energy Board (NEB) hearings, Stó:lō and other Indigenous communities raised a host of concerns over the threat the pipeline posed to the local ecology (should there be a spill) as well as to sacred and heritage sites due to its construction.[4] The Stó:lō made eighty-nine recommendations outlining how their concerns could be mitigated. These included a guarantee that they would have input on future fishing management plans, an assurance that they would be involved in determining the location of water-testing facilities, and a commitment that there would be river-bank restoration wherever negative impacts were anticipated. Condition 77 required a detailed archaeological and cultural heritage study to guide the creation of a mitigation plan to protect intangible heritage transformer sites along with tangible archaeological and physical heritage sites. When neither the NEB nor the federal cabinet adopted a single one of the conditions, the Indigenous leaders and their allies chose to go to court to try to block the development.

The federal court proved sympathetic to the Stó:lō concerns. In her 2018 ruling, Justice Eleanor Dawson stated, "For the most part, Canada's representatives limited their mandate to listening to and recording the concerns of the Indigenous applicants and then transmitting those concerns to the [corporate] decision-makers. . . . The law requires Canada to do more than receive and record concerns and complaints." The judge was particularly disappointed by the federal government's disregard for the Stó:lō's recommendations. "These measures," Dawson wrote, "are specific, brief and generally measured and reasonable." In failing to acknowledge them, let alone meet them, the Canadian government "fell well short of the minimum requirements imposed by the case law of the Supreme Court of Canada" in its efforts to consult. As a result, pipeline construction was put on hold pending the government's revision of its consultation process and a commitment to consider Indigenous concerns (Dawson). Additionally, in 2018, in an attempt to soften international corporate power and to reassure Canadians that the government's principal objective was to ensure that any pipeline development was in the public interest, the federal government purchased the pipeline project from the Texas-based Kinder Morgan Corporation and created the TransMountain Corporation. TransMountain is a wholly owned subsidiary of the Canadian Development Investment Corporation, which in turn is directly accountable to the Canadian Parliament.

But these changes have not allayed the Stó:lō people's worries nor addressed their concerns. As of October 2020, pipeline construction is underway despite the fact that the eighty-nine recommendations the Stó:lō made have not been met to the Stó:lō leaders' satisfaction. Chief Dalton Silver of the Sumas First Nation is especially exasperated that the TransMountain Corporation is proceeding with plans to build the pipeline adjacent to a transformer stone known as Lightning Rock (and an associated archaeological site that elders have described as the site of a mass burial created following the smallpox epidemic of 1782) (Barrera). Silver and other Stó:lō have not ruled out direct action if the pipeline project is not either canceled or at a minimum adjusted to respect their eighty-nine conditions—including small-scale rerouting to avoid sacred sites.

Similar contemporary developments elsewhere in western Canada suggest that, as with corporations and governments, the Canadian courts are only listening selectively to those Indigenous peoples' concerns that can be "validated" or "authenticated" by Western science. A few short weeks before the federal court issued its 2019 injunction against the pipeline construction, the Supreme Court of Canada rejected an effort by the Ktunaxa people of British Columbia's interior region to block the $1 billion development of the massive "Jumbo Glacier" ski resort on a mountain they understand to be the sacred place where the Grizzly Bear Spirit resides. The Supreme Court ruled that while the community's concerns over environmental impacts were worthy of further investigation, they could not agree to support the Ktunaxa assertion that construction of the resort facilities would irreparably damage the Indigenous spiritual landscape and therefore constitute an infringement on the community's religious freedom.

Put another way, the court determined that under settler Canadian law, the right to worship was protected for Indigenous people as it was for all groups, but that did not include a fiduciary obligation on the part of the Canadian state to protect against the development of particular sites on the land that Indigenous people regarded as integral to their ancestral identity and contemporary collective spiritual health. While tangible heritage sites could be justification for such protections (i.e., sites associated with verifiable archaeological remains or those that science could validate were ecologically vulnerable), ones that could only be known and measured by means outside Western scientific epistemology could not (K. Harris; MacCharles). A journalist covering the proceedings noted, "The B.C. government, in its brief to the top court, said that giving protection to the meaning of a subjective belief could end up affecting laws on abortion and same-sex marriage," thus effectively equating an ancient collective belief system with arbitrary individual beliefs (MacKinnon). This reasoning has a tradition in the United States, too. [5]

What all this suggests is that despite the protection of preexisting Aboriginal rights in the Canadian Constitution, the various arms of the settler colonial government continue to situate collective Indigenous rights within the context of the protection of individual rights as would be applied to members of settler minority groups more generally. By extension, the perceived necessity for government and the courts is in balancing such interests against those that elected officials regard as being in the broader societal interest.

Conclusion

Settler colonialism has been facilitated by a specific way of seeing the landscape that is imperviously insensitive to Indigenous cultural and historical hermeneutics and epistemologies. Thus, in addition to what it has represented in terms of land alienation, settler colonialism in the lower Fraser River watershed includes a process of ontological oppression through both the incidental as well as the intentional destruction of Indigenous spiritual places. It is not to suggest, however, that settler colonial cultures were culturally or historically incapable of identifying and valuing intangible spiritual sites, as their protection of such sites in their colonial homelands, mentioned at the beginning of this chapter, so vividly illustrates. While Judeo-Christian (or indeed pre-Christian, "pagan") sacred places in the "Old World" were in no need of scientific confirmation to deserve protection, a similar practice of inscribing the land with spiritual meaning was ignored in Indigenous North American cultures. As Roderick Nash has pervasively argued, European settlers transported their understandings of a nature inscribed with meaning to North America; but other than that, North America was a topological tabula rasa, ready to be inscribed by Canadian and American society with political myths such as Dominion and Manifest Destiny. The British and European landscapes, in this view, metaphorically remained North American settler colonialists' natural *and* supernatural archives and museums—places where both great things and miraculously local things had happened that were worthy of preserving. To this day, the descendants of the European settlers travel to Europe to visit the great ancient sites of religion, spirituality, and history. They rest easy knowing that European governments and societies protect sites such as Lourdes, Stonehenge, the Irish fairy homes, and Fatima, regardless of whether archaeological or environmental science can prove their religious validity. Meanwhile, Indigenous people such as the Stó:lō continue to be denied even approximations of a similar security and comfort for the sites that they regard as inherently, if intangibly, valuable for their own individual and collective spiritual well-being. Ongoing efforts by the Stó:lō and other Indigenous communities to protect their lands and their rights are therefore as much about challenging settler society to open itself to alternative ontologies and belief systems (and all this implies) as they are about restoring destroyed environments, returning alienated lands, and building genuinely respectful cooperative systems of co-management and governance.

Notes

The senior author, Keith Carlson, is especially grateful to his longtime friend Naxaxalhts'i (Sonny McHalsie) for the thoughtful and sustained conversations and collaborations over the past twenty-eight years. Together, Carlson and Naxaxalhts'i both extend their thanks to the various Stó:lō knowledge keepers who generously trusted us and patiently provided us with exposure to Stó:lō sacred sites and Stó:lō ways of knowing and relating to the land, in particular, Matilda Gutierrez, Agnes Kelly, Nancy Philips, Rosaleen George, P. D. Peters, and Andy Commodore. We are also appreciative of comments and feedback on earlier drafts provided by Gesa Mackenthun and other participants of the 2018 symposium where Carlson first presented a draft of this chapter. Likewise, we thank Colin Osmond and Alessandro Tarsia for their thoughtful suggestions on an earlier draft. Finally, we would like to thank Sheila McMahon for her careful copyediting skills.

1. Owing some debt of gratitude to Lubbock's legislation are recent efforts by both Christians and neo-pagans in the British Isles working to preserve sites they believe to be associated with the apparition of the Virgin Mary (as Walsingham) or with fairies and other ethereal beings (Cheallaigh).

2. North American salvage ethnography, led first by social Darwinists such as Lewis Henry Morgan and later by adherents of historical particularism such as Franz Boas and his students, regarded Indigenous cultures as ahistorical and frozen in time. Change, it was believed, was by definition a result of external pressures rather than internal innova- tions. In this view, change in Indigenous societies resulted from contact with Western European/British society and could only be reactionary and degenerative.

3. Indigenous people in Canada sometimes also find allies among the non-Indigenous population when the endangered geographical feature is regarded as geologically unique and distinctive, and therefore scientifically verifiable as deserving of natural heritage status. For a discussion of similar processes in Europe as related to Fin Mc- Cool's causeway in Ireland, see Cohen and Cohen.

4. In 2018 the Canadian government replaced the NEB with the Impact Assessment Agency of Canada (IAAC) and the Canadian Energy Regulator (CER). The IAAC was described as an attempt to make the processs of assessing development im- pacts more responsive to Indigenous people and other noncorporate interests. The CER, meanwhile, has the mandate of "keep[ing] energy moving safely and efficiently through our country's pipelines and powerlines." CER home page, cer-rec.gc.ca/en/ index.html, accessed 2 Nov. 2020.

5. See the infamous U.S. Supreme Court decision on a sacred area in northern California, *Lyng v. Northwest Indian Cemetery Protective Association* (U.S. Supreme Court 1988) (discussed in Echo-Hawk, chapter 12).

References

Barker, A. J., and E. Lowman Battell. *Settler: Identity and Colonialism in 21st Century Can- ada*. Fernwood, 2015.

Barrera, Jorge. "Stó:lō First Nation Eyes Claim over Lightning Rock Site in Path of Trans- Mountain." *CBC News*, 13 May 2020, cbc.ca/news/indigenous/sumas-first-nation -lightning-rock-tmx-1.5566941.

Boas, Franz. *Indianische Sagen von der Nord-Pacifischen Küste Amerikas*. Verlag von A. Asher & Co., 1895. [Available in English translation by Dietrich Bertz in Randy Bouchard and Dorothy Kennedy, eds., *Indian Myths & Legends from the Pacific North Coast of America*. Talonbooks, 2001.]

Boyd, Robert. *The Coming of the Spirit of Pestilence: Introduced Infectious Diseases and Population Decline Among Northwest Coast Indians, 1774–1874*. University of Washington Press and University of British Columbia Press, 1999.

Carlson, Keith Thor. "The Numbers Game: Interpreting Historical Stó:lō Demographics." *A Stó:lō-Coast Salish Historical Atlas*, edited by Keith Thor Carlson, Douglas and McIntyre, 2001, pp. 76–83, plate 27.

Carlson, Keith Thor. "Orality About Literacy: The 'Black and White' of Salish History." *Orality and Literacy: Reflections Across Disciplines*, edited by Keith Thor Carlson et al., University of Toronto Press, 2011, pp. 43–69.

Carlson, Keith Thor. *The Power of Place, the Problem of Time: Aboriginal Identity and Historical Consciousness in the Cauldron of Colonialism*. University of Toronto Press, 2010.

Chamberlin, Edward. *If This Is Your Land, Where Are Your Stories? Finding Common Ground*. Knopf Canada, 2003.

Cheallaigh, Máirín Ní. "Ringforts or Fairy Homes: Oral Understandings and the Practice of Archaeology in Nineteenth- and Early Twentieth-Century Ireland." *International Journal of Historical Archaeology*, vol. 16, no. 2, 2012, pp. 367–84.

Cohen, Paul S., and Brenda H. Cohen. "Giant's Causeway, County Antrim, Northern Ireland: A Rare and Superlative Natural Phenomena." *Journal of College Science Teaching*, vol. 31, no. 6, 2002, pp. 412–14.

Coqualeetza Media Production Centre for the Alliance of Tribal Councils. *The River Is Our Home*. Video, 1984.

Dawson, J. A. "Reasons for Judgement." *Tsleil-Waututh Nation et. al. V. Canada et al.*, Federal Court of Appeals, FCA 153, 30 Aug. 2018.

Dippie, Brian D. *The Vanishing American: White Attitudes and U.S. Indian Policy*. Wesleyan University Press, 1982.

Echo-Hawk, Walter. *In the Courts of the Conqueror: The 10 Worst Indian Law Cases Ever Decided*. Fulcrum, 2012.

Evans, Illtud. "Lourdes: A Place of the Gospels." *Life of the Spirit*, vol. 12, no. 143, 1958, pp. 482–86.

Harris, Cole. *The Resettlement of British Columbia: Essays on Colonialism and Geographical Change*. University of British Columbia Press, 1997.

Harris, Cole. "Voices of Disaster: Smallpox Around the Strait of Georgia in 1782." *Ethnohistory*, vol. 41, no. 4, 1995, pp. 591–626.

Harris, Kathleen. "Supreme Court Ruling Removes Barrier for Year-round Ski Resort on Sacred First Nations Land." *CBC News*, 2 Nov. 2017, cbc.ca/news/politics/indigenous-rights-ski-resort-1.4381902.

Jansen, Willy, and Catrien Notermans. "From Vision to Cult Site: A Comparative Perspective." *Archives de sciences sociales des religions*, vol. 55, no. 151, 2010, pp. 71–90.

MacCharles, Tonda. "Supreme Court Approves B.C. Ski Resort Development on Indigenous Lands." *Toronto Star*, 2 Nov. 2017.

MacKinnon, Leslie. "SCC Picks B.C. Ski Hill Project over Indigenous Spirituality." *iPolitics*, 2 Nov. 2017, ipolitics.ca/2017/11/02/scc-picks-b-c-ski-hill-project-over-indigenous-spirituality.

McHalsie, Albert "Sonny" [aka Naxaxalhts'i]. "We Have to Take Care of Everything That Belongs to Us." *Be of Good Mind: Essays on the Coast Salish*, edited by Bruce Granville Miller, University of British Columbia Press, 2008, pp. 82–130.

Mohs, Gordon. "Spiritual Sites, Ethnic Significance, and Native Spirituality: The Heritage and Heritage Sites of the Sto:lo Indians of British Columbia." MA thesis, Simon Fraser University, 1987.

Morgan, Lewis Henry. *League of the Ho-dé-no-sau-nee or Iroquois*. Rochester, N.Y., 1851.

Nash, Roderick. *Wilderness and the American Mind*. Yale University Press, 1967.

O'Sullivan, John L. "The Great Nation of Futurity." *United States Democratic Review*, vol. 6, no. 23, 1839, pp. 426–30.

Pratt, Angela. "Treaties vs. *Terra Nullius*: Reconciliation, Treaty-Making and Indigenous Sovereignty in Australia and Canada." *Indigenous Law Journal*, vol. 3, 2004, pp. 43–60.

Pratt, Julius W. "The Origin of 'Manifest Destiny.'" *American Historical Review*, vol. 32, no. 4, 1927, pp. 795–98.

Rabson, Mia. "Indigenous Groups Have 'Specific' Requests That Could Save Trans Mountain." *Globe and Mail*, 7 Sep. 2018.

Richardson, Boyce. *People of Terra Nullius: Betrayal and Rebirth in Aboriginal Canada*. Douglas & McIntyre, 1993.

Sage, Walter. "Some Aspects of the Frontier in Canadian History." Report of the Annual Meeting of the Canadian Historical Association, 1937.

Sax, Joseph L. "Is Anyone Minding Stonehenge? The Origins of Cultural Property Protection in England." *California Law Review*, vol. 78, no. 6, 1990, pp. 1543–67.

Spivak, Gayatri Chakravorty. "Can the Subaltern Speak?" *Colonial Discourse and Post-Colonial Theory: A Reader*, edited by Patrick Williams and Laura Chrisman, Columbia University Press, 1988, pp. 66–111.

Suttles, Wayne. "Central Coast Salish." *Handbook of North American Indians*, vol 7, *Northwest Coast*, edited by Wayne Suttles, Smithsonian Institution, 1990, p. 15.

Todhunter, Rodger. "Preservation, Parks and the Vice-Royalty Lord Dufferin and Lord Grey in Canada." *Landscape Planning*, vol. 12, no. 2, 1985, pp. 141–60.

Turner, Frederick Jackson. "The Significance of the Frontier in American History." Paper read at the annual meeting of the American Historical Association, Chicago, 12 July 1893, historians.org/about-aha-and-membership/aha-history-and-archives/historical-archives/the-significance-of-the-frontier-in-american-history.

Veracini, Lorenzo. *The Settler Colonial Present*. Palgrave Macmillan, 2015.

Wolfe, Patrick. "Settler Colonialism and the Elimination of the Native." *Journal of Genocide Research*, vol. 8, no. 4, Dec. 2006, pp. 387–409.

7

Indigenous Knowledge, Archaeological Thought, and the Emerging Identity Crisis

Jeff Oliver

A RECENT BBC DOCUMENTARY, *Masters of the Pacific Coast*, provides British TV viewers with a fascinating window on the Indigenous cultures of North America's rugged western periphery. The host of the program, the affable British Museum archaeologist Jago Cooper, takes the audience on an exhilarating journey through the striking coastal landscapes of the Alaskan panhandle, British Columbia, and Washington State while recounting the story of "how a cultural tradition that began over 10,000 years ago survived against the odds" (*Masters*). The program demonstrates its postcolonial credentials by positioning Indigenous spokespersons to comment on aspects of this story; and it is through their voices that we learn how ancient artifacts— such as chipped stone tools and cedar zoomorphic carvings—have become touchstones linking the present with the deep past. Those familiar with the history of first peoples will recognize this form of historicizing and understand its significance for cultural revitalization. More intriguing is that this narrative is also actively embraced and woven into the archaeological plotline. The message for the British audience is clear: the people who live on the coast today are the same people who have lived on the coast since ancient times.

Archaeological practice has clocked a shift in the twenty years since I left British Columbia for Britain, and particularly in how it relates to indigenous communities. Although archaeology has traditionally focused on "ancient peoples"—the biological and cultural antecedents of North America's indigenous populations—over much of its history, it has had a somewhat dismissive attitude toward its living descendants. Decolonization movements the world over are beginning to alter this approach, and archaeology in turn has started to shed its top-down image. Indeed, many archaeologists now aspire to do "indigenous archaeology," that is, archaeology by, for, or with indigenous communities. Even those not working directly with indigenous groups are increasingly integrating indigenous knowledge into their work, to the degree that much archaeological research is increasingly pitched at a new register of cultural sensitivity associated with the concerns and insights of contemporary first peoples.

This chapter provides an annotated tour of this changing scholarly landscape, focusing specifically on the development of indigenous-inflected archaeologies and how the "identity crisis" (Brubaker and Cooper 2) of our current historical moment has encouraged archaeologists to turn inward and to see the past, recent or ancient, through the prism of identity. Identity work within the humanities and social sciences developed as an outgrowth of postmodernism and postcolonialism. It sought to challenge hegemonic discourses that marginalized minorities and others "without history," providing them with voices and spaces of resistance that allowed them to "write back," so to speak, from the margins of their oppression. But identity work can have unintended consequences. Its dominance in the literature, combined with the increase of identity politics in civil society, can encourage us to surrender to the demands of identity at the cost of everything else. In archaeology, it can encourage the veneration of ancestors, but it may also lead to an overemphasis on cultural persistence and even the identification of ancient archaeological cultures with contemporary groups. Such counterintuitive claims make identity politics odd bedfellows with the decolonial emphasis on cultural diversity, multivocality, and change (Liebmann; Oliver, "Native-Lived" 79–80).

While the objectification of identity has been much critiqued, notably the ethnonationalisms of nineteenth- and early twentieth-century Europe (Jones), the North American experience must be understood on its own terms. The history of archaeological thought has not unfolded in a vacuum but is fundamentally grounded within its social milieu (Trigger). I use the distance gained through my positioning on the other side of the Atlantic to provide a critical analysis of the nature of work that might be termed "identity history" (Oliver and Edwald 209) and its appeal for archaeologists working in the Pacific Northwest along with some of the challenges it possesses for our global discipline. Distance is traditionally a quality attributed to colonizers, in the way that it can encourage the abstraction and dehumanization of people. I need to be wary of this potential. However, distance also provides a means for assessing the relationships that lend archaeology in this part of the world its unique character. It is commonly asserted that archaeology is haunted by its colonial past and must be decolonized, but few have acknowledged that archaeological practice cannot be adequately reinvented until we acknowledge the material legacies of colonialism, which help shape the world around us. The solution to this double bind is found in developing a deeper, more reflective and honest engagement with the different communities with which we interact. This includes recognizing the continuing effects that colonial power structures have on how we see ourselves as well as the inherent limitations of archaeology to address who we think we are. While many of the details of this discussion relate to my experience of archaeology in British Columbia, the broader sweep of the argument is relevant to the wider region as well.

Archaeology in the Twentieth Century

To understand the present, we need to start with the beginning. Archaeological interest in the Pacific Northwest began in the late nineteenth century (R. Carlson, "History"). As an arm of ethnology, early practitioners of archaeology were quick to identify the links between indigenous peoples and excavated remains of material culture. However, the discipline's evolution over the twentieth century served mainly to distance archaeology from the living descendants of those remains. Its increasing reliance on field observations and recording assisted the creation of new scientific taxonomies. This allowed material traces of past societies to be described and compared, but it also turned them into cultural abstractions and "specimens" produced and controlled by an academic elite.

Much of archaeology's formative period was focused on defining and chronologically ordering excavated cultural sequences. In company with archaeologists working in other parts of the Americas and Europe, migration was seen as a key instigator of change. For example, Charles Hill-Tout's discoveries of stratigraphic layers of differently shaped human crania near the mouth of the Fraser River allowed him to promote the now-discredited idea of an invasion of hostile people based on the sequence of a "broad headed" population succeeding a "longheaded" one (Hill-Tout). Its early history helped build its colonialist legacy. Although indigenous peoples were sometimes relied upon as informants and wage laborers, questionable ethics surrounding the excavation of sites and desecration of graves confirmed archaeology's reputation as a cultural appropriator, a practice that served to divorce native peoples from their cultural legacy (Roy).

Later developments around midcentury pushed the temporal and cultural distance between living descendants and archaeological cultures even further.

By the 1940s, it was recognized that many archaeological sites could have deep cultural stratigraphy and complex chronologies. Cultural horizons were labeled using abstract terms like *Archaic* and *Palaeoindian* not only to demonstrate temporal distinctiveness but also to show their connections to other parts of North America. For example, Arden R. King's research at the Cattle Point site on San Juan Island in Washington led him to believe the deepest chronological phase was culturally related to Archaic cultures occupying the continent's interior. New dates revealed over subsequent decades at Ground Hog Bay, in Alaska, and Namu, on the central coast of British Columbia, confirmed that human occupation on the coast could be pushed back to at least 10,000 years before the present (BP) (R. Carlson, "History").

The final decades of the twentieth century saw archaeologists change their interpretive models. Many swapped theories of diffusion for the scientific rigor of what became known as the New Archaeology. By the 1980s, the New Archaeology not only used scientific methods to produce and control data; it placed science at the root of its questioning. Central to this effort was a new interest in the role that evolutionary theory played in directing cultural change. Understanding why cultures had developed from simple hunter-gatherer societies into the culturally complex ones of the ethnographic period was fundamental to the history of cultural evolution. Its advocates linked social change to ecological diversity and the question of whether past societies were successful in harnessing this abundance (Ames and Maschner 249–50). It was at the tail end of this period that I undertook my own undergraduate training in archaeology, at Simon Fraser University in British Columbia. We learned that to understand human decision-making, you had to appreciate the guiding hand of the environment. Growing up in a place dominated by dramatic geography—cue high granite mountains cloaked in rainforest and hemmed in by the Pacific—such views, on reflection, were not difficult to accept.

Given the general narrative plotline of Pacific Northwest Coast archaeology in the twentieth century and its increasing confidence in the explanatory power of science, it is perhaps not surprising that archaeologists tended to underplay, ignore, or look dismissively on the use of alternative forms of evidence, such as native oral traditions (Lepofsky 24). This is because the past was seen as being fundamentally different from the present. It was a place shrouded in the mists of time and only accessible through the cool neutrality of scientific objectivity. The implications for the living descendants of this cultural legacy were largely unambiguous: the most valuable indigenous peoples were those long dead whose traditions, as revealed archaeologically or in ethnographic volumes, were untainted by the cultural filters of the present.

The Emergence of Indigenous Archaeology

The turn of the twenty-first century marked something of a watershed for archaeology's relationship with indigenous peoples. Where they were once largely dismissed as irrelevant to the discipline, the new century has witnessed reflection and increasing calls for engagement. To be sure, calls for change had begun earlier with the rise of decolonization movements in certain quarters of academic and civil society. However, more palpable signs of change would take longer. In British Columbia, this was marked in the 1990s with the establishment of a number of important legal precedents. These included the revising of the Heritage Conservation Act of 1996 and a 1997 court decision, the now-historic land claims negotiation, *Delgamuukw v. British Columbia*. To make a long story short, it not only made consultation with First Nations a legal requirement; it also empowered them by acknowledging their connections with the past (Nicholas 356–57). The case resulted in a subtle but discernible shift in how archaeology was approached. Similar legal changes in the United States, notably with the introduction of the Native American Graves Protection and Repatriation Act (NAGPRA) in 1990, have helped chip away at older attitudes there as well, though its impact is by no means homogeneous.

The new social responsibility toward indigenous peoples initially gained traction within the archaeology of the forest industry (Klassen et al; Nicholas 357). Archaeological contractors began to employ First Nations regularly in mitigation surveys to identify archaeological sites in areas scheduled for felling. Such changes were becoming established around the time I was finishing my bachelor's degree and getting my foot in the door of professional archaeology and cultural resource management (CRM). The brief was straightforward: identify archaeological sites and other places of cultural significance at risk of being mauled by a feller buncher, a motorized tree-harvesting vehicle (see figure 7.1). The task, of course, was more difficult in practice.

If "ways of seeing" are culturally contingent, then they depend on who is doing the seeing. What *seemed* like a dark, tangled understory—nature par excellence to one set of eyes—could be seen in a different light when indigenous crew members were entrusted with their own insights: how features in the landscape were used in the times of their grandparents or more distant ancestors, what plants might have attracted people to particular locations, and how place-name evidence could aid our search for new sites. This was knowledge of human-environment relationships that might otherwise have remained hidden. At best, these relationships provided an important context for nurturing mutually beneficial knowledge exchanges. While the Western

FIGURE 7.1. The author and an indigenous crew member stand alongside a bark-stripped western red cedar, a form of culturally modified tree (CMT) in coastal British Columbia. Bark was collected from red cedar to make baskets, rope, and fishing nets. CMTs are one of the most common but least appreciated archaeological features in the Pacific Northwest. Private collection of Jeff Oliver.

agendas of CRM are far from aligned with those of first peoples (Budhwa and McCreary 204), it has nevertheless set the stage for the placement of indigenous knowledge and archaeology on a more equal footing.

However, it was in the context of academic archaeology where the most significant changes occurred, notably in the late 1990s when the term *indigenous archaeology* entered the conversation. It was based on the premise that New World archaeology was fundamentally part of the heritage of local indigenous communities because archaeological sites bridged past and present, creating a timeless cultural landscape that mattered to first peoples (Nicholas 363). It therefore follows that archaeologists have an obligation to address these concerns. There is not one formula for doing indigenous archaeology, but it is generally accepted to mean that archaeologists and cognate scholars relinquish their monopoly on authority and open up decision-making processes to include first peoples and instill meaningful collaboration wherever possible (Atalay; Budhwa and McCreary; K. Carlson et al.; Nicholas).

Changes in legal, professional, and academic quarters have all helped transform the agenda. Where the meaning of archaeology was once the preserve of archaeologists, it is now increasingly shaped by the values and knowledge of contemporary first peoples (Kelley 187). Relationships between archaeology and indigenous knowledge can range widely. Many have drawn on indigenous environmental knowledge to make sense of archaeological assemblages that remain imperceptible to conventional frames of reference, notably identifying past land use (e.g., Reimer) and subsistence patterns (e.g., Menzies). At the other end of the spectrum, they have helped open up new questions and entirely new ways of using the past. Some projects have shown how the use of "sound science" and a collaborative approach to archaeological discovery can add value to places already viewed as culturally significant to first peoples for other reasons (Lepofksy 25). Others have noted how archaeological finds can help kindle cultural revitalization, from the relearning of lost skills to the remembering of forgotten dancing (Hillerdal). Particularly remarkable is that these sorts of outcomes are often the unforeseen consequences of collaboration, especially where coproduced and relational methodologies prevail, a feature applicable to other forms of community archaeology as well (e.g., Vergunst et al.).

A final point to consider is that although archaeology in the twenty-first century has changed, so have indigenous peoples. The novelty of the relationships I have described is put in sharper relief when we consider that the ways in which first peoples value the material past has not remained constant. For example, during ethnology's formative years, the digging of graves for "specimens" was not always viewed controversially. Indeed, when sites were "so old" that their histories "were no longer known," local groups could show indifference to their excavation (Roy 44). The developing relationship between archaeologists and indigenous peoples is not a one-way street but a dual carriageway; it has done as much to alter how indigenous peoples see archaeology as well.

Indigenous Archaeology and the New Presentism

While the turn toward indigenous perspectives is often viewed positively, it is not without controversy. A more contested area, and one I shall develop more fully, is their use to guide archaeological interpretation of the identities of those responsible for creating the archaeological record. Quite literally, who were the makers of these objects? If archaeological discoveries were once seen through the prism of culture history labels—abstractions of people who were long dead and buried—they are now often seen as evidence of continuity between past and present. It is increasingly common to see the names, values, and even territories of present indigenous communities used to give meaning to excavated material culture. Where it tends to capture our imaginations is where signs of the past impinge on the present, such as the archaeology of coastal settlements. In these places, the remains of iconic cedar plank houses and deeply stratified shell middens are conspicuous and evocative. This is also true where the remains of continuous occupation culminate in the recent past, where "the archaeology of us" is inscribed within living memory. In the face of colonialist narratives that saw the Pacific Northwest as a landscape ruled by nature rather than culture (Oliver, *Landscapes*), archaeology and other historical sciences have played an important role in establishing a degree of historical legitimacy for first peoples. In this context, acknowledging that a particular kin group, tribe, or nation has occupied their land for "countless generations" or "thousands of years" might be seen as pushback against more than a century of colonial writing that frequently served to marginalize or deny their existence.

More recently, others have sought to add empirical rigor to such statements. A few examples will outline the character of this work. Within the present territory of the Gitxaala Nation, on the northern coast of British Columbia, archaeologists have identified shell midden profiles that show a similar pattern of shellfish gathering and consumption dating back over a timespan of at least two thousand years. This sequence, they argue, shows clear continuity from the twentieth century, when the Gitxaala were increasingly impacted by settler colonialism, to a period contemporary to the Roman invasion of Britain. For the excavators, "empirical data documenting Gitxaala *bilhaa* harvests extending back in time at least two millennia" (Menzies 136) not only give credence to a long-standing material tradition but also push the historical existence of a First Nation into deep time. In this context, as indigenous archaeologist Charles Menzies explains, archaeology becomes both "object and metaphor of the Gitxaala" (130), an apparent material symbol of their historical continuity.

In the Fraser Valley, home of the Stó:lō Nation, a collaboration of archaeologists, cognate scholars, and indigenous peoples has discovered a distinctive architectural pattern coupling plank houses with semisubterranean square houses preserved through a huge sweep of time commencing around 5,000 years BP and continuing until the late nineteenth century. For the collaborators, the evidence demonstrates "the unique character . . . and long-term importance of the Stó:lō" in this region (Lepofsky et al. 621). Translated into a Western timescale, this is the span of time that commences with the later Neolithic when Stonehenge was being constructed and culminates when it was taken into care as a scheduled monument by the British state.

A final example of indigenous archaeology takes us to Haida Gawaii and the lands of the Haida Nation, where archaeologists have been studying the seabed in the area of Skidegate Inlet. The picture emerging is of a landscape of changing sea levels at the end of the Ice Age. In the early Holocene, the inlet was dry land, part of the continental shelf and likely an important migratory route for the human colonization of North America. Archaeological sites on present land surfaces dating to 12,000 BP, along with the possibility that now-submerged sites could date to 14,000 BP, have given archaeologists cause not only to establish an early baseline of human activity but to suggest "it is probable that the ancestors of the Haida occupied this landscape" (Millennia Research 10).

If archaeology in the twentieth century evoked the past as a "foreign country," in the current century it has become increasingly familiar, even personal territory. As archaeologists speaking on behalf of the Hul'qumi'num Treaty Group on Vancouver Island have put it: "Archaeological heritage is valued for its relation to 'people,' rather than as 'objects' of material value," and "sites are perceived not as abstract scientific resources, but as the 'cemeteries' of family Ancestors" (McLay et al. ii). While many archaeologists will be familiar with the anthropological significance of narratives of unbroken historical continuity and accept their importance for contemporary indigenous ontologies, of interest here is the way such historicizing is increasingly influencing how the discipline of archaeology constructs the past.

The Emerging Identity Crisis and Its Critique

The integration of indigenous viewpoints has produced a richer set of optics for exploring deep time. However, important questions remain about the role of the present in understanding the past. This is a challenge for scholars who see the value of engaging with indigenous perspectives and collaborative and relational forms of working but who also feel bound to certain academic principles of critical inquiry. What is particularly controversial is the idea that archaeological remains can be seen as empirical evidence of the historical antiquity of a given contemporary "people," because embedded within such attributions are ahistorical convictions about the very nature of these social groups (Jones 321).

In a context where the study of identity has reached "crisis" proportions in the humanities and social sciences (Brubaker and Cooper 2), and where identity politics have become all consuming, one wonders whether we are seeing the emergence of an identity crisis in indigenous-inflected archaeology as well. What does the future hold? Will it see the prioritizing of indigenous identities taking precedence over all other questions, turning archaeologists into little more than "ethnographers of earlier eras" (Kelley 186)? While there are routine calls by archaeologists to uncouple our interpretive lens from the ethnographic present (e.g., Ames and Maschner 29; Birch; Grier), the often-politicized nature of archaeological practice can mean that we are more comfortable fence-sitting than critically engaging with these issues.

Globally speaking, archaeology is an extremely broad field, and as such, archaeologists have addressed identity in different ways. Among those who study the recent past, there is broad and growing awareness of the need to historicize and contextualize identities whether we are considering gender, race, class, or nationality. This is partly because written sources and oral testimony can provide important clues about processes of identity construction and the fault lines upon which identities shift, especially given their contingent natures (Jenkins). Awareness of these issues among those who study prehistory or deep history is far patchier (Stahl 490). Despite changes in archaeological theorizing over recent decades, archaeology's materialist outlook continues to present a heavy burden for many prehistorians. In this context, it can be tempting to elide the idea of a "cultural continuum"—the patterning of artifacts and features over long time periods—with the concept of ethnicity or other social identities. This can be irresistible when archaeological patterns, each phase apparently giving rise to the next as if a genetic lineage, appear to share internal consistency with the traditions and ethnonyms of descendant populations (Hall 88).

Such arguments resonate with the earlier history of archaeological thought where culture historians focused on grouping artifact types into "Peoples" and documenting their persistence over time. The "Beaker People" of European prehistory, named after a conspicuous pottery type and associated set of artifacts, is perhaps one of the most famous examples of this. While theorists have strongly discredited the idea of one-to-one relationships between material culture and identity (Jones), the situation is further complicated in North America due to the legacy of salvage ethnography and the parallel development of the culture area concept.

Culture areas are based on the idea that cultural variation can be expressed geographically as well as temporally (Trigger 122). If colonial-era ethnologists busied themselves by documenting the variability of "Indian culture" across space, typically through the use of detailed culture area maps, archaeological cultural historians focused on the chronological expression of culture over time. Culture area thinking has had an indelible impact on archaeological expressions of history and identity. Using the "direct historic approach," North American prehistorians often begin with ethnographically known peoples and "work backwards" to infer similarities and differences preserved in the archaeological record. An unintended outcome is that we sometimes speak about "archaeological cultures," using a shorthand based on ethnonyms derived from the subjective experience of broadly contemporary descendant communities (Borgstede and Yaeger 103). In other words, it is so very easy for pots to become "People."

The transformation of *cultural* continua into *ethnic* antecedents of living groups reveals a number of paradoxical assumptions at odds with postmodern and postcolonial social theory more generally, despite their role in giving voice to indigenous perspectives. This is often bound up with ideas of a shared past, a distinct role within history, and that this shared existence has a common purpose or shared fate (Harmon 30). Words like *persistence* or *resilience* are often used within contemporary archaeological narratives to assess the status of indigenous social groups, past and present, in a way that curiously conflates social identity with the objectifiable notion of physical health (Kuper 390). However, the problem is not solely that of creating essentialist identities, strategically or otherwise, which can share features with nationalist accounts of history (e.g., Dietler; Trigger 174), particularly where colonial violence and its resulting power structures have reshaped the social fabric (more on this later). An archaeology that gives precedence to the history of contemporary people is a good way to silence the possibility of other histories. What about those groups that were snuffed out by events like the eighteenth-century smallpox epidemic (Boyd)? Or those who perished in environmental calamities such as the tsunami that hit the Pacific Coast in 1700, who were subsequently not around to be noticed by ethnographers and linguists, their traditions having been either largely forgotten or appropriated by their neighbors? One estimate suggests that the tsunami alone may have extinguished around 95 percent of the oral traditions on the west coasts of Vancouver Island and Washington State (Ludwin et al. 140) due to the untimely deaths of storytellers. And what about events unknown to us today? Can we even fathom the forgetting that has occurred between the present age and five hundred years ago, never mind five thousand years ago? Can we *really* speak for the social identities of the dead? Assuming we know who these people were and what they valued can result in something closer to hubris than elucidation. At best, overemphasizing identity (as in the examples of the Gitxaala, Stó:lō, and Haida given here) smothers the past with sameness; at worst, it confuses the processes of identity construction in the present and recent past with those that were operating in deep time.

Assessing the theoretical assumptions of archaeologists provides a partial critique; a historical approach to identity provides further lessons. Studies of colonialism in western North America focusing on issues like power and the material effects of inequality help underline the historical and contingent nature of identity. Particularly relevant here is the idea that the colonial landscape was not only a destructive force but also a creative one (Gosden, *Archaeology*). A now well-established analysis suggests that contemporary expressions of indigenous identity (whether local, regional, or pan-national) are not objective givens but are dependent on a bundle of shifting social and material relationships that exert influence on how indigenous peoples see themselves and how others see them (Hill). "National," "tribal," and "band" identities have been shaped through a two-way process: by the sharp end of colonial relations, notably practices of representation and the materialization of inequality within the landscape, and the ways in which indigenous peoples have negotiated these circumstances. These things range from the large-scale dispossessions of traditional lands and the naturalization of first peoples within the engineered spaces of Indian reserves in Canada (Brealey) or reservations in the United States (Colson), to the ways that recognition by the state, usually to guarantee certain rights or benefits, requires indigenous peoples to provide "proof" of descent to an ancestral territory or allegiance to an enduring tribal polity (Harmon 46). The power of states to shape social identities is well acknowledged (Anderson). Less well-known but equally powerful influences include the timing and spacing of the landscape of capitalism, which reformed the ways in which people could or could not interact (Oliver, *Landscapes* 188–89); or the creation and circulation of cultural maps by anthropologists and government agencies charged with welfare or treaty work, which have helped anticipate the creation of ethno-territoriality (Nadasdy). Rather than giving undue weight to cultural continua, a historical approach encourages us to ask questions about the complex nature of identity, helping us see that culture alone is a poor predictor of past social categories (e.g., Hodder). In our enthusiasm to assign identities to the makers of the archaeological record, a question we might ask is: Are these our categories or theirs?

The Changing Political Landscape of Archaeology

If the critical points I have marshalled in this chapter seem like well-worn ground to scholars of a more theoretical or historical bent, why do they have such limited appeal among indigenous-inflected archaeologies? Archaeologists are not simply shaped by matters of theory or method; as good historiographers know, we are also products of our wider social milieu. Two factors at play deserve further review.

The first is the establishment of first peoples as modern political entities tied to distinct territories. The history of this development is incredibly complex. It is at least in part shaped by the colonial process previously described, though it is also linked to an increasingly active interest by indigenous peoples in asserting their "place" within the evolving geography of contemporary political and economic boundaries. The confiscation of indigenous lands in the preceding two centuries has helped impel acts of "reterritorialization," a process that works at a variety of scales and in different social arenas. Perhaps its most powerful expression is in the development of indigenous cartographies: mapping projects undertaken by, or in collaboration with, First Nations. These projects deploy painstaking research to visually display the precontact cultural landscapes inhabited by local groups. They can take the form of reports and atlases (e.g., K. Carlson) or digital reconstructions of place available online (e.g., *Native Land*). They can include place-names and place-based narratives associated with the history of their traditional geographies. Sometimes they can be concerned with the definition of boundaries and the demarcation of territory—even if ethnographic data cast doubts on the significance and stability of ideas like territory in favor of concepts like borderless kin networks (Thom).

Such geographical statements have more than just historical use. On the one hand, they can be seen for their value in reasserting indigenous presence in landscapes once shown on colonial maps as empty space (Sparke). On the other hand, they are manifestations of how indigenous peoples have had to reform themselves to accept the dominant cultural idiom of territorial sovereignty within British Columbia, Canada, and the United States. The visual culture of mapping has probably done more to bring first peoples into our collective consciousness as ethno-territorial entities than almost any other scholarly output (Nadasdy).

Cultural maps of one form or another have played an important role in archaeological work in British Columbia, notably by professional archaeologists in advance of heritage mitigation work as a means of understanding whose cultural inheritance might be at stake. Yet while indigenous cartographies effectively challenge popular assumptions about colonial geographies, because maps are also artifacts, they tend to fossilize our understandings of place and space and can be further implicated in archaeological decision-making about whose past traces archaeologists expect to find when digging beneath the turf.

Second, this all takes a new dimension when we consider that first peoples continue to deal with the legacies of colonialism, including modern land grabs or other transgressions across their traditional lands—Canada's new bitumen pipeline to the Pacific being a recent example (Jubas). The difference from the "bad old days" is that First Nations are increasingly articulate and persuasive political actors in defending what they view as their cultural heritage, and they now employ their own experts, including archaeologists, in these defenses. As new cohorts of archaeologists emerge from graduate school, they are more and more being employed by indigenous governments (Kelley 187–88). In contexts where government institutions and university departments are no longer funded in ways that allow them to be the sole arbiters of knowledge production, we see a transition toward more decentered ways of knowing, evening up the playing field.

With archaeological field projects more commonly being co-designed, co-managed, and even led by indigenous peoples, archaeology can be an active form of resistance against state or corporate actors (e.g., Menzies; Nicholas 362). Keeping in mind that identity politics can cause people to become invested in their marginalization, it is not surprising to see history and heritage elided. This is not an indigenous issue but a human one, with a colonial legacy that easily predates indigenous-inflected archaeologies. Indeed, the Canadian government has been implicated in reproducing the same kinds of essentialized models of history and identity, from the creation of a heritage industry that valorizes Canadian history as white and European (Klimko) to its own legal rulings on indigenous land rights (Martindale). Where land claims are live issues, archaeology can become a way to prove in the courts what indigenous peoples have been saying all along. As Daniel L. Boxberger suggests, litigation can therefore profoundly alter the nature of knowledge claims in these areas.

Conclusion

Archaeology is not a neutral technique for studying the past, despite occasional claims that the evidence "speaks for itself." Archaeology has always been political, though not always acknowledged as such. But occasionally, challenges to the status quo come along that help unsettle a gaze that has become fixed. Indigenous perspectives and the rise of indigenous-inflected archaeology in North America have exposed Western misconceptions for what they are, with some going as far as to suggest there is no longer a binary choice between indigenous ways of knowing and Western science. Indeed, first peoples have much to teach archaeologists, and here we should be listening. This approach takes advantage of the significant epistemological overlaps between archaeological and indigenous knowledge that can serve as a basis of cooperation, mutual learning, and "federated knowledge," providing opportunities for deeper and more complex analyses (Martindale and Nicholas 450).

At the same time, certain tensions remain. As the acute observer Daryl Stump notes, there are areas where overlap may not exist. This is because Western and indigenous epistemologies and ontologies are different in respect to certain formative assumptions. Perhaps one of the more notable areas of divergence is in the construction of temporality. It may be impossible to reconcile indigenous notions of the past, which can emphasize stability over change, with those held by Western historical disciplines, which emphasize diachrony and causality. Indeed, this is where there may be little common ground between archaeologists, who are wont to temporalize identities (Gosden, "Commentary" 477) by historically situating the causal relationships behind their emergence, and indigenous communities, who recognize continuities with the past based on other cultural criteria such as storytelling and placemaking. This observation is hardly novel. Of greater interest is why such a premise might so far have been overlooked. The fact that most Pacific Northwest archaeologists accept that living indigenous communities share cultural affiliations with the region's archaeological sequence, and commonly use historical analogies to help shed light on the ancient peoples of the coast, is certainly a powerful stimulus—as it is elsewhere (Borgstede and Yaeger). Another reason relates to the contemporary political landscape with its fractious and polarizing colonial legacy in which archaeologists are themselves deeply entangled. As compelling as these suggestions may be, we should not fail to recall or minimize our discipline's own theoretical developments. Archaeology can be very effective in identifying the material dimensions of cultural continuity across time and space, but it is much less convincing at "digging up" social identities without credible corroborating historical evidence. Quite simply, one cannot infer "People" from an archaeological cultural pattern because social groups coalesce around a kaleidoscopic set of historical factors far more complex than the superficial unities implied by the stylistic character of wood, bone, or stone artifacts (Hodder 103). Although archaeological interpretation should stay open to what indigenous knowledge can provide, it does not follow that archaeologists should remain oblivious to the limits of the interpretive process.

Can one do "decolonial" archaeology and yet maintain the formative logic of Western historical disciplines? In my experience, disagreement need not spell the end of collaboration. If there is one thing that participating in community archaeology has taught me on the other side of the Atlantic (Vergunst et al.), it is that disagreement along with respectful exchanges of different standpoints actually helps build trust. This is what Richard Sennett refers to as dialogical conversations, where people can have very different outlooks but, through an empathetic commitment to understanding other perspectives, can begin to mitigate differences and manage disagreement, "getting things done" by way of cooperation (6). A more open and critical perspective might help enrich the quality of our discussions about identity, allowing us to identify material similarities between past and present, such as cultural or technological continuities, without letting *social identity* get in the way. Of course, if we are to promote dialogue, we should also be accepting that archaeological standpoints might well be rejected (Joyce 65). This is partly about recognizing the situated nature of audiences, whether they are indigenous peoples, archaeologists, or others; they will respond very differently depending on their respective positionality. In these contexts, we should, naturally, respect the role of pasts that are alternative to those created by the disciplinary structures of archaeology. Given that the purpose of collaborative archaeologies is often to make the past accessible to local communities, beyond the interests of professionals, they should be more than capable of accommodating contrasting views. What is required for a decolonial archaeology deserving of its name is a willingness to engage colleagues, collaborators, and the wider public in a respectful dialogue that seeks to listen, take on views from outside the discipline, and improve our own understanding through such dialogue. But it also has an obligation to educate about archaeology and its limitations (González-Ruibal et al.). Respectful collaborations should therefore be places where these kinds of debates are tolerated and even encouraged.

The project of "decolonizing prehistory" should not be limited to addressing contemporary indigenous voices and perspectives, although this is important. Archaeology is also beholden to its own frameworks for creating knowledge. As John and Jean Comaroff have argued in the context of South African colonial history, colonialism "altered everyone and everything involved, if not all in the same manner and measure" (5). If we are serious about removing the misconceptions of the colonial past, then we also need to think more critically about the legacy of colonialism on the world around us. To do these things, archaeologists have an incredible challenge. They must be as effective at untangling the historical conditions of the present as they are in reconstructing deep time, all the while balancing the concerns of contemporary communities.

Note

I would like to thank the participants of the symposium "Decolonizing 'Prehistory': Deep Time and Topological Knowledge in the Americas" (2018) and Aberdeen's Department of Anthropology Seminar Series (2019) for their perceptive comments and valuable feedback on earlier versions of this chapter. I am particularly grateful to Ana Jorge, the volume editors, and the external readers for their critical engagement with the text and for pointing out inconsistencies. All errors are my contribution.

References

Ames, Kenneth, and Herbert D. G. Maschner. *Peoples of the Northwest Coast: Their Archaeology and Prehistory*. Thames and Hudson, 1999.

Anderson, Benedict. *Imagined Communities: Reflections on the Origin and Spread of Nationalism*. Verso Books, 1991.

Atalay, Sonya. *Community-Based Archaeology: Research with, by, and for Indigenous and Local Communities*. University of California Press, 2012.

Birch, Jennifer. "Rethinking the Archaeological Application of Iroquoian Kinship." *Canadian Journal of Archaeology*, vol. 32, no. 2, 2008, pp. 194–213.

Borgstede, Greg, and Jason Yaeger. "Notions of Cultural Continuity and Disjunction in Maya Social Movements and Maya Archaeology." *Archaeology and the Postcolonial Critique*, edited by Mathew Liebmann, Altamira Press, 2010, pp. 91–107.

Boxberger, Daniel L. "The Not So Common." *Be of Good Mind*, edited by Bruce Granville Miller, University of British Columbia Press, 2007, pp. 55–81.

Boyd, Robert T. "Demographic History, 1774–1874." *Handbook of North American Indians*, vol. 7, *Northwest Coast*, edited by Wayne Suttles, Smithsonian Institution, 1990, pp. 135–48.

Brealey, Kenneth G. "Mapping Them 'Out': Euro-Canadian Cartography and the Appropriation of the Nuxalk and Ts'ilhqot'in First Nations' Territories, 1793–1916." *Canadian Geographer*, vol. 39, no. 2, 1995, pp. 140–56.

Brubaker, Rogers, and Frederick Cooper. "Beyond 'Identity.'" *Theory and Society*, vol. 29, no. 1, 2000, pp. 1–47.

Budhwa, Rick, and Tyler McCreary. "Reconciling Cultural Resource Management with Indigenous Geographies: The Importance of Connecting Research with People and Place." *A Deeper Sense of Place: Stories and Journeys of Indigenous Collaboration*, edited by Jay T. Johnson and Soren C. Larson, Oregon State University Press, 2013, pp. 195–214.

Carlson, Keith Thor, ed. *A Stó:lō-Coast Salish Historical Atlas*. Douglas and McIntyre, 2001.

Carlson, Keith, et al., eds. *Towards a New Ethnohistory: Community-Engaged Scholarship Among the People of the River*. University of Manitoba Press, 2018.

Carlson, Roy. "History of Research in Archaeology." *Handbook of North American Indians*, vol. 7, *Northwest Coast*, edited by Wayne Suttles, Smithsonian Institution, 1990, pp. 107–15.

Colson, Elizabeth. *The Makah Indians*. University of Manchester Press, 1953.

Comaroff, John, and Jean Comaroff. *The Dialectics of Modernity on a South African Frontier*. University of Chicago Press, 1997.

Dietler, Michael. "'Our Ancestors the Gauls': Archaeology, Ethnic Nationalism, and the Manipulation of Celtic Identity in Modern Europe." *American Anthropologist*, vol. 96, no. 3, 1994, pp. 584–605.

González-Ruibal, Alfredo, et al. "Against Reactionary Populism: Towards a New Public Archaeology." *Antiquity*, vol. 92, no. 362, 2018, pp. 507–15.

Gosden, Chris. *Archaeology and Colonialism: Cultural Contact from 5000 BC to the Present*. Cambridge University Press, 2004.

Gosden, Chris. "Commentary: The Archaeology of the Colonized and Global Archaeological Theory." *Rethinking Colonial Pasts Through Archaeology*, edited by Neil Ferris et al., Oxford University Press, 2014, pp. 476–82.

Grier, Colin. "Consuming the Recent for Constructing the Ancient: The Role of Ethnography in Coast Salish Archaeological Interpretation." *Be of Good Mind*, edited by Bruce Granville Miller, University of British Columbia Press, 2007, pp. 284–307.

Hall, Martin. "The Burden of Tribalism: The Social Context of Southern African Iron Age Studies." *Histories of Archaeology: A Reader in the History of Archaeology*, edited by Tim Murray and Christopher Evans, Oxford University Press, 2008, pp. 72–93.

Harmon, Alexandra. "Coast Salish History." *Be of Good Mind*, edited by Bruce Granville Miller, University of British Columbia Press, 2007, pp. 30–54.

Hill, Jonathan. *History, Power, and Identity: Ethnogenesis in the Americas, 1492–1992*, edited by Jonathan Hill, University of Iowa Press, 1996.

Hillerdal, Charlotta. "Integrating the Past in the Present: Archaeology as Part of Living Yup'ik Heritage." *Archaeologies of "Us" and "Them": Debating History, Heritage and Indigeneity*, edited by Charlotta Hillerdal et al., Routledge, 2017, pp. 64–79.

Hill-Tout, Charles. "Later Prehistoric Man in British Columbia." *Transactions of the Royal Society of Canada*, 2nd series, vol. 1, no. 2, 1895, pp. 103–22.

Hodder, Ian. *Symbols in Action: Ethnoarchaeological Studies of Material Culture.* Cambridge University Press, 1982.

Jenkins, Richard. *Social Identity.* 2nd ed., Routledge, 2005.

Jones, Sian. "Ethnicity: Theoretical Approaches, Methodological Implications." *Handbook of Archaeological Theories*, edited by R. Alexander Bentley et al., Altamira, 2008, pp. 321–33.

Joyce, Rosemary A. "Critical Histories of Archaeological Practice: Latin American and North American Interpretations in a Honduran Context." *Evaluating Multiple Narratives: Beyond Nationalist, Colonialist, Imperialist Archaeologies*, edited by J. Habu et al., Springer, 2008, pp. 56–68.

Jubas, Keala. "Alberta's Shameful Pipeline Politics Ignores First Nations." *The Conversation*, 28 Mar. 2018, theconversation.com/albertas-shameful-pipeline-politics-ignores -first-nations-93721.

Kelley, Jane H. "Presentism? Balderdash." *Canadian Journal of Archaeology*, vol. 32, no. 2, 2008, pp. 186–93.

King, Arden R. *Cattle Point: A Stratified Site on the Southern Northwest Coast.* Memoirs of the Society for American Archaeology 7. Society for American Archaeology, 1950.

Klassen, Michael, et al. "First Nations and the Transformation of Archaeological Practice in British Columbia, Canada." *Heritage Management*, vol. 2, no. 2, 2009, pp. 199–238.

Klimko, Olga. "Fur Trade Archaeology in Western Canada: Who Is Digging Up the Forts?" *The Archaeology of Contact in Settler Societies*, edited by Tim Murray, Cambridge University Press, 2004, pp. 158–75.

Kuper, Adam. "The Return of the Native." *Current Anthropology*, vol. 44, no. 3, 2003, pp. 389–401.

Lepofsky, Dana. "Deconstructing the Mccallum Site." *BC Studies*, no. 158, Summer 2008, pp. 3–31.

Lepofsky, Dana, et al. "Exploring Stó:lō-Coast Salish Interaction and Identity in Ancient Houses and Settlements in the Fraser Valley, British Columbia." *American Antiquity*, vol. 74, no. 4, 2009, pp. 595–626.

Liebmann, Mathew. "Postcolonial Cultural Affiliation: Essentialism, Hybridity, and NAGPRA." *Archaeology and the Postcolonial Critique*, edited by Matthew Liebmann and Uzma Z. Rizvi, AltaMira, 2010, pp. 73–90.

Ludwin, Ruth S., et al. "Dating the 1700 Cascadia Earthquake: Great Coastal Earthquakes in Native Stories." *Seismological Research Letters*, vol. 76, no. 2, 2005, pp. 140–48.

Martindale, Andrew. "Archaeology Taken to Court." *Rethinking Colonial Pasts Through Archaeology*, edited by Neil Ferris et al., Oxford University Press, 2014, pp. 397–422.

Martindale, Andrew, and George Nicholas. "Archaeology as Federated Knowledge." *Canadian Journal of Archaeology*, vol. 38, no. 2, 2014, pp. 434–65.

Masters of the Pacific Coast. BBC 4, 28 July 2016, bbc.co.uk/programmes/b07m771x.

McLay, Eric, et al. "A'lhut tu tet Sulhween—Respecting the Ancestors: Report of the Hul'qumi'num Heritage Law Case Study." Summary report, 2004, polisproject.org/ PDFs/HTG%20Report%202004_Summary.pdf.

Menzies, Charles R. "Revisiting 'Dm Sibilhaa'nm da Laxyuubm Gitxaala (Picking Abalone in Gitxaala Territory).'" *BC Studies*, no. 187, Autumn 2015, pp. 129–53.

Millennia Research. "Gwaii Communications Subsea Fibre Optic Cable Archaeological Overview Assessment." Non-permit report prepared for Gwaii Communications, 2018.

Nadasdy, Paul. "Boundaries Among Kin: Sovereignty, the Modern Treaty Process, and the Rise of Ethno-Territorial Nationalism Among Yukon First Nations." *Comparative Studies in Society and History*, vol. 54, no. 3, 2012, pp. 499–532.

Native Land. native-land.ca. Accessed July 2019.

Nicholas, George. "Decolonizing the Archaeological Landscape: The Practice and Politics of Archaeology in British Columbia." *American Indian Quarterly*, vol. 30, nos. 3 & 4, 2006, pp. 350–80.

Oliver, Jeff. *Landscapes and Social Transformations on the Northwest Coast: Colonial Encounters in the Fraser Valley*. University of Arizona Press, 2010.

Oliver, Jeff. "Native-Lived Colonialism and the Agency of Life Projects: A View from the Northwest Coast." *Rethinking Colonial Pasts Through Archaeology*, edited by Neil Ferris et al., Oxford University Press, 2014, pp. 76–102.

Oliver, Jeff, and Ágústa Edwald. "Between Islands of Ethnicity and Shared Landscapes: Re-thinking Settler Society, Cultural Landscapes and the Study of the Canadian West." *Cultural Geographies*, vol. 23, no. 2, 2016, pp. 199–219.

Reimer, Rudy. "Extreme Archaeology: The Results of Investigations at High Elevations in the Northwest." MA thesis, Simon Fraser University, 2001.

Roy, Susan. *These Mysterious People: Shaping History and Archaeology in a Northwest Coast Community*. McGill-Queen's University Press, 2011.

Sennett, Richard. *Together: The Rituals, Pleasures and Politics*. Penguin Books, 2012.

Sparke, Mathew. "A Map That Roared and an Original Atlas: Canada, Cartography, and the Narration of Nation." *Annals of the Association of American Geographers*, vol. 88, no. 3, 1998, pp. 463–95.

Stahl, Ann B. "Afterward: Vantage Points in an Archaeology of Colonialism." *Rethinking Colonial Pasts Through Archaeology*, edited by Neil Ferris et al., Oxford University Press, 2014, pp. 481–99.

Stump, Daryl. "On Applied Archaeology, Indigenous Knowledge, and the Useable Past." *Current Anthropology*, vol. 54, no. 3, 2013, pp. 268–98.

Thom, Brian. "The Paradox of Boundaries in Coast Salish Territories." *Cultural Geographies*, vol. 16, no. 2, 2009, pp. 179–205.

Trigger, Bruce. *A History of Archaeological Thought*. Cambridge University Press, 1989.

Vergunst, Jo, et al. "Shaping Heritage in the Landscape Among Communities Past and Present." *Heritage as Community Research: Legacies of Co-production*, edited by Helen Graham and Jo Vergunst, Policy Press, 2019, pp. 27–50.

8

Lilies, Ice, and Oil

INDIGENOUS LANDSCAPES, SETTLER COLONIALISM, AND DEEP
TIME AROUND THE SOUTHERN SALISH SEA

Coll Thrush

ON 26 JANUARY 1700, AT around 9 p.m.—well within the realm of
"prehistory" in this part of the world—much of the northwest coast of North
America slipped and shuddered, causing a massive earthquake and a violent
tsunami that inundated the region's coastal areas and reached as far as Asia.
It devastated communities from what is currently known as Oregon to what
is for the moment British Columbia. The fact that we can time this event to
the specific day and hour speaks to a rich diversity of archives: archaeological
horizons, ghost forest dendrochronology, Japanese clerks' records, and, most
importantly, accounts from the Nuu-chah-nulth, Makah, Alsea, Yurok, and
other Indigenous peoples of the region. The story of this most recent Cascadia
Subduction Zone megathrust earthquake has captured the attention of the
broader public throughout the Pacific Northwest and British Columbia, to the
extent that the anniversary is typically now observed every 26 January through
stories in local newspapers and the occasional safety drill. Several books have
been published about it (Clague and Turner; Doughton; Thompson), and the
New Yorker ran a story in 2015 about what a subduction zone rupture might do
to Seattle (Schultz). The article quickly went viral on social media platforms,
suggesting the extent to which historical and "prehistorical" earthquakes and
tsunamis are becoming part of public interest and local knowledge beyond
Indigenous, scientific, and risk management communities.

However, the politics of the 1700 event—the ways in which Indigenous
knowledge was ignored for decades and then more recently deployed in a
primarily corroborative register—remain largely obscured. Geologist Ruth S.
Ludwin and I tried to speak into this relative silence several years ago with

our piece "Finding Fault: Seismology, Colonial Science, and the Rediscovery of Earthquakes and Tsunamis in Cascadia," which looked critically at the relationship between Western science and Indigenous knowledge on the Northwest Coast, and focused on the events of 1700. We wrote that seismologists, historians, and other researchers must engage with the ongoing power relations between two profoundly different ontologies and social and political systems. We also discussed the implications of settler society, through its scientific institutions, extracting knowledge from published or other Indigenous sources without any sort of reciprocity with the communities in which that knowledge originated.

This chapter is not about earthquakes and tsunamis, although it is about the politics of the deeper, precolonial past in one small part of the Northwest Coast. Building from our work on the January 1700 disaster, I want to extend some of the arguments we made in "Finding Fault" to the lands and waters around and immediately to the south of Seattle. These ancient places, I argue, must be understood as imbricated with the more recent politics of settler colonialism. Borrowing from Tonawanda Seneca scholar Mishuana Goeman, I illustrate how settler "grammars of place" in the region have historically required both a maladaptive rejection of Indigenous knowledge—by which I mean Coast Salish ontologies and practices on the land—and a disavowal of ongoing Indigenous presence and the complex politics that emerge from that presence. With "maladaptive," I am referring to the devastating environmental consequences of settler colonialism in this place: the loss of ancient forests, the pollution of waterways and the disappearance of salmon runs, and top-of-the-food-chain orcas cruising toward extinction, all within the context of possibly irreversible climate change. In short, settler society is only just learning the foundational realities of the place it has so quickly, so utterly transformed (Goeman 235–65).

Meanwhile, the "prehistory" of the lands around the Salish Sea has all too often been cut off from their "history," the latter often said to begin in 1792 with the arrival of British captain George Vancouver and his crew. This is partially a result of the compartmentalization of scholarly disciplines, a form of intellectual segregation that has distilled and legitimized the notion that some people have "history," while others merely have something called "culture." This splitting of the past has also historically been undergirded by a deeply held European belief in the superiority of alphabetical text: if it was not written down, it may as well never have happened. Without the written word, *terra nullius*. It is also related to Enlightenment-derived developmental theories of human history, which placed people such as Vancouver and the Mowachaht Nuu-chah-nulth leader Maquinna at different places along an

imagined line of "progress" toward "civilization," despite the fact that the
men were not only contemporaries but, inherently, equals. This constellation
of epistemic and ontological frames comprises the regional manifestation of
Goeman's settler colonial grammars of place and continues to have effects on
Indigenous lives and nations. Stories do work, and the divorce of deep time
from the colonial past has ramifications.

The invasion of Indigenous territories around the Salish Sea has been an
imperfect process, in no small part because of the active resistance of Coast
Salish peoples, practices, beliefs, and systems of governance. As historian
Laura Ishiguro has written, "the emerging settler order . . . [is] both powerful and partial, inconsistent in its imposition, complicated in its effects, and
never inevitable or without resistance" (125). Indeed, the ascendancy of settler
colonialism has been paralleled by the fact that, as Mohawk anthropologist
Audra Simpson puts it, "the condition of Indigeneity in North America is to
have survived" (205). It is in the tension between accounts of settler colonialism and accounts of Indigenous survivance that we can see the ways in which
deep time continues to animate, and be animated by, ongoing relations of
Indigenous and settler peoples.

In this investigation of settler colonialism and survivance in Coast Salish
territories, the landscape itself is the antiquity in question, whether in the
form of anthropogenic spaces, places of deep memory, or sites of ongoing
contestation. Rather than a passive canvas upon which history happens, the
landscape is itself agentive in the ways it does (and sometimes does not) support and respond to life. Landscape is also agentive in the sense that it is good
to think with: it can transform our understanding of things. Lenape scholar
Joanne M. Barker, for example, has argued for territory as an analytic in its
own right, while Yellowknives Dene political scientist Glen Sean Coulthard
makes a case for "grounded theory," in which relations with the land can—
and indeed must—inform intellectual and political projects of person- and
peoplehood, resistance, and sovereignty. The land teaches.

This chapter uses particular places in the Coast Salish territories around
the southern Salish Sea, also known as xʷəʼlč ("hwultch") or Puget Sound, to
offer a trio of regional microhistories that take the fine-grained textures of
locality and link them to broader questions about the politics of "prehistory"
and "history" as well as to larger ecological and historical scales. Together,
three places—prairies, an ancient ice dam, and the waters of xʷəʼlč itself—call
for the interpenetration, porosity, and weave of past, present, and future. This,
I suggest, is the proper mode for understanding "prehistory" in the southern
Coast Salish world. To "decolonize" prehistory and deep time, we must understand it as colonized in the first place.[1]

∴

The first of these places is one of the more important and endangered landscapes found in the territories around the southern Salish Sea. While many
people imagine the precolonial Puget Sound lowlands as a wilderness of end-
less old-growth coniferous forests, it was in fact a patchwork of forests, wet-
lands, and open prairies. The prairies in particular captured the imagination
of many early European and American visitors. As early as the late eighteenth
century, British explorers were impressed with the area's prairie landscapes,
which they interpreted as parklands created by the hand of Providence. Archibald Menzies, a physician and botanist on Vancouver's ship, described local
places in 1792 in language both enraptured and anticipatory: "I ascended the
Bank with one of the Gentlemen & strolled over an extensive lawn, where
solitude rich pastures & rural prospects prevaild [sic] . . . a pleasant & desirable
tract of both pasture & arable land where the Plough might enter without the
least obstruction" (23). Meanwhile, despite seeing Indigenous women culti-
vating these landscapes and even being offered prairie-grown foods, foreign
observers had little understanding of the ways those ecosystems worked and
were worked. Early American settlers, for their part, sometimes commented
on the vast crops of food plants and flowers found only in these places, and
which included c̓ábid ("tsah-beed") or camas (*Camassia* spp.) lily, whose bulb
was an essential staple in Coast Salish foodways.

But these are no providential landscapes. Rather, the prairies near the
southern Salish Sea—known as báqʷab ("bah-quahb") in the local xʷəlšucid
("hwull-shoot-seed") language—are the results of human knowledge, kinship, governance, and work. Kept healthy and open by intentional burning,
the prairies provide diverse foods and medicines found nowhere else. They are
carefully cultivated remnants of a landscape that once dominated the region
when the climate was colder and drier, and without human effort, the prairies
would have been swallowed up by encroaching forests of fir and cedar. Prairies
force us to consider the history of human occupation and horticultural labor
in the region as central to its deep history. No wilderness, but a garden.[2]

The prairies of southern Puget Sound country also have had a very specific
kind of postcontact history, bound up in contestation and violence. Prairies
were often the first places chosen by American settlers, so it is not surprising that they played a central role in conflicts between settlers and Coast
Salish people. In what would become southern King County and northern
Pierce County in Washington State, for example, Americans quickly established homesteads on prairies and began changing them through intensive
agriculture while extracting labor, sometimes through coercion and violence,

from communities with ancestral ties to those places. Settler encroachment, combined with a fractious treaty process, led to war across southern Coast Salish territories and beyond in 1855 and 1856. Many of the most important battles and killings of the so-called Puget Sound Indian War—known in local Indigenous communities as the First Treaty War—took place on prairies that had been taken over by settlers in what Patrick Wolfe has called the "lethal interlude" between squatting and legal dispossession (qtd. in Nichols 20). With the ascendancy of settler colonialism, many prairies changed from places of sustenance and healing to strategic sites of violent conflict.[3]

This transformation has continued into the first decades of the twenty-first century. Only a handful of the region's prairies survive; some of the most intact ones, ironically, can be found on the Fort Lewis-McChord Military Base near the southernmost reaches of the Salish Sea, where regular burning by explosive ordnance has to some degree mimicked Indigenous firing practices, resulting in relatively healthy prairies. While a handful of other prairies can be found in nonmilitarized sites, I would argue that there is a through line between the initial settler occupation of prairies and its resulting violent conflicts and today's military occupation of some of the most important remnants of this ecosystem. Fort Lewis, after all, began as an installation meant to protect settlers from Indigenous combatants during and after the First Treaty War. Even though some cooperative management between local tribes and the U.S. military has begun to take place, the fact remains that the prairies of the territories around the southern Salish Sea are profoundly endangered, and must be understood not just as artifacts of Indigenous labor but also as artifacts of settler colonialism. I should point out, though, that not all prairies of the region have experienced this history; a handful are sites of active cultural resurgence, in which tribal members are relearning practices of care, connecting land use to issues of food sovereignty and community health. In this way, "prehistoric" landscapes remain vital and contested in the present.

∴

If the prairies around the Salish Sea have fared poorly under American settler colonialism, the region's estuaries have not done much better, and the places where rivers flow into xʷəlč have been transformed in profound and destructive ways. The Duwamish River, which debouches at Seattle, is perhaps the most transformed of all. Straightened in the 1910s, its mouth stopped up with what was, in the early twentieth century, the world's largest man-made island, and filled with heavy industry, the Duwamish, home to the Coast

Salish people of the same name, is one of the most polluted places in Washington State and a federally designated Superfund site.[4]

Sometime in the 1920s, Major Hamilton, a man of Duwamish ancestry living on the Muckleshoot Reservation southeast of Seattle, sat down with Arthur C. Ballard, the town clerk of Auburn, Washington, a town that sidles up against the reservation. The story he told the clerk went something like follows.

A boy named South Wind lived with his people at sqʷəlac ["skwuh-lots"]. North Wind, who had built a weir of ice across the river that prevented the salmon from coming up, came to sqʷəlac and killed all but the old lady and the boy. The boy grew, killing pheasants as he did. The old people told him, "Forbidden to go downriver, they killed your ancestors, only go upriver walking, Grandson." South Wind grew to be a man. His grandmother was making baskets to hold rain, and told him he would go downriver to see the North Wind people who had decimated his people. South Wind went downriver, and as he did, the North Wind people began to melt. He went back to his grandmother, and as she poured her baskets of rain into the river, he threw large trees into it. The rain caused the river to rise, and the trees caught up on the fish weir. All the North Wind people were melted, and North Wind himself agreed to stay away except for brief visits. The remains of the ice weir were turned to stone and can still be seen in the river today (Ballard 55–64).

Other knowledge keepers told slightly different versions of the story to Ballard. Sukwálasxt from the Green River described how the fish weir was turned to stone and the grandmother's home into a hill, introducing the character of Mountain Beaver Woman into the story. Sotaiakub from the Duwamish described another hill named after North Wind, and put it simply: "if the young man [South Wind] had not been born," he told Ballard, "we would still have the ice here now" (Ballard 59). Together, these and other versions of the story make up what is often referred to as "The Epic of the Winds," an account of the world becoming the way it is: of the climate warming, of the salmon coming up, and of geological changes in the land. They are also understood today by most local Coast Salish people and their listeners as a memory of the end of the last Ice Age, of the withdrawal of the massive sheets of ice to the north. They are examples of sx̌ʷiʔáb ("shwee-ahb"), tales of creation and transformation in deep time.

Major Hamilton and the others interviewed by Ballard had seen and experienced transformations almost as significant as those described in the sx̌ʷiʔáb. They were each born in the years after the treaties of 1855 ceded most of their lands to the settlers, and the changes that soon followed altered the landscapes on which they lived. Forests were cut down, salmon runs were decimated through overfishing and habitat loss, other wildlife populations were nearly wiped out, and Indigenous communities were battered by epidemic diseases that had continued from earlier generations. Indeed, one Duwamish and Suquamish headman named siʔaɬ—better known to most as Chief Seattle— even referred to the newcomers as "changers" during the 1855 treaty process, employing the same word used to describe the powerful beings that made many things the way they are in the sx̌ʷiʔáb.[5]

But this was also a generation that resisted settler colonialism. Relatives of many of the same elders who shared sx̌ʷiʔáb with outsiders in the 1920s shared their knowledge in other ways, as witnesses in a land claims case involving many of the region's tribes. They gave detailed accounts of prairies, potato gardens, fish weirs, longhouses, and other cultural landscapes and, in doing so, asserted their territoriality against a hostile State of Washington. Their testimonies remain one of the most important archives of Coast Salish inhabitance in the region and a resource used by scholars both within and outside Indigenous communities.[6]

Two years after the publication of these knowledge keepers' testimonies, in 1929, Ballard published "Mythology of Southern Puget Sound," the first written account of the Epic of the Winds and other sx̌ʷiʔáb from the area's Indigenous communities. We might think, then, of the choice made by Major Hamilton and the others to share the Epic of the Winds when they did, at a time of profound change to their traditional territories and treaty lands. These are more than "legends" or "myths"; they are accounts of deep time that assert and affirm topological heritage—an Indigenous "antiquity"—and the continued connections between Indigenous people and places beyond the reservation. They speak back to the narrative logics of elimination and the vanishing Indian, so common in the early twentieth century, that sought to reduce Indigenous people to relics of a primitive and placeless past.

Several decades after the Epic of the Winds found its way into print, the stony remains of the ungenerous fish weir became the focus of attention once again. Under a 1997 public arts project funded by King County, the x̌ʷməθk-ʷəy̓əm (Musqueam) Coast Salish artist Susan Point, from Vancouver, British Columbia, installed six large carvings near the site, which together tell the Epic of the Winds. They feature each of the major characters—South Wind; his grandmother, North Wind; and of course the salmon that are at the center of the story. Just out of sight of the fish weir itself, along a bike trail that follows the Duwamish for several miles, the carvings reanimate the site and re-emplace the Epic within its specific landscape rather than leaving it in the realm of displaced "myth."

Susan Point's work, meanwhile, is just across the Duwamish from Cecil Moses Memorial Park, which includes ecologically restored riverbanks that overlook the remains of North Wind's weir. Moses, a member of the Muckleshoot Tribe, was a leading activist during the Second Treaty War of the 1960s and early 1970s, also known locally as the "Fish Fights." Facing regular arrest by state fish and wildlife agents for exercising treaty rights to the salmon runs on the Duwamish and its tributaries, Moses and his compatriots throughout the lands around the southern Salish Sea brought attention to the ongoing presence of the Muckleshoot, Duwamish, Puyallup, Nisqually, and other tribes, and to the continued relevance of the treaties. Ultimately, their efforts led to a victory in the 1974 case *United States v. Washington*, which affirmed that federally recognized tribes have rights to half the harvestable salmon runs in the waterways within the boundaries set by treaties. This ruling, which remains a watershed moment in Indigenous rights and in regional history, is commemorated at Cecil Moses Park, connecting the Epic of the Winds to a recent history of contestation and resistance.[7]

Meanwhile, not far upriver from the weir, another site associated with the sx̌ʷiʔáb also asserts Indigenous presence. Just south of the Seattle city limits and just upriver from the fish weir, a hill of bedrock emerges from the flat floodplain of the Duwamish Valley. This is stəqaxʷ ("stuh-kah-hw"), another site featured in the Epic of the Winds and a place where sentinels would watch for canoes coming upriver. With a name that means "dammer" but was known to settlers for much of the twentieth century as Poverty Hill, stəqaxʷ is hemmed in by a highway off-ramp and a shooting range, and houses creep up its eastern slope. And yet the hill has played a key role in two local communities: a group of neighborhood environmentalists and the Duwamish Tribe. Beginning in the 1990s, a group calling itself Friends of Duwamish Hill began to organize a campaign to preserve the prominence, which was at the time slated for further development. They envisioned its scrubby top, infested with invasive English ivy and Scotch broom, restored to a healthy native ecosystem. More than simply creating an ecological space free of human history, however, they also worked closely with the Duwamish Tribe, many of whose members continue to call Seattle and its environs home.

The Duwamish are a federally unrecognized tribe, meaning that the United States government does not regard them as Indigenous, although they do have a longhouse near the river that bears their name. Throughout the tumultuous changes of the nineteenth and twentieth centuries, some Duwamish maintained their community despite lacking a land base of their own, while others moved to area reservations or blended into settler society. Despite these transformations, since the 1970s, the Duwamish have been savvy and highly visible activists on the Seattle cultural scene, making use of archaeological excavations, the city's 2001 sesquicentennial, and other events to call attention to their legal situation and their community's history. The campaign to preserve stəqaxʷ was no different; almost from the beginning, non-Indigenous organizers linked it to the Duwamish Tribe's efforts toward federal recognition, and Duwamish people often participated in storytelling events at the hill as it was being restored.[8]

Today, the Tribe remains unrecognized by the federal government, but the work to protect stəqaxʷ has paid off: it is now officially a park called Duwamish Hill Preserve. The ivy and broom are gone and trails wind through a forest of madrone, ferns, fir, and other native plants. Around the base of the hill, restorationists have constructed a nascent prairie ecosystem, with camas and other food plants, as well as a tule marsh. Throughout the site, interpretive signage speaks to the Epic of the Winds and to Indigenous and settler histories of the place, and provide information on traditional uses and xʷəlšucid names of numerous plant species. That the story of the Duwamish and their ongoing quest for recognition, however, is not told there may speak to the influence of federally recognized tribes such as Muckleshoot, who generally oppose Duwamish recognition and have their own historic claims on landscapes in and around Seattle. But this also makes my larger point: deep-time sites like stəqaxʷ remain active, contested locations of memory, culture, and politics for local Indigenous communities.

All of this is to say that in the lands around the southern Salish Sea, stories of deep time cannot easily—or perhaps, even, logically or ethically—be divorced from more recent forms of resistance to settler colonialism, as well as ongoing tensions between Indigenous communities, themselves largely a product of that colonialism. In locations where the Epic of the Winds took place, stories from the beginning of the world have been sutured onto more contemporary Coast Salish accounts of resistance, survivance, and futurity, ensuring that the Epic of the Winds, like other sx̌ʷiʔáb, remain culturally, politically, and even legally relevant. Here, "prehistory" is still happening. It is almost as if the ice never fully melted.

∴

On the matter of melting ice, we might now turn to the onrushing climatic transformation of the planet and its local manifestations. Most of the glaciers that feed the rivers of the Salish Sea are melting, while precious and delicate alpine ecosystems are being pushed ever higher in elevation, with scientists and others fearing that they will literally run out of room and seemingly evaporate into the skies above the increasingly ice-free volcanic peaks. Most of this is the result of what many have come to call the Anthropocene, a new geological period in which some human societies have irreparably transformed the Earth's climate and left their marks in its soil. Without distracting from the basic truth of climate change, I want to acknowledge the different formations among scholars about the extent, nature, and history of the Anthropocene, and indeed, whether "anthropo-" is in fact the proper term for it. Some have deepened the case for the Anthropocene, while others have argued for terms that put a finer point on the matter; examples include influential theorist Donna Haraway's Chthulucene. But whose Anthropocene is it, after all? Métis anthropologist Zoe Todd, Heather Davis, and Potawatomi philosopher Kyle Powys Whyte each note that Indigenous peoples in North America have been living in a postapocalyptic world for the past five hundred and some years, describing settler society's awakening to the potentially apocalyptic implications of climate change as a deeply problematic form of "discovery."

These matters were clearly on the mind of the hundreds of people who lit out onto the Salish Sea at Seattle in the summer of 2015. They were there to protest the docking in xʷəّlč of a massive oil rig destined for the Arctic. What became known as the "shell no!" actions and was made up of non-Indigenous activists referred to as "kayaktivists" but centered on Indigenous land and water protectors in traditional canoes dominated headlines for days in the Seattle area (Associated Press). Similar protests had happened before (and will continue to happen) around coal depots, oil refineries, and liquefied natural gas facilities around the shores of xʷəّlč. The shell no! actions garnered international attention, in no small part because Indigenous voices were at the center of the action, with Coast Salish and other Indigenous people positioning themselves at the helm as spokespeople for the planet. Throughout the protests, Indigenous people and their allies asked observers to consider not only the present but the past (Brownstone). Many, including members of the Duwamish Tribe, drew attention to the local treaties of 1855 and to the longer history of settler colonialism in this place.

Simultaneously, they leaned into the future, pointing toward the multigenerational ethics at the core of Indigenous belief systems and practices and the matter of being good relations across time. Eric Day of the Swinomish Tribe, a Coast Salish community whose territory lies to the north of Seattle, told reporters that "this is our livelihood. . . . We need to protect it for our children" (Associated Press). Other speakers invoked the language of seven generations, asking listeners what sort of ancestors they wanted to be. In doing so, they connected the Permian era with the present and the Carboniferous with the colonial. In this, their actions linked "prehistory" to what has come, refracted through the political battles of the current moment.

We might go so far as to borrow a term from Indigenous studies scholar Mark Rifkin and think of this as a form of "temporal sovereignty," in which Indigenous communities and individuals challenge linear Western teleologies of progress by asserting different time frames and framings based in their own ontologies and histories. Indigenous land and water protectors and their allies on the Salish Sea, in place of the short-term temporalities of corporate profit margins, set what seemed like a brief and sudden moment of protest in an Indigenous *longue durée* that both reached into the deep past and gestured toward the distant future, another manifestation of temporal sovereignty.

There is a sort of spatial sovereignty at work here as well. By "spatial sovereignty," I mean the capacity of Indigenous activists and their non-Indigenous compatriots to assert connections between the Salish Sea and further-flung sites of Indigenous resistance and settler resource extraction. The shell no! actions were explicitly connected, for example, to tribal journeys that are made every summer with the very same canoes, linking communities around the Coast Salish world and beyond through the work of traveling protocols. Meanwhile, the canoeists and kayaktivists mirror the land and water defenders that took place at Standing Rock, North Dakota. As Chief Arvol Looking Horse, nineteenth keeper of the sacred bundle of the Lakota, Dakota, and Nakota peoples, has written: "Standing Rock is everywhere." In the same way, the Coast Salish world reaches out transnationally through hard-won linkages between social and political movements and the broader discourses of a resurgent indigeneity. The microgeographies of the Salish Sea are thus simultaneously planetary in scale, just as they are vast in their temporal dimensions.

∴

One last deep-time story. Around 5,600 years ago, təqʷuʔbəʔ ("tuh-quoo-buh," also known as Mount Rainier) lost 1,500 feet of its summit due to either an earthquake or a small volcanic eruption. The gargantuan lahar that resulted flowed all the way to xʷəʔlč, filling in a saltwater inlet and creating a new valley floor. This event may be referenced in local Coast Salish stories of whales carving river paths through the mud, or the numerous stories of floods that once covered the land and killed many people. Today, that lahar is generally known as the Osceola Mudflow, named after a tiny and largely forgotten settler community that was founded on land it covered and is one of the inspirations for evacuation signs and drills throughout the nearby valleys.[9]

Settler colonialism, Lorenzo Veracini writes, "is not somewhere else" (49). Nor is it someone else. I want to end on a personal note, to imbricate myself into the landscapes I have been discussing in this chapter. I am a white settler who was raised on a hillside above the valley of the lahar, just a short distance from the Muckleshoot Reservation, in the town where Arthur Ballard, the man who recorded the Epic of the Winds and so many other sx̌ʷiʔáb, served as clerk. My mother, like many lower-class white children in the area, worked as stoop labor in the berry fields around town in the 1950s and 1960s, alongside families from Muckleshoot and other reservations. My doctoral work and first book focused on the urban transformation of Coast Salish landscapes in Seattle, including the Duwamish River. After completing my PhD, I worked for the Muckleshoot Tribe for three years, conducting oral histories and constructing a tribal history of the Green River, which becomes the Duwamish in its lower reaches. My mother's ashes lie scattered on a high ridge on təqʷuʔbəʔ, overlooking a shrinking glacier at the head of the valley down which the lahar once flowed.

All of this is to say that as a settler scholar, I am implicated in these histories. This is not to make myself the center of the story; rather, it is to situate myself within processes that have shaped place and peoplehood around the Salish Sea. Those of us who are not of this place but who, uninvited, have come to call it home, have a responsibility to engage the deeply complicated and ongoing colonial histories of the lands and waters we inhabit. "Deep time" is as much about the present as it is about the past, and we must not shy away from bringing the politics and analytics of settler colonialism and Indigenous survivance into our discussions of "prehistory," so that we might engage meaningfully with our contested now and our shared time to come.

But does this sort of work contribute to "decolonizing" the sciences? Many Indigenous scholars have been wary of the growing claims of "decolonization" in academic and activist discourse, expressing concern than the term can become eroded through overuse until it is little more than a buzzword or, as Alutiiq scholar Eve Tuck and collaborator K. Wayne Yang have noted, a metaphor. Decolonization, they argue, is emphatically *not* a metaphor. It instead "must involve the repatriation of land simultaneous to the recognition of how land and relations to land have always already been differently understood and enacted; that is, *all* of the land, and not just symbolically. This is precisely why decolonization is necessarily unsettling, especially across lines of solidarity" (7). So how might the scholarly "decolonization" of "prehistory" contribute to this more radical (as in getting to the root of things) agenda?

And to return to an earlier question: Who benefits from such "decolonization"? How might scholarly research be conducted by non-Indigenous people
in meaningful solidarity with Indigenous peoples and in defense of and sovereignty over their land and water?

In her canonical 1999 work *Decolonizing Methodologies*, Māori scholar Linda
Tuhiwai Smith sets out a typology of twenty-five decolonizing projects. Some
of these involve direct community participation, or even community direction, while others are more in the vein of solidarity. These latter include,
among others, *indigenizing* ("a centering of the landscapes, images, themes,
metaphors and stories in the indigenous world and the disconnecting of many
of the cultural ties between the settler society and its metropolitan homeland.
This project involves non-indigenous activists and intellectuals") and *reading*
("the genealogy of colonialism is being mapped and used as a way to locate
a different sort of origin story, the origins of ideas and values. These origin
stories are deconstructed accounts of the West") (Smith 146–47, 149). Indigenizing and rereading "prehistory" in Coast Salish territories involves work
that reaches across disciplines and seeks to understand settler colonialism as
much as it tries to "figure out" the "native."

Those of us who work in and with Indigenous histories must actively engage with the tangles of settler colonialism. As a historian, I am committed
to the idea that stories matter, and that amplifying the good old stories and
imagining promising new ones opens conversations that can ripple out from
edited volumes to classrooms to a newspaper read on the morning bus to a
bill introduced in Congress—and ultimately to social change. The story of the
January 1700 Cascadia Subduction Zone megathrust earthquake, with which
I started this chapter, is an exemplar of what can happen when science and
Indigenous knowledge, prehistory and history, and academia and the public
all intersect: a settler culture can begin to learn where it really is, and then
act from that understanding.

The precarity of lavender-blue c'ábid lilies, ice disappearing both in the
ancient past and in the troubled present, and the dangerous flow of fossil
fuels can all be teachers. I believe that this happens through attention not
only to the grand sweep of more than five centuries of settler colonialism
and survivance but to the details of local places and lives. We live in places,
not concepts, and paying attention to where we are might help understand who we are and who we are with. Getting there, whether on the
lands around xʷə́lč or elsewhere, will be a crucial, difficult, and exciting
conversation that is both a long time coming and, in the context of deep
time, just beginning.

Notes

The bulk of the research and writing for this piece took place on the traditional, ancestral, and unceded territory of the hən̓q̓əmin̓əm̓-speaking xʷməθkʷəy̓əm (Musqueam) First Nation, where I live and work. I also want to acknowledge the Coast Salish peoples, tribes, and nations whose territories surround and include the southern Salish Sea, and most notably the Muckleshoot Indian Tribe, in whose treaty lands I was raised.

1. "Coast Salish" has origins as a colonial term, emerging primarily from early twentieth-century anthropology and linguistics. However, it has more recently become an important term of use within Indigenous communities of the region, one that asserts patterns of kinship between different communities and articulates shared political and cultural agendas, including those that cross the boundary between two settler states. The moniker "Salish Sea," meanwhile, was first coined by a settler scholar from Bellingham, Washington; it includes the Gulf of Georgia, the Strait of Juan de Fuca, Hood Canal, and Puget Sound. Made official in 2009 and 2010, the name quickly gained support from Tribes and First Nations on both sides of the U.S.-Canada border.

2. For discussions of prairies within the larger regional context, see Deur and Turner. For citizen advocacy, see South Puget Sound Prairies, southsoundprairies.org, accessed 15 Jan. 2019.

3. For the First Treaty War and its legacies, see Blee; Eckrom.

4. For overviews of changes to the Duwamish River, see Klingle; Sato.

5. For this framing in the broader context of Seattle's development, see Thrush, "City of the Changers."

6. Such proof of inhabitance occasionally features in legal discourse. See, e.g., *Duwamish et al. v. the United States of America*.

7. For the Second Treaty War, see American Friends Service Committee; Cohen; Wilkinson.

8. For Duwamish histories, see Allain; Thrush, *Native Seattle*.

9. Let us stop for a moment and think about the implications of that settlement's name: Osceola, a Seminole military leader whose head was sent to the Smithsonian after his death in prison in 1838, offers an opportunity to consider the more nefarious practices of anthropological science, many of which grew up alongside, or were constitutive of, violent settler colonialism—as well as a chance to ponder the appropriative nature of colonial place-naming.

References

Allain, Julia, "Duwamish History in Duwamish Voices: Weaving Our Family Stories Since Colonization." PhD diss., University of Victoria, 2014.

American Friends Service Committee. *Uncommon Controversy: Fishing Rights of the Muckle-shoot, Puyallup, and Nisqually Indians.* University of Washington Press, 1970.

Associated Press. "'Shell No': Hundreds Take to Boats in Seattle to Protest Arctic Drilling." *The Guardian,* 16 May 2015.

Ballard, Arthur C. "Mythology of Southern Puget Sound." *University of Washington Publications in Anthropology,* vol. 3, no. 2, Dec. 1929, pp. 31–150.

Barker, Joanne M. "Territory as Analytic: The Dispossession of Lenapehoking and the Subprime Crisis." *Social Text,* vol. 36, no. 2, 2018, pp. 19–39.

Blee, Lisa. *Framing Chief Leschi: Narratives and the Politics of Historical Justice.* University of North Carolina Press, 2014.

Brownstone, Sydney. "Why Descendants of Chief Seattle Led the Protest against Shell on Saturday." *The Stranger,* 18 May 2015.

Clague, John J., and Bob Turner. *Vancouver, City on the Edge: Living with a Dynamic Geological Landscape.* Gordon Soules, 2005.

Cohen, Fay G. *Treaties on Trial: The Continuing Controversy over Northwest Indian Fishing Rights.* University of Washington Press, 1986.

Coulthard, Glen Sean. *Red Skin, White Masks: Rejecting the Colonial Politics of Recognition.* University of Minnesota Press, 2014.

Davis, Heather, and Zoe Todd. "On the Importance of a Date, or Decolonizing the Anthropocene." *Acme: An International Journal for Critical Geographies,* vol. 16, no. 4, 2017, pp. 761–80.

Deur, Douglas, and Nancy J. Turner, eds. *Keeping It Living: Traditions of Plant Use and Cultivation on the Northwest Coast of North America.* University of Washington Press, 2005.

Doughton, Sandi. *Full Rip 9.0: The Next Big Earthquake in the Pacific Northwest.* Sasquatch Books, 2013.

Duwamish et al., Claimants, vs. the United States of America, Defendant, Consolidated Petition No. F-275. Argus Press, 1933.

Eckrom, J. A. *Remembered Drums: A History of the Puget Sound Indian War.* Pioneer, 1988.

Goeman, Mishuana. *Mark My Words: Native Women Mapping Our Nations.* University of Minnesota Press, 2013.

Haraway, Donna. *Staying with the Trouble: Making Kin in the Chthulucene.* Duke University Press, 2016.

Ishiguro, Laura. *Nothing to Write Home About: British Family Correspondence and the Settler Colonial Everyday in British Columbia.* University of British Columbia Press, 2019.

Klingle, Matthew. *Emerald City: An Environmental History of Seattle.* Yale University Press, 2009.

Looking Horse, Chief Arvol. "Standing Rock Is Everywhere: One Year Later." *The Guardian,* 22 Feb. 2018.

Menzies, Archibald. *Menzies' Journal of Vancouver's Voyage, April to October 1792,* edited by C. F. Newcombe, William H. Culling, 1923.

Nichols, David Andrew. *Engines of Diplomacy: Indian Trading Factories and the Negotiation of American Empire.* University of North Carolina Press, 2016.

Rifkin, Mark. *Beyond Settler Time: Temporal Sovereignty and Indigenous Self-Determination*. Duke University Press, 2017.

Sato, Mike. *The Price of Taming a River: The Decline of Puget Sound's Duwamish/Green Waterway*. Mountaineers Books, 1997.

Schultz, Kathryn. "The Really Big One." *New Yorker*, 20 July 2015.

Simpson, Audra. *Mohawk Interruptus: Political Life Across the Borders of Settler States*. Duke University Press, 2014.

Smith, Linda Tuhiwai. *Decolonizing Methodologies: Research and Indigenous Peoples*. Zed Books, 1999.

Thompson, Jerry. *Cascadia's Fault: The Deadly Earthquake That Will Devastate North America*. HarperCollins, 2011.

Thrush, Coll. "City of the Changers: Indigenous Peoples and the Transformation of Seattle's Watersheds." *Pacific Historical Review*, vol. 75, no. 1, 2006, pp. 89–117.

Thrush, Coll. *Native Seattle: Histories from the Crossing-Over Place*. University of Washington Press, 2007.

Thrush, Coll, and Ruth S. Ludwin. "Finding Fault: Indigenous Seismology, Colonial Science, and the Rediscovery of Earthquakes and Tsunamis in Cascadia." *American Indian Culture and Research Journal*, vol. 31, no. 4, 2007, pp. 1–24.

Todd, Zoe. "Fish, Kin, and Hope: Tending to Water Violations in amiskwaciwâskahikan and Treaty Six Territory." *Afterall: A Journal of Art, Context and Inquiry*, vol. 43, no. 1, 2017, pp. 102–7.

Tuck, Eve, and K. Wayne Yang. "Decolonization Is not a Metaphor." *Decolonization: Indigeneity, Education and Society*, vol. 1, no. 1, 2012, pp. 1–40.

Veracini, Lorenzo. *The Settler Colonial Present*. Palgrave Macmillan, 2015.

Whyte, Kyle Powys. "Our Ancestors' Dystopia Now: Indigenous Conservation and the Anthropocene." *The Routledge Companion to the Environmental Humanities*, edited by Ursula K. Heise et al., Routledge, 2017, pp. 206–18.

Wilkinson, Charles. *Messages from Frank's Landing: A Story of Salmon, Treaties, and the Indian Way*. University of Washington Press, 2006.

9

Yucatec "Maya" Historicity and Identity Constructions

THE CASE OF COBA

Jessica Christie

THIS CHAPTER CRITICALLY INVESTIGATES THE historicity of "Maya"-
ness through ethnographic fieldwork in the small town of Coba in Quintana
Roo, Mexico, which has grown next to the archaeological site of Coba in the
twentieth century. Cobaneros self-identify as "Maya" because they speak Yucatec Maya, were born on the Yucatec peninsula, and own land. But are there
deep-time connections that would affiliate today's Cobaneros with the classic
"Maya" people who built and lived in the archaeological zone? Archaeologists
have not found any material evidence in the archaeological zone dating later
than about 1550 CE and concluded that people largely abandoned the area
until resettlement of the present town in the middle of the twentieth century.
Ethnohistory says otherwise. After the Spanish invasion, Maya culture adjusted and reorganized, was shaken by the Caste War, and then was reshaped
with many outside forces on regional, national, and eventually global levels,
building the notion of heritage that Cobaneros practice today.

The focus in this chapter is on heritage politics, practice, and identity
constructions. The first section comprises a chronological overview of the
precontact site based on its physical remains and of the postcontact town. It
presents the academic or scientific definition for "Maya," derived from the
discipline of archaeology. This narrative is the historical reconstruction of the
Coba zone by archaeologists, art historians, and epigraphers derived from the
physical precontact remains using colonial methodologies of the top-down
forces of science funded by government institutions. I link this archaeological
definition with the colonially sanctioned, top-down power structures from
which academic disciplines derive their authority.

The second section mines linguistic and colonial sources, historical records, and ethnographic fieldwork conducted by myself and others to highlight the mechanisms of interplay across the top-down authorities of the federal government in Mexico City, the state of Quintana Roo, the tourism industry, and the town of Coba organized as a bottom-up ejido.[1] This section also discusses examples of visual culture as living case studies of how the Coba Maya connect the present with the past. I suggest that the processes of coming together and disjuncture of the top-down authorities and bottom-up movements are played out in a fragmented "third space" of discordance and juxtaposition that is structured in ambivalence (Bhabha 310–11). In this dynamic interplay, ingrained structures of colonialism are contested, at times adopted and altered; and heritage politics and identity constructions are formulated. In Coba, I argue, this third space is the space between the scientific narrative and Maya identity constructions and what it means to be Maya today.

It is in this fluid, dynamic, and often-contested realm that the potential for making Maya heritage evolves. Ultimately, this study fine-tunes the discourse between academic, political, and economic top-down forces anchored in colonialism and the community-based, bottom-up ejido in Coba, and it argues that the land base is pivotal to Maya heritage practice as well as contemporary notions of Maya identity.

It is important to state from the outset that the scientific, archaeological narrative is what has defined "Maya culture" in the twentieth century. This academic definition was formulated in the southern lowlands of the Petén (Guatemala) and of Chiapas (Mexico) and then applied throughout the Maya area. There, researchers classified sets of material remains that they later used to identify a site as Maya. This is the origin of most discussions of Maya identity and heritage to this day. Most stakeholders have accepted this "Maya" definition uncritically, ignoring the Indigenous perspective. It is this scientific narrative of history, which carries the colonially based authority of Mexican and U.S. academia as well as of the Instituto Nacional de Antropología e Historia (INAH, National Institute of Anthropology and History), the federal arm responsible for the administration of national cultural patrimony, that I wish to interrogate here.

The Scientific Narrative from Archaeology and History

Coba is situated in the Yucatán peninsula in the state of Quintana Roo, inland from the coastal town of Tulum. The archaeological site grew around several lakes and was first settled during the Late Formative Maya period (ca. 50

BCE–100 CE).[2] During the Classic Maya period (250 CE–900 CE), population growth and control over trade routes turned Coba into a powerful city-state in the cultural landscape of the northern peninsula with access to ports in the east. The material evidence of monumental temples, ballcourts, roads, and most notably stela iconography and hieroglyphic writing link Coba with Classic Maya culture as defined by archaeologists and epigraphers.

The main building groups in the core archaeological area are known as Coba or Group B, Nohoch Mul or Group C, and Macanxoc or Group A. They were constructed in the Late and Terminal Classic Maya periods (ca. 600–800/900 CE). The Coba group is situated between Lakes Coba and Macanxoc. Structures were arranged around a wide plaza fronting Lake Coba. The tallest building is La Iglesia, which rises nine levels to a height of twenty-four meters (see figure 9.1). It was originally faced with a thick layer of carved, polychrome stucco motifs. Several staircases ascend to different heights. A small ballcourt with rings and two stelae fragments is situated to the north of La Iglesia. Archaeologists have surmised that these extensive building complexes constituted the religious and political power center of Coba.

FIGURE 9.1. Coba, Group B, La Iglesia, Late Classic, ca. 600–800 CE.

The tallest temple structure in the Nohoch Mul group is Structure I or Ixmoja (see figure 9.2), which meets the twenty-four-meter height of La Iglesia. It is situated on the northeastern corner of an enormous terrace that forms the main avenue of approach and may have functioned as a plaza and market area. Structure I / Ixmoja grew in two principal construction phases: during the Late Classic, the seven-level pyramidal base of the temple was constructed. The summit temple was added during the Post-Classic. Access to the temple is provided by a wide stairway that rises on the southern side to the base of the final terrace, where it divides into two small flights of stairs leading to the top platform.

The third building group is Macanxoc or Group A, which is situated between Lake Macanxoc and Lake Xkanha. It is reached by Sacbe 9, which branches off Sacbe 8 at the northeastern bend of Lake Macanxoc to connect with the architectural group. A *sacbe* (pl. *sacbeob*) is an elevated roadway constructed on a bed of roughly shaped stones arranged so that larger-sized stones form a foundation and smaller ones rest on top. Sacbeob are reinforced by two retaining walls and topped off with a covering of *sascab*, a whitish layer of

FIGURE 9.2. Coba, Group C, Ixmoja, Late Classic, ca. 600–800 CE.

naturally occurring mineral material described as decomposed limestone or
a lime-gravel mixture used as mortar and pavement (Benavides Castillo, *Los
Caminos* 70; Folan et al. 81–87; Villa Rojas, "Yaxuna-Cobá Causeway" pl. 9a).
The light color of the sascab infill led to the name *sacbe*, "white road." Sacbe 9
at Macanxoc forms an exceptionally wide causeway (19–22 m) that provides
a formal public approach to Group A (Benavides Castillo, *Los Caminos* 120).
The Macanxoc group was built on an asymmetrical platform. The arrangement of its buildings is not as orderly as in the Coba and Nohoch Mul groups
(see Thompson et al. 88–96, pl. 17).

The monumental center was surrounded by concentric residential zones
that were surveyed by William Folan and colleagues in the late 1970s and
early 1980s. They documented that the typical household unit was constituted by an irregular platform supporting at least one or more vaulted or
unvaulted rooms, possible ancillary room(s) below the platform, and possible
houselot walls. The spatial distribution of these households fit and supported
the concentric model in the sense that larger platforms with a greater number
of vaulted buildings are present in a higher frequency in the inner suburban
zone, whereas smaller platforms supporting unvaulted structures are more
common in the outer suburban zones (Benavides Castillo, "Coba y Tulum"
213–15). Folan's team also registered that the structures varied considerably
in form and were clearly socially stratified (Kintz, "Social Organization" 66–
157). Such data shed light on precontact Coba residents as individuals and
social agents with personal "Maya" identities, in contrast to the previously
simplified interpretations of "Maya" commoners as an egalitarian mass. The
great variety and stratification of household units suggests some degree of
hierarchies and social organization within the residential zones in addition to
or perhaps independent from the central administration in the monumental
core.

Vital links between the downtown core zone and the inner and outer suburban zones and the region were provided by the sacbeob or roads (see figure
9.3). The people of Coba built close to fifty sacbeob, which divide the city
and its surrounding area into multiple sections. It is supposed that a majority
of sacbeob originate from the Coba / Group B and the Nohoch Mul / Group
C. They represent part of the infrastructure of the urban area and manifest
its control. The intrasite sacbeob primarily functioned as high-status arteries
between the central core and its peripheral zones. The intersite sacbeob, on
the other hand, seem to represent commercial and military right-of-ways
(Folan et al. 53). Most significant are two longer sacbeob: one connected Coba
with Yaxuna in a line due west over a distance of one hundred kilometers; the
second led from Coba twenty kilometers southwest to Ixil.

FIGURE 9.3. Coba, road (sacbe).

Carved stelae were part of many of the building complexes. In the early twentieth century, Eric Thompson et al. documented twenty-four sculpted stelae monuments (131); eight were found in Coba or Group B, eight at Nohoch Mul, and eight in Macanxoc.[3] According to Folan (81), most stelae had been removed from their original sites and set up in new shrines during Post-Classic times (Peniche Rivero and Folan 49; see also Thompson et al. 132–33). Many of the sculpted monuments with recognizable imagery depict a single principal personage holding a sloping ceremonial bar and standing on the backs of subdued figures (see figures 9.4 and 9.5).

Similarities with iconography on the stelae of specific sites in Petén state in northern Guatemala are noted by Thompson et al. (187, 194; see also Benavides Castillo, *Los Caminos* 23; Folan et al. 80–81). Researchers have invested great efforts to reconstruct dates from any readable text, placing the Coba stelae between about 613 CE and 780 CE (Benavides Castillo, *Los Caminos* 22; Gronemeyer; Stuart; Thompson et al. 182), dates that also firmly tie the Coba stelae to the Late Classic Maya historical monument tradition shared with the cities in the Petén.

After 900 CE, Coba began a slow decline; major buildings in the Coba and Nohoch Mul groups were altered by Post-Classic additions, usually of summit

FIGURE 9.4. Coba, Late Classic stela, original.

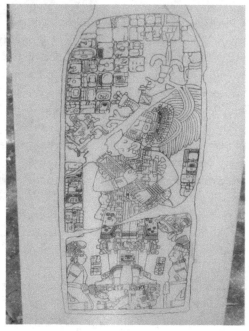

FIGURE 9.5. Coba, Late Classic stela, drawing.

temples. A small new building complex, "Las Pinturas," was added. Another Post-Classic strategy was to reset and ceremonially reuse most stelae from the Late and Terminal Classic in small platform shrines. Some of these stelae shrines line the east side of the wide platform leading up to Structure I / Ixmoja, and numerous examples accent the Macanxoc group. The act of reusing ancient stelae implies an active engagement by the Post-Classic occupants with the past. Most Post-Classic people could probably not read the Classic Maya texts but nonetheless acknowledged the ruler portraits as potent ancestors. Such context is supported by ethnographic work done in the nineteenth century (for example, Villa Rojas, *Estudios etnologicos* 587–89). I extend it back to the Post-Classic.

The site was abandoned around 1550 CE. From then on, the area of Coba lay at the periphery of political events set in motion by the Spanish invasion. The Mexican War of Independence ignited in 1810, lasting more than ten years, and in 1823, Yucatán's leaders of European descent, Yucatecos, joined the Mexican Republic as the Federated Republic of Yucatán, which included the entire peninsula (see Picas in this volume). Nonetheless, strong pro-independence currents and ethnic factionalism remained, sentiments that were unleashed in the Caste War of Yucatán (1847–1901), which began as a revolt of native Maya peoples in the peninsula's southeast against the Yucateco elite and their Yucateco forces in the northwest. Chan Santa Cruz, situated south of Coba, became the political and religious center of Maya resistance, and followers of the "Talking Crosses" there created new forms of social organization. Military, political, religious, and cultural practices centered on the crosses, which eventually became the core of distinct and independent self-identifications (see Picas in this volume).

The Coba area was situated in the sparsely populated border zone between the Yucatecos and independent Maya forces and probably served as a hideout and temporary shelter for many Maya groups throughout the nineteenth and early twentieth centuries (see Kintz, *Life Under* 104). The local Maya perspective is best assessed by Ellen R. Kintz, who emphasizes continuities of subsistence-based lifestyles under the tropical canopy (*Life Under*), or as moral ecology in José E. Martínez-Reyes's terms (21–23). What this means is that Maya people have always known how to live from the resources the tropical forest has provided. Their self-sufficient, bottom-up lifestyles had supported them no matter whether top-down authority was enforced by Late Classic Maya rulers, the Spanish, the Mexican nation-state, or the Republic of Yucatán. In the Coba case study, it is this bottom-up view that begins to break down the academic "prehistory"/history divide (see Matthew 3–4).

Maya oral histories attest that the modern community of Coba began to be formed in the 1950s by families from Kanxoc, Tixhualatun, Chemax, and

FIGURE 9.6. Town of Coba, main road to the archaeological site.

Valladolid, Yucatán, who migrated east to cut chicle (gum resin), hunt, and eventually plant milpas (cornfields) (Kintz, *Life Under* 41). Families from Kanxoc settled on the south side of Lake Coba and people from Tixhualatun on the north side (Kintz, *Life Under* 105). The chiclero camps grew into the small current-day town that has approximately 1,300 inhabitants (Litka 352) (see figure 9.6).

The Politics of Colonialism, Maya Heritage, and Identity as Performed in Coba

The politics of Maya heritage begin with the term *maya* itself. Matthew Restall has traced the origin of the word to the colonial period, establishing that it has only recently been used by the Indigenous population of the Yucatán peninsula to self-identify (80–81). Before, *maya* was primarily used to refer to the Yucatec language and to Indigenous material items with sacred and/or historical associations. When applied to people, it referenced small groups defined by region or class but never implied a macroregional ethnic identity. While the Spanish introduced and then altered numerous designations for social groups from the sixteenth through the nineteenth centuries, Indigenous self-identity was instead grounded in two fundamental units of social organization: the municipal community the Maya call *cah*, and the patronym group called *chibal*. Identity was loosely defined and negotiated at their meeting point, with cah functioning as the geographical entity comprising the residential core and agricultural territories, and chibal acting as the social entity of extended families (Restall and Gabbert, 101–2).

On the Yucatán peninsula, the formation of a modern Maya ethnic identity has to be seen in correlation with the development of Cancún and the Riviera Maya as a tourism corridor in the 1970s (Picas in this volume). The federal government and state agencies marketed "Maya culture" as the tangible and highly profitable remnant of Mexico's unique national patrimony. As their response, the Maya, often with non-Maya allies, constructed their historical roots and adopted elements of the top-down "Maya" paradigm in order to mobilize the mostly underprivileged Maya population (Taylor 5). The great majority of Cobaneros proudly and readily self-identify as Maya because they speak the Yucatec language, own property, and were born on the peninsula. I will focus on two elements of Maya heritage I deem most relevant: first, the ejido system as the present Coba meeting point of cah and chibal; and second, selected examples of Maya-produced visual culture.

The Ejido System

The ejido system lies at the heart of the notion of Maya heritage in Coba today with regard to land, control of space, and social network. The Mexican Revolution in the 1910s initiated the process of agrarian land reform, during which the lands of former colonial haciendas were distributed to Indigenous groups. At this time, *ejido* was used to refer to all types of land restored to agricultural communities under this land reform process and to designate the landed communities themselves. Under this system, individual residents, *ejidatarios*, received plots of land meant to remain in their families for generations under the rubric of "use rights," as opposed to private ownership (Taylor 66–67). Under the ejidal law, land had to be worked by the ejidatario and could not be rented, sold, or left unused. Ejidatarios could not possess more than one piece of land. Communal decisions regarding land tenure were made by the ejidal assembly, composed of all ejidatarios in a given ejido, a body with the authority of reassigning a plot if it felt the laws were insufficiently followed. In addition to individual plots, an ejido maintains extensive common-use areas. At a basic level, ejidal land provides food security as well as access to government-sponsored programs, such as the Programa de

Apoyos Directos al Campo (PROCAMPO, Program for Direct Assistance in Agriculture) (Taylor 68).

Only in the 1930s, under President Lázaro Cárdenas, were the land reform and its ejidos fully implemented. Cárdenas believed that land should form a basis of subsistence for peasant families rather than be an economic commodity. This initial concept of the ejido began to be modified under President Luis Echeverría, who legalized collective ejidos organized as large foreign-owned private farms under the Federal Agrarian Reform Law of 1971. In the 1980s, international pressures on the Mexican government began to mount regarding the low productivity of its ejidal system. The World Bank, specifically, observed that the ejido system had become "obsolete" due to its "productive inflexibility and increasing non-compliance with the . . . legal framework" (Taylor 71). World economic agencies encouraged Mexico to completely restructure its ejidal system. Eventually, the Agrarian Law of 1992 replaced the 1971 law as part of major reforms required for Mexico's participation in the North American Free Trade Agreement (NAFTA). This resulted in a number of important changes to the ejido system: no additional lands could be expropriated to create new ejidos or enlarge existing ejidal holdings; ejidatarios would have permission to rent, sell, buy, or lease land; ejidatarios could work with private enterprises and individual investors; and ejidatarios could receive individual land titles.

In the early 1970s, Coba became an ejido and its community lands were parceled out to approximately 132 original ejidatarios (Kintz, *Life Under* 105–7; Litka 353–54). These ejido lands (*terreno*) encompass around 3,800 acres, which are largely used for milpa (cornfield) cultivation and chicle (gum resin) production. The ejidal assembly meets every few months and is the voice and de facto government of the community. Most families have at least one relative who is an ejidatario; nonlocal community members have to rent or buy a piece of land from an ejidatario to build their homes, but they do not become ejidatarios. The ejido functions as the sociohistorical mechanism that binds each ejidatario family to the community, assuming the present-day functions of cah and chibal (Litka 360).

The social and economic benefits of maintaining use rights to ejidal land versus private ownership are played out in daily lived reality, as most ejidatarios today use their land in a number of ways. Few continue to plant corn in the milpa, but most ejidatarios have at least one family member who cultivates some type of crops on their land; other sections of ejido lands grow back to *monte* (uncultivated land, symbolically associated with wild forces of nature) or are sold to newcomers or other outsiders (Litka 358–61). However, many ejidatarios hold on to at least some of their ejido terreno as a land-based security: if tourism fails, they will have a potential livelihood or at least an economic asset to go back to. Further, they may need it for subdivision among their children.

From the ejido perspective, engagement with the archaeological zone and the associated tourism industry is primarily an issue of land tenure. After the Coba ejido was created, officials realized that some tracts of ejido lands overlaid the large archaeological site. According to Mexican laws of cultural patrimony from the 1980s, however, all archaeological monuments belong to the nation and are managed and protected by the INAH. Coba, like many other Indigenous towns in Mexico, thus faced a dilemma: the ruins are the property of the government, whereas the land belongs to the ejido. In response, Coba ejidatarios organized and negotiated mutually beneficial relations with the federal authorities. Now, the INAH collects entrance fees to the archaeological site but community members maintain the right to operate several businesses within the archaeological zone. This is a unique arrangement because the INAH typically has full control over federally recognized archaeological sites.

Most notable among these community enterprises is the tricycle transport business that offers shuttle services to visitors who do not want to walk the long forest trails tracing the sacbeob (see figure 9.7). The business started around 1990, when a local resident by the name of Hipolito first spread the idea of organizing and building a transport business. When I met Hipolito at the bicycle rental stand in 2014, he was a man around fifty years old with a calm smile who seemed to enjoy overlooking the growth of ejido enterprises within the archaeological zone (see figure 9.8). After his friends, who gave me most of the information about the tricycle business, told me he mostly speaks Maya, Hipolito then looked me in the eyes and said loudly and clearly: "¡Ser Maya es un orgullo!" (To be Maya is a matter of pride!).

Hipolito's motivation was to offer work opportunities in town to curb the out-migration of young people. He and some friends started by purchasing bicycles with their own funds. Now the enterprise runs about 130 tricycles assigned to registered operators who are overseen by an administrative committee (author's ethnographic consultations, 2014–17). This committee issues licenses to the tricicleros (tricycle riders), provides maintenance services on site, and secures income for their tricicleros at a level roughly double the national minimum wage. It exempts community employees from paying income tax; instead, a business tax is paid to the municipio in Tulum by the ejido tricycle organization (ethnographic consultations, 2014–17).

Near the site entrance is a thatched house, where bicycle rental is offered to tourists who do not wish to walk along the sacbeob or use the tricycle

FIGURE 9.7. Coba, tricycle transport business.

FIGURE 9.8. Coba, Hipolito.

shuttle service. Cold drinks are sold in another thatched house at Nohoch Mul plaza. In the tourism business, Coba's Ixmoja temple and Ek Balam in Temozón are the only Maya pyramids on the peninsula visitors are still allowed to climb. This constitutes another special deal the ejido has worked out with the INAH. One guide told me that the INAH threatened twice to close the pyramid for security reasons but the ejido spoke against it and so far has prevailed in keeping it open (ethnographic consultations, 2014).

At the parking lot, the Coba community runs the Ki-Hanal Restaurant, the largest and most attractive nearby eating venue. The menu offers international and local food options cooked and served by ejido-trained personnel. Since approximately 2015, the restaurant has hosted tourist groups upstairs, offering a package that includes a lunch buffet and performances of the Classic Maya ballgame and associated rituals.

The most surprising attraction on the parking lot is a zip line that spans the north to the south shore of Lake Coba (see figure 9.9). In 2014 Joel, a staff member at the zip line, explained that a wealthy Argentinian who owns another zip line in Tulum put up the initial capital and keeps both zip lines on an inspection schedule. Such a collaboration was made possible by the Agrarian Law of 1992, which provides that ejidatarios can work with private enterprises and individual investors. Joel and other staff confidently proclaim that the zip line is viewed as the property of Coba.

FIGURE 9.9. Coba, zip line.

From the road leading south out of town are turnoffs to three cenotes also situated on ejido lands. Cenotes are sinkholes with icy-cold and crystal-clear groundwater formed in the characteristic karst terrain of soluble limestone in the Yucatán peninsula.[4] They constitute the only natural groundwater sources and played vital roles in the economy and cosmology of traditional Maya subsistence-based lifestyles. Ejidatarios have built changing rooms, showers, some drink stands, and small ticket offices, which collect entrance fees around the cenote openings.

In sum, the challenge for the Coba ejido lies in staying organized at a community level to confront the top-down mechanisms by the INAH, state institutions, and the tourism industry to take control of the archaeological zone and collect its profits. So far, the Coba ejido has been remarkably successful in maintaining a strong presence at the site by operating multiple businesses that provide jobs for the younger generation and thereby reduce out-migration to the coast.

Today, the Coba ejido actively engages with international tourists who come to explore the ruins. Visitors have learned that the archaeological site presents the physical remains of Maya culture, and by extension they identify the local people in some ways as Maya descendants, although there is no direct line of descent. In broad terms, Cobaneros feel that the ruins are their heritage. Their documented history, however, goes back only to the beginnings of the town and the ejido in the mid-twentieth century.

Visual Culture

One form of newer heritage making is the erection of contemporary stelae throughout the Maya area. In 2016 and 2017, the Yucatec Maya artist Luis May Ku, myself, and several individuals affiliated with Mayas for Ancient Mayan (MAM) discussed the project of erecting a contemporary stela at the school in Coba.[5] Work began in the summer of 2016 and the stela was unveiled in a ceremony at the school on 21 March 2017, the equinox and founding date of the primary school, which is located on the southern shore of Lake Coba. Unlike the Classic Maya limestone stelae in the archaeological zone, May Ku's stela is an oversized concrete slab with visual accents of inlaid pieces of colored glass, tiles, and mirrors (see figure 9.10a). The frontal image depicts the "Crocodile God" *ayiin* rising in an upright position within a blue frame symbolizing Lake Coba.

On the back side (see figure 9.10b), Maya hieroglyphs record the text, here translated into English:

FIGURE 9.10. Coba, Luis May Ku and his stela, front side [a] and back side [b]. Courtesy Luis May Ku.

On 21 March 2017,
    Deep under the land of Coba,
    The Crocodile God [referring to the famed local crocodile(s) living in the lake]
    In the water [referencing Lake Coba],
    Sat up and opened
    His mouth and wisdom flowed out
    Over the school

The idea and design of the stela were the creation of May Ku, who lives in Coba as an artist and teacher. The text was translated into Maya glyphs with the collaboration of Bruce Love, then president of MAM, and other epigraphers. The Crocodile God and glyphs are terracotta reliefs that were first shaped in plaster molds by May Ku, who then brought them to a ceramic workshop in Ticul for firing (see figure 9.11).

FIGURE 9.11. Ticul, Luis May Ku working with a pottery workshop.

Ticul, situated in the western part of the state of Yucatán approximately one hundred kilometers south of the state capital, Mérida, has a long history of pottery production, documented through the lifelong work of anthropologist Dean Arnold ("Changes in Ceramics"; *Maya Potters'*).[6] Ticul specialists approach the process of pottery making through a close intimacy with the land. They believe the forest to be the living portion of their landscape: they know the different ecological zones of the peninsula, which tree species each supports, and the qualities of the wood of each species for ceramic firing. Ticul potters categorize the Earth as a nonliving landscape that provides the raw materials of clay, temper, and water through openings in the ground. They know the soils and minerals in the varying ecological zones and their usefulness for shaping vessels (Arnold, *Maya Potters'* 50, 54–78). May Ku has collaborated and engaged on several projects with Ticul potters, who use traditional Maya clay types and techniques.

The pre-Hispanic settlement of San Francisco de Ticul was situated a short distance north of the present town of Ticul. Both precontact and postcontact potters have gone to the cave of Aktun to obtain temper for pottery used for cooking; both have perceived this and other caves as gateways to the underworld. To find temper for pottery not used for cooking, they accessed the temper mines of Yo'Sah Kab, now an archaeological site where the feathered serpent has been sighted. The primary source for raw materials has been the clay mine Yo'K'at, again for both, pre- and post-Hispanic potters, until about the 1960s.[7] Firewood is collected in the forest known as K'ash. Present-day potters perceive the forest as the location of nature spirits; they differentiate guardians of the forest from those of the fields. Non-Christian rituals are always performed in the forest. Water for mixing clay and temper comes from wells, che'en. All these culturally significant landscapes are located no more than five kilometers from Ticul or the ancient San Francisco de Ticul.

The cultural landscape of contemporary Ticul potters builds on that of their local ancestors, while adding and amending as circumstances shift and change. Arnold (*Maya Potters'* 215–26) refers to this process as the Indigenous knowledge that creates and defines Maya heritage and identity. This is very different from the essentialized notion of "authenticity" central to the outside colonial construction of Maya culture and Maya-ness. May Ku accesses and integrates this Indigenous knowledge as he has some of his clay sculptures fired in the Ticul method; in this way, May Ku connects the local Maya heritage of Ticul with Coba.

In what ways does May Ku's stela challenge colonialism as related to Maya heritage and identity? In Coba, cultural colonialism is practiced by the tourism industry, which has adopted the top-down academic definition of Maya culture as materialized in the monuments at the archaeological site. May Ku resists these practices, definitions, and materializations in subtle but deliberate ways. His upright slab stela form makes conceptual reference to Classic Maya carved stone stelae, but his is constructed of modern materials. Text and iconography are also the creations of May Ku, and the image of the Crocodile God and the hieroglyphic inscription closely resemble Classic Maya prototypes. As a self-identified Yucatec Maya man, May Ku strives to learn what he can about ancient Maya culture from scientific sources, to apply this knowledge to his artistic work, and to pass it on as Maya heritage to his students in curricular and extracurricular activities. This is also why he engaged the help of Bruce Love, a respected U.S. epigrapher, in the writing of the text. Moreover, his collaboration with Ticul potters integrates Indigenous knowledge derived from regional ancestral practices.

In the eyes of May Ku and the potters, their works bring to life ancient Maya knowledge. At the same time, May Ku's concrete stela as well as the vessels that Ticul potters offer for sale are deliberately different from Classic Maya stelae or Codex-style cylinder vessels from northern Guatemala, the forms of "art" most widely circulated as identifiers of Maya culture in textbooks, coffee-table books, and tourism literature composed by academic writers immersed in colonial mindsets (this includes many *National Geographic* articles). May Ku's art does not strive for the goal of "authenticity" as defined by external constructions of Maya culture.

The polarization between Indigenous knowledge and "authenticity" is still a poorly addressed but important point of new, bottom-up heritage constructions that defy rigid scientific rubrics of style (see Galinier and Molinie). Shaping new and more popular heritage through ceramic art and stelae creates a visual culture based on Indigenous knowledge as well as alternative experiences, different from those described in the travel literature, when tourists interact with Maya artists and their work. What matters is that these constructions of what is "Maya" are controlled by the artists and transpire on their terms.

What matters in tourism encounters is that visitors obtain objects they believe are authentically "Maya" and that the Maya vendors boost their income. Tourism has surely increased the production of embroidered huipiles, the colonial-era garment traditionally worn by Indigenous women on the peninsula (see figure 9.12). It is a loose-fitting tunic with openings for the head and arms. The Yucatec huipil is white, made of light cotton, and is the length of a dress.

The top section is embroidered with colorful floral arrangements; the amount and quality of the embroidery as well as the cotton layers determine its value. In the colonial period, Maya women adopted the flowery designs from the dresses of Spanish women who looked to Europe for the latest fashion

FIGURE 9.12. Piste, Yucatec Maya women wearing their huipiles.

FIGURE 9.13. Coba, woman embroidering a huipil in front
of her house on the road to the cenotes.

trends precisely to differentiate themselves visually from the Indigenous population, who ended up copying them after all (Scott 221). In fact, the huipil
constitutes a Spanish-imposed dress code designed by the Catholic friars but
one that most likely resembles a type of huipil Nahua and Maya women wore
before the Spanish invasion (Hervik 39, 56). Most Maya women in rural Yucatán continue to wear huipiles on a daily basis.

In Coba, every morning around 11 a.m., the woman who lives in the
corner house on the south side of the lake where the main road leaves town
and leads to the cenotes sets up her Singer sewing machine outside. In her
yard facing the road, she busily embroiders huipiles, wearing a very artful
one herself (see figure 9.13), while female family members hang finished
huipiles and other garments for sale on clotheslines and from tree branches.
Inevitably, tour buses stop and groups of visitors enter the backyard to look,
start conversations, and—hopefully—purchase a huipil.

FIGURE 9.14. Coba, Ki-Hanal Restaurant, performance of the Classic Maya ball game.

Tourist groups who opt for the lunch buffet at Ki-Hanal Restaurant enjoy reenactments of Classic Maya rituals and ball games by groups of young actors from the region (see figure 9.14). They perform on a stage with a miniature copy of the Classic ballcourt from the archaeological site. Performers dress as Maya ballplayers and manipulate a ball with their bodies without kicking or catching it by hand.

Other actors wear elite costumes and open and close the game. This newly reinvented form of Maya heritage works to re-create Classic Maya ritual, music, and dance based on the study of academic sources. It demonstrates a growing interest by the younger generation in learning about the lives of their ancestors. The costumes are handmade with great care and many hours are spent rehearsing. Actors clearly invest part of their heart and soul and do not merely perform for monetary gain.

Conclusion

I have discussed the Coba ejido system and the artistic work of Luis May Ku as a type of "third space," the place between the scientific narrative and living Maya heritage. A third space of enunciation, as theorized by postcolonial literary scholar Homi K. Bhabha, is a split-space of enunciation [which] may open the way to conceptualizing an *inter*national culture, based not on the exoticism of multiculturalism or the *diversity* of cultures, but on the inscription and articulation of culture's *hybridity*. . . . We should remember that it is the "inter"— . . . the *inbetween* space—that carries the burden of the meaning of culture. . . . By exploring this Third Space, we may elude the politics of polarity and emerge as the others of our selves. (56)

What is new about this version of international space are its discontinuous historical realities or nonsynchronous temporalities of global and national cultures. This space of "thirdness" in postmodern politics opens up an area where the newness of cultural practices and historical narratives are registered in generic discordance, or unexpected juxtaposition (Bhabha 310–12). As part of the disjointed signifier of the present, this supplementary third space introduces a structure of ambivalence that eludes colonial power systems (Bhabha 143–44). This space opens up to both sides of binaries and adopts and reshapes elements selectively through conscious agency.

In the Coba case, the ejido may be such an example: it is a land division and management structure imposed by the federal government that the local ejidatarios have shaped into the dominant sociopolitical network in the community. It follows a model of cooperative entrepreneurship (Simonelli and McClanahan 221–25) and as such can hold this third space unless or until those ejidatarios driven by individual and competitive, capitalist, profit-driven interests may reach a majority. Since the neoliberal changes to the ejido system went into effect in the early 1990s, the ejido has been a dynamic, oscillating third space cloaked in ambivalence. The ejido has been in a push-and-pull state as ejidatarios sell part of their lands to outsiders but so far has maintained its status based on a majority solidarity.

May Ku is viewed by Cobaneros as a cultural broker who eagerly learns about Maya history, art, and culture to pass on this heritage to schoolchildren, his artistic audience, academic friends, and other outside contacts. His sculptures link ancient and present techniques and subjects. Thus his professional life constructs and secures this place of thirdness through active agency and on his terms. It is particularly noteworthy that in the stela monument discussed here, iconography and text are anchored in the local Coba landscape through reference to the crocodile and thus keep his message Coba Maya specific as opposed to Yucatec Maya specific, as in the huipiles.

In sum, Cobaneros have sustained their notion of Maya heritage and identity that is anchored in the ejido lands and tied to the archaeological site. Such notions of heritage and identity are contested within and challenged from the outside as part of the human condition of cultural hybridity.

Notes

1. An ejido is a form of federal land grant given to rural communities.
2. Lakes are sought-after features in the geology of the Yucatán peninsula because it has a mainly limestone karst topography in which rivers are absent and lakes are few; where they do form, they are likely the result of the collapse of several sinkholes or faulting (see Folan et al. 21–34).
3. In 1981 Benavides Castillo (*Los caminos* 22) counted thirty-four stelae, twenty-three of which were sculpted and eleven plain. Archaeologists assume that more stelae will come to light; thus the history of Coba is in the process of being put together.
4. Chaak has been the god of rain among contemporary and ancient Maya; he inhabits the cenotes.
5. MAM is a public charity founded by U.S. Americans in 2005 to raise travel funds for Indigenous Maya scholars to attend the Workshops on Hieroglyphic Writing at the University of Texas at Austin. In the late 1980s, U.S. Maya linguists and epigraphers Linda Schele and colleagues encountered great eagerness among Maya speakers to participate in their work and learn about the writing, calendar system, and iconography of their ancestors. Schele and colleagues began to hold workshops for Maya speakers and invite them to Schele's workshops at UT Austin. I introduce MAM here to support my argument for decolonization. It surely began as a top-down relationship of U.S. scholars teaching Maya people their own history and culture. Maya speakers have mobilized themselves and taken strong initiatives to pursue teaching and learning about their culture on their own terms. Today, many Maya have completed their own academic education in Maya history, archaeology, and epigraphy and teach other Maya. Speakers of all Maya languages participate. May Ku has connections with MAM members.
6. Arnold (*Maya Potters'* 198–214) reconstructs a well-organized but complex "taskscape" (a landscape constructed of spatially conditioned tasks) of the present and ancient potters in Ticul with religious associations that are materialized in pottery. Following Tim Ingold, Arnold (*Maya Potters'* 198–99) reasons that pottery is a taskscape that distills those features of the landscape that yield raw materials possessing the most suitable performance characteristics for making pottery.
7. Yo'K'at had St. Peter as its patron saint and a novena was said in his honor until 1978.

References

Arnold, Dean. "Changes in Ceramics as Commodities in Ticul, Yucatán, Mexico (1965–2008) and What They Tell Us About Ancient Maya Ceramic Production." *The Value of Things*, edited by Jennifer Mathews and Thomas Guderjan, University of Arizona Press, 2017, pp. 193–214.

Arnold, Dean. *Maya Potters' Indigenous Knowledge: Cognition, Engagement, and Practice*. University Press of Colorado, 2018.

Benavides Castillo, Antonio. *Los caminos de Cobá y sus implicaciones sociales*. Colección científica: Arqueología. Instituto Nacional de Antropología e Historia, 1981.

Benavides Castillo, Antonio. "Cobá y Tulum: Adaptación al medio ambiente y control del medio social." *Estudios de Cultura Maya*, Universidad Nacional Autónoma de México, 1981, pp. 205–22.

Bhabha, Homi K. *The Location of Culture*. Routledge, 1994.

Folan, William, et al. *Coba: A Classic Maya Metropolis*. Coba Archaeological Mapping Project, National Geographic Society, Academic Press, 1983.

Galinier, Jacque, and Antoinette Molinie. *The Neo-Indians*. University Press of Colorado, 2013.

Gronemeyer, Sven. "A Preliminary Ruling Sequence at Coba, Quintana Roo." *Wayeb Notes*, vol. 14, 2003, wayeb.org/wayebnotes/archive.php.

Hervik, Peter. *Mayan People Within and Beyond Boundaries*. Harwood Academic, 1999.

Kintz, Ellen R. *Life Under the Tropical Canopy: Tradition and Change Among the Yucatec Maya*. Holt, Rinehart and Winston, 1990.

Kintz, Ellen R. "The Social Organization of a Classic Maya City: Coba, Quintana Roo, Mexico." PhD diss., State University of New York, Stony Brook, 1978.

Litka, Stephanie. "The Maya of Coba: Managing Tourism in a Local *Ejido*." *Annals of Tourism Research*, vol. 43, 2013, pp. 350–69.

Martínez-Reyes, José E. *Moral Ecology of a Forest*. University of Arizona Press, 2016.

Matthew, Laura. *Memories of Conquest: Becoming Mexicano in Colonial Guatemala*. University of North Carolina Press, 2012.

Peniche Rivero, Piedad, and William J. Folan. "Coba, Quintana Roo, Mexico: Reporte sobre una metropolis Maya del noroeste." *Boletin de la Escuela de Ciencias Antropológicas de la Universidad de Yucatán*, no. 30, 1978, pp. 48–74.

Restall, Matthew. "Maya Ethnogenesis." *Journal of Latin American Anthropology*, vol. 9, no. 1, 2004, pp. 64–89.

Restall, Matthew, and Wolfgang Gabbert. "Maya Ethnogenesis and Group Identity in Yucatán, 1500–1900." *"The Only True People": Linking Maya Identities Past and Present*, edited by B. J. Beyyette and I. J. LeCount, University Press of Colorado, 2017, pp. 91–130.

Scott, Mary Katherine. "Meaning in the Making: Locating Value in the Production and Consumption of Maya Tourist Arts." *The Value of Things*, edited by Jennifer Mathews and Thomas Guderjan, University of Arizona Press, 2017, pp. 215–34.

Simonelli, Jeanne, and Lupita McClanahan. "Interpreting Canyon de Chelly: Sacred Sites and Human Rights." *Artisans and Advocacy in the Global Market: Walking the Heart Path*, edited by Jeanne Simonelli et al., School for Advanced Research Advanced Seminar Series, School for Advanced Research Press, 2015, pp. 197–225.

Stuart, David. "Notes on Accession Dates in the Inscriptions of Coba." *Mesoweb*, 20 Jan. 2010, mesoweb.com/stuart/notes/Coba.pdf.

Taylor, Sarah. *On Being Maya and Getting By: Heritage Politics and Community Development in Yucatán*. University Press of Colorado, 2018.

Thompson, Eric, et al. *A Preliminary Study of the Ruins of Cobá, Quintana Roo.* Carnegie Institute of Washington, 1932.

Villa Rojas, Alfonso. "The Yaxuna-Cobá Causeway." *Contributions to American Archaeology,* vol. 2, no. 9, 1934, pp. 187–208.

Villa Rojas, Alfonso. *Estudios etnológicos: Los Mayas.* Universidad Nacional Autónoma de México, 1995.

10

The Plurivocality of Tulum

"SCIENTIFIC" VERSUS LOCAL NARRATIVES ABOUT MAYA SITES IN QUINTANA ROO

Mathieu Picas

ON 21 MARCH 2017 I was undertaking participant observation fieldwork to document possible celebrations related to the spring solstice at the archaeological site of Tulum, Mexico. At 9 a.m., a private tourist guide led a group of visitors to the area where about thirty people from different regions of the world—all dressed in white clothes—were standing in a circle. They were dedicating chants and copal incense to the Vírgen de Guadalupe and the four directions of the universe. Immediately, one of the visitors asked the guide about the performance, and the guide's answer, surprisingly to me, was that they were observing "an Indigenous tradition. They still practice their old rituals according to their beliefs, and they still wear their ancient white outfit." Even though this explanation of the celebration was not addressed to me, I realized that the ceremony performed by a group of so-called Indigenous people was somehow giving an added value to the visit of the pre-Hispanic remains, a site believed to "belong" to a remote past. Given that only one of the ceremony participants was Maya, and that most of the Maya present at the site are usually custodians, I asked myself: Are there any religious or spiritual linkages between Tulum and Maya peoples today? Is Tulum part of Maya communities' history and memory?

In my fieldwork, I investigated the possible sacred and political values attached to archaeological sites through the collection of present-day oral histories in the Mexican state of Quintana Roo. I found that, due to the growth in tourism during the 1970s–1980s, Maya communities have increasingly perceived archaeological sites as places that have been taken from them and made into private property. This rupture is the continuation of a colonialist and nationalist dimension of archaeology that had previously served to distance Indigenous people—including the Maya—from the archaeological remains present in their landscapes (Bueno 18; Díaz-Andreu 7; McAnany 21). But studying the sacred values attached to archaeological remains in Quintana Roo shows that this rupture is only partial. In this chapter, I focus on Tulum—a sacred place for the Cruzo'ob Maya during the Caste War (1847–1901) that was converted into a nationally administered tourist destination in the twentieth century—because of its prevalence in the archaeological literature and because, as was demonstrated by the solstice celebration, current-day tourist use of the remains seemingly continues to fix Tulum and the Maya in a remote past.[1]

The conversion of archaeological remains into national heritage since the late nineteenth century provoked numerous ruptures, changes, and adaptations in the way Indigenous peoples interacted with the pre-Hispanic sites.[2] Historian and geographer David Lowenthal explains that interacting with heritage modifies its original meaning and context (379), while archaeologist Alejandro Haber notes that the scientific setting of archaeological remains or artifacts in the past implicates a negation of its possible use in the present (15). Indeed, as expressed by Māori scholar Linda Tuhiwai Smith, the scientific research on Indigenous peoples has generally been related to Western imperialism and its constant will to convert Indigenous knowledge into Western "discoveries" (120). One of the main colonialist and imperialist ideas perpetuated by science regarding the Maya is that they all disappeared after the so-called Maya collapse at the end of the Classic Period (250–900 CE). The archaeologist Patricia McAnany sees in this recurrent idea the evidence of archaeology's deep-colonial roots (4). According to David Webster, this so-called collapse is part of a "Maya mystique" based on "uniqueness and mystery" (131), which is also commonly referred to in travel literature and accepted by visitors, as noted by Traci Arden (105). Such scientific statements regarding this mysterious disappearance legitimate the common idea that present-day Maya have no relation with the builders of the pre-Hispanic cities and, consequently, have no reason to engage with archaeological heritage.

In Quintana Roo, archaeological mounds known locally as *múulo'ob* (hill) in Yucatec Maya are perceived as part of a living landscape or, as Henri Lefebvre would define it, as the "space of representations" or "lived space" that allow people to engage with the objects present in the physical space. This conception of space contrasts with representations made by scientists whose interactions with space are usually analytical and not experiential (Lefebvre 97–98). Local Maya knowledge related to the múulo'ob remains at Tulum, and elsewhere in Quintana Roo, indicates that they are perceived as the dwelling places of more-than-human entities and ancestors who are present in ritual activities related to agriculture, healing, and sacred land tenure. Some of these entities are the *aluxo'ob* (guardians of cornfields), the *iiko'ob* (winds/spirits), the *cháako'ob* (responsible for rain), the *báalamo'ob* (guardians of villages), and the *itzá máako'ob*—also known as "itzaes" in Spanish—or ancestors related to a pre-Hispanic lineage. The system of interdependence between the human and more-than-human entities depends on rituality and ceremonial offerings, and it is in this context that the archaeological remains are held as important ritual places by several communities, especially when it comes to petitioning for rain (*ch'a' cháak*), performing healing rituals (*k'eex*), thanksgiving (*janli kool*), and asking for permission to use the ancestors' land (*looj* and *jets' lu'um*).[3]

In this chapter, I focus on the ethnopolitical, spiritual, and sacred values attached to the múulo'ob and on the changes in use and perceptions of the remains at Tulum from the nineteenth century to the present day. I compare current "scientific" literature to Maya oral narratives and the other information on Maya rituality and prophecy that I collected during ethnographic work in Quintana Roo undertaken in the spring of 2017 and in 2018. My fieldwork research allows me to analyze the emergence of important socio-cultural changes regarding the use and interpretation of the site of Tulum and how both "scientific" and local use and knowledge about the remains have been interacting and influencing each other during the past century. I ultimately propose that the evident ruptures caused by colonialism, science, and tourism are only partial, and that the use and understanding of archaeological remains in Quintana Roo, including those of Tulum, question the nationalist and hegemonic setting of the site in pre-Hispanic times. I argue that archaeological sites, such as the one of Tulum, are plurivocal spaces that allow Mayas' representation and legitimation of the present in a specific socio-historically built territory. However, this lived space seems to have a limited capacity of creating a sense of belonging because of its transformation into a scientific and tourist site.

The Plurivocality of Tulum: From a Local Sacred Site to the Heritage Era

From La Montaña to Quintana Roo

The remains of Tulum are located on the Caribbean coast of Quintana Roo, an area that was densely inhabited until the European invasion and where most of Post-Classic Period (900–1521 CE) settlements are located (Con Uribe, "East Coast" 15; Roys 143). From then on, different causes— including diseases and cultural and political conquest—provoked import- ant changes to the region's demography. While the colonial system mainly focused on the northern and western regions of the Yucatán peninsula, in the east, a wide territory almost free from colonization and evangelization remained controlled by a few independent Indigenous groups (Bracamonte y Sosa 20). This region was named "La Montaña" (the Mountain) by Euro- pean inquisitors and chroniclers. It is there that the Itzá, the pre-Hispanic lineage that the Cruzo'ob Maya conceive as their ancestors, resisted the Spaniards until 1697 in the Petén region in Guatemala (Bartolomé and Barabas 61; Bracamonte y Sosa 33).

The year 1847, two decades after Mexico's independence, marks the beginning of a period of long-running conflict known as the Caste War between Maya peasants and the Mexican Army in the area of the former colonial border between the independent region of La Montaña and the sugar and henequen plantations owned by Yucatec landowners of European descent (Bartolomé and Barabas 21; Villanueva Mukul and Suárez Méndez 56). Three years later, the Cruz Parlante (Talking Cross) appeared, an event that marks the ethnogenesis of the Cruzo'ob Maya (Barabas). The town of Noh Kaj Báalam Nah Chan Santa Cruz (today's Felipe Carrillo Puerto) became the sanctuary of this oracle and the de facto Cruzo'ob capital. Al- though the Caste War officially ended in 1901 with the storming of this locality, its capture by the Mexican Army did not mean that the conflict ended immediately. Indeed, according to Cruzo'ob collective memory, the Caste War continues today.

The invasion of the Maya region by the Mexican Army during the Caste War and the deliberate campaign of Mexican colonization afterward caused different migrations within the peninsula. Anthropologists Miguel A. Bar- tolomé and Alicia M. Barabas describe the early twentieth century as the start of the Mexican colonization of Cruzo'ob territory, especially from the year 1915, with the beginning of the chicle industry (52). Since then, the demography of Quintana Roo has changed and numerous groups of Maya from the state of Yucatán and peasants from other regions of the country have settled in the eastern part of the peninsula (Bartolomé and Barabas 93–95). The Cruzo'ob mainly settled in the central region of today's Quintana Roo. The resulting reconfiguration of Indigenous settlements led to the creation of a sacred and political Cruzo'ob territory in Quintana Roo, articulated around the different Talking Cross ceremonial centers of Chancah Veracruz, Xcacal Guardia, Chumpóm, and Tulum.

The Sacred Value of Tulum up to the "Heritage Era"

Ethnographic information present in both explorers' and archaeologists' works from the mid-nineteenth century to the late 1930s indicates that Maya communities from the central region of Quintana Roo attached a particular importance to Tulum's remains (Catherwood 23; Villa Rojas 51). The British explorer Frederick Catherwood documented evidence of recent ritual activity in a structure of the pre-Hispanic city in 1842 (23). In 1863 the village of Tulum became one of the most important political and ceremonial centers for the Cruz Parlante worship, and so did the pre-Hispanic remains (Goñi; Santana Rivas). Indeed, the Cruzo'ob gave particular importance to the structure of El Castillo, where they placed a cross in order to use it as a sanctuary (Dumond 548).

In the late nineteenth and early twentieth centuries, foreign explorers and archaeologists came to study the "mysterious" ancient city of Tulum. However, even if the Caste War had officially ended in 1901, in the collective Maya memory, the site of Tulum still needed to be protected from invaders. Nonetheless, the British archaeologist Thomas W. Gann, part of the 1916 and 1922 Carnegie expeditions, managed to establish some relations with the Maya from the region of Tulum. He even attended two ceremonies dedicated to the Talking Cross held within the structure of El Castillo in 1922 and during a later visit to Tulum in 1926 (Con Uribe and López Portillo Guzmán 121). During the latter, he observed that the participants asked "his god" to protect him from the iiko'ob (Gann 119), the wind/spirits that dwell in the remains. Gann also documented the fear caused by an "idol" located in a small temple outside the archaeological site (132). He decided to leave it there but he finally "took" another idol, which is today part of the British Museum of London collection (Goñi 154).

In the 1930s, Mexican anthropologist Alfonso Villa Rojas collected information on pilgrimages to Tulum among the inhabitants of Tusik and Xcacal Guardia, all of whom worshipped a cross inside El Castillo (51).[4] In 1937, however, while Tulum hosted the first Mexican archaeological project, the governor of the Territory of Quintana Roo, Rafael Melgar, forbade the Maya from accessing Tulum's Castillo, forcing them to change their ritual customs (Goñi 163–65). In 1939 the Instituto Nacional de Antropología e Historia (INAH, National Institute of Anthropology and History)—the entity in charge of all activities related to pre-Hispanic archaeological administration, conservation, and research—was created. Both this institutionalization of heritage administration and the restriction of access for religious purposes marked the beginning of a new era in which Tulum's remains became Mexico's state property.

Although the 1930s saw transformations in Maya rituality, we also know that Tulum continued to be of great significance for Cruzo'ob from Chumpóm and Felipe Carrillo Puerto until the 1950s (Con Uribe and López Portillo Guzmán; Peissel). The ethnologist Michel Peissel collected valuable information regarding this specific matter during his visit to Quintana Roo in 1958, and in 1963 he explained that the Maya from Felipe Carrillo Puerto held a pilgrimage to Tulum, where they performed a ceremony "in homage to the crosses which are set into the cliff at the foot of the Castillo" (143–44). These pilgrimages and ritual practices illustrate continuity in the symbolism attached to the ancient city beyond the off-limits structure of El Castillo.

In Tulum, no archaeological projects were run between 1940 and 1974. During this period, it seems that the relations between the local communities and the INAH were peaceful, especially considering that around that time, there was only one custodian and his position was honorary until the year 1974 (Con Uribe, personal communication). However, this situation changed in the late 1970s and early 1980s when the Tulum National Park was decreed, and the institution started to take a closer look at the site visitors and their activities.

Internal Colonization and Heritage Making

In the 1930s, Mexico's president, Lázaro Cárdenas, visited Quintana Roo several times, and he envisioned a new future for that remote and disputed land: economic riches grown through tourism (Verdayes Ortiz). The first national excavation of Tulum took place in 1937 and was connected to that vision. In 1939 Las Ruinas (the Ruins) became Tulum's first hotel, and it was located right next to the archaeological site. Quintana Roo's tourism industry grew steadily, but with the emergence of Cancún as an international tourist destination in the 1980s, the pace of touristification significantly increased (Castañeda 264). One result of Cancún's growth was the emergence of another tourist region in the ensuing years: the Riviera Maya, where Tulum is located. During recent decades, Tulum has become a small city of eighteen thousand inhabitants. With its beaches and archaeological site, it is one of the main tourist areas of the region. In 2018 more than two million people visited the remains, making Tulum the third-most-visited archaeological site in Mexico, after Teotihuacán and Chichen Itzá.[5]

In this later period, the religious and spiritual maps of Tulum have also changed, and a diversity of sacred places have appeared. Several churches as well as the Maya Ceremonial Center are now located in the center of the city (see figure 10.1). The latter is the only place where religious activities

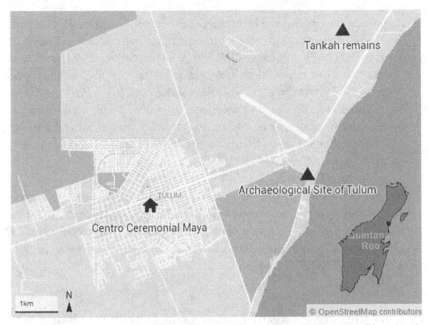

FIGURE 10.1 Ceremonial Center and Tulum and Tancah's remains, 2019. Photograph by the author.

related to the Talking Cross are currently allowed. Yet nowadays the remains also attract New Age groups who perform ceremonies—usually on equinox and solstice days—as well as groups from the Church of Latter Day Saints, who connect the archaeological site to the Book of Mormon (McDannell 74). The conversion of Tulum into a location of national heritage, international cultural tourism, and alternative spiritual destination has modified Cruzo'ob's territoriality and rituality.

Nowadays, it seems that the sacred value attached to the remains by the Maya from the nineteenth and early twentieth centuries has completely disappeared. The only remembrance of the site is political, and sacred use is the one presented on a discrete plaque along one of the paths that lead to the exit of the archaeological site (see figure 10.2).

In 1847 an armed uprising called the Caste War began and a new religion, known as the Cult of the Talking Crosses, developed. The rebel capital was Noh Cah or Chan Santa Cruz (now Carrillo Puerto), with smaller centers like Tulum adjutant to the military and religious headquarters. When the capital fell, the Villa Grande de Santa Cruz Tulum became an important center, directed by María Uicab, known as the Queen of Tulum. The rebels (cruzoob) recognized that the ruins were sacred and placed a cross in the temple known as El Castillo (the Castle). At the beginning of the 20th century, the Mexican army put down the rebellion, although the worship of the cross was maintained at Tulum's Castillo. Archaeological expeditions were initiated at that time. In the mid-1930s the Mexican government took charge of the site and assumed responsibility for investigation, conservation, and tourist visits. (translation by INAH / Consejo Nacional para la Cultura y las Artes)

In this passage, the use of the term *responsibility* legitimates the scientific and national interventions that have led to the conversion of a sacred site into a historic and tourist one. In other words, it was Mexico's duty to fight against the Maya "rebels" and to preserve archaeological heritage in order to include it in the nation's heritage inventory.

At the Crossroads of Sciences and Local Knowledge

All Paths Lead to Tulum

We know from colonial documents and archaeological research that the site of Tulum was inhabited at least until the late seventeenth century (Miller 85; Roys 147). At that time, the site was known as Tzamá. There are different

FIGURE 10.2 INAH "historical viewpoint" board on Cruzo'ob's use of the site at Tulum, 2017. Photograph by Amilcar Vargas.

hypotheses regarding the meaning of this name, one of the most accepted being the one suggested by archaeologist Arthur G. Miller, who linked it to the word *sáamal*, which means "dawn," and thus to the concept of *rebirth* as related to the east (85). In 1842, when U.S. explorer John Lloyd Stephens and his companion Frederick Catherwood visited the archaeological remains there, the local Maya knew the site by the name of Tulum. This change of toponym may indicate other transformations regarding its use: by then, the local Maya were visiting the site for ritual purposes, as suggested by offerings reported in Catherwood's writings (23). The most common hypothesis regarding the name of Tulum is that it refers to the defensive wall that surrounds the archaeological site (Roys 146).

Another hypothesis for the name change, based on linguistic and oral tradition, relates to Tulum's ethnopolitical and prophetical dimensions. According to historian Marco Antonio León Diez, the correct way of writing the name of the site is *Tuulum* and its meaning might be "place of resurgence," potentially a reference to the local oral tradition that evokes the return of the "Ancient ones" from the East (León Diez 105). León Diez's hypothesis connects to Miller's earlier translation of the city's former name, Tzamá, as "dawn" (Miller 85).

In the Yucatán peninsula, including Quintana Roo, the prophecy that a group of Itzá people escaped from the Spaniards by moving toward the east—from which they are expected to appear again one day—is common, especially among elders. In 1937 the U.S. anthropologist Robert Redfield was told by informants from Chan Kom, a village in the state of Yucatán, that the archaeological remains of Oxkin Kiuic were the place where the Ancient ones, the Itzá, would someday reappear (156). In the same period, Villa Rojas documented a similar narrative in Tusik, Quintana Roo. There, the remains were supposed to be the dwelling places of the Itzá people, the "wise ancestors" of the Maya who live underground for an "unknown reason" (439). Villa Rojas also published a conversation with the Maya general Captain Cituk, in which the latter told a story of the European invasion. Cituk recounted that, before the arrival of the Spaniards in the area, the "king" Don Juan Tutul Xiu used to visit Tulum to pray. However, the European colonization of the area caused him and some of his followers to run away through an underground path that led eastward and passed under the site of Tulum (441). This oral testimony is a clear reference to the Itzá prophecy of reappearance that, according to Bartolomé and Barabas, led the Cruzo'ob Maya to fight against Mexico during the Caste War (177).

Continuity in the ritual use of the archaeological site at Tulum during the last quarter of the twentieth century was confirmed to me by five people in interviews I undertook at the different Maya villages of Señor, Uh May, Chumpón, Felipe Carrillo Puerto, and Tulum in 2017 and 2018. Their histories highlight a correspondence in the historical perception of Tulum among the elders of several Maya villages, and especially in the remains' prophetical dimension.

In Señor, a village near the Xcacal Guardia ceremonial center, an elder remembered going to Tulum to deposit offerings and pray in the archaeological site until the 1980s. He explained that he stopped going because the entrance fee had become too expensive for him. He told me during the interview that Tulum was the place of the *china'an kaab* people, a name that refers to the ancestors believed to live beneath the earth.[6] In addition, in another interview, a former member of the Tulum Ceremonial Center told me that he had witnessed offerings in the stairway of El Castillo until the year 1978. According to him, the custodians forbade this practice after that year. An elder from Felipe Carrillo Puerto informed me that a ritual expert from Tulum used to avoid the official entrance to the ruins and preferred to reach them through the jungle for ritual purposes. Another elder from Tulum confirmed this information and added that the *jmeen* (ritual expert; pl. *jmeeno'ob*) continued using this jungle path until the 1990s. Moreover, an elder inhabitant of Uh May, a village related to the Chankah Veracruz Ceremonial Center—more than one hundred kilometers away from the Tulum remains—remembered visiting the ruins during a pilgrimage in the late 1970s. That was the only time he visited the archaeological site, but the Uh May elder recalled what he was told during this pilgrimage.

> There is a pathway that connects Xcacal Guardia to Tulum. Where the pathway starts there are ruins that look like houses. It is an ancient path and the *aluxo'ob* goes through it. But this is not a normal road, you must go under the earth. The walls are painted. But I think it is dangerous, there are a lot of snakes. (personal communication, 6 May 2017)

There is clearly a connection between the oral testimony of Capitan Cituk, collected in Tuzik by Villa Rojas in the 1930s, and this memory from a present-day Maya elder.

During my interviews, different people, including jmeeno'ob, also mentioned underground paths that lead to Tulum from the different Cruz Parlante ceremonial centers of Chankah Veracruz, Xcacal Guardia, and Chumpón. In Kantulnikín, a Maya village in the northern region of Quintana Roo, the local chronicler Gaspar Maglah Canul explained that the *abuelos* (grandfathers/

ancestors) had a prophecy in which the *beelo'ob yáanal lu'um*, the underground paths that connect Chichén Itzá to Coba and Tulum, would "open" again someday. Other testimonies from the central region of the state evoke the fact that, at a place where monoliths and "ancient statues" appear in abundance, an underground tunnel was made by the Antiguos, the "Ancient ones," who also painted its walls. According to oral history in the region, the tunnel was closed by the INAH in the 1970s–1980s.[7]

In March 2018, the INAH Center located in Chetumal (CINAH Quintana Roo) allowed me to consult reports from the different archaeological projects undertaken in Tulum. There I found a reference to the closure of a *sac-be*, a pre-Hispanic path, in a report from a 1974 INAH project. However, the underground nature of the path was not mentioned. It seems that this path probably communicated from Tulum to Muyil, another archaeological site thirty kilometers away from the Chumpóm Ceremonial Center. The archaeologist María José Con Uribe remembers being told by fellow archaeologists and biologists that in the 1970s and 1980s, the pilgrimages to Tulum used to go through the Sian Ka'an Reserve and the archaeological site of Muyil, where pilgrims prayed each 3 May—the day of the Holy Cross—in front of an image of the Virgin Mary located outside these remains (Con Uribe, personal communication). Clearly, in both oral history and archaeological records, Tulum is related to real and mythological pathways that connect the past to the present as well as to the history of the Itzá and the political identity of the Cruzo'ob and their descendants.

Modern Enshrinements

Because of the sociocultural changes of recent decades, relations between archaeological structures and Maya communities are difficult to document today, especially in archaeological sites administrated by the INAH. Usually, the ancient cities remained part of local communities' oral history and ritual practices until a few decades ago. The linkages between the pre-Hispanic structures and Indigenous inhabitants of the region have changed because there has been an increase in the institutionalized management of archaeological heritage and because of Maya labor migration to tourist regions. Despite this, archaeological remains, especially múulo'ob not administered by the INAH, have continued to be places where jmeeno'ob, hunters, and farmers communicate with supernatural entities through offerings and ceremonies. Indeed, I have collected information about ceremonies performed in several archaeological mounds in different villages of the region.

Although more difficult to document, ceremonies are also performed in archaeological sites managed by the INAH. A former jmeen from Chunyaxche explained to me that he performed a *looj* (land protection/blessing) ceremony at the site of Muyil in order to appease an unhappy *alux* who was causing trouble among visitors and custodians. He said that the alux was the owner of the site and that an offering had to be made so that people would be allowed to visit and use the alux's land. Until approximately fifteen years ago, the rain petition ceremony of *ch'a' cháak* used to be performed inside the archaeological site of Coba, and the offerings used to be deposited in front of stela number 11, as previously documented by Con Uribe and Octavio Esparza Olguín (3) and confirmed during my fieldwork.

Tulum's conversion into such a tourist place—along with the high entry price and the prohibition of ritual activities there—have influenced the local Maya to progressively detach themselves from the site. In fact, actual Maya offerings or ceremonies seem to be nonexistent in Tulum today. To perform such a ritual activity, it is necessary to fill out an official request form and send it to the Centro INAH Quintana Roo in Chetumal, with no guarantee of acceptance. Practical knowledge about this process is very scarce between local communities. During fieldwork, I encountered some cultural promoters from the Felipe Carrillo Puerto region whose *fuego sagrado* (sacred fire) spiritual ceremony request was denied because it involved fire and was interpreted as a risk to archaeological heritage. The local communities' scant knowledge about the application system contrasts with the permissions regularly granted to different New Age groups, who often meet for specific dates—in some cases every twenty-first day of the month—to perform ceremonies in Tulum or the sites of Coba, Muyil, Xel-Há, and El Meco.

Even if ritual practices are now restricted in the archaeological area of Tulum, I was able to document that some inhabitants of the region believed the entities who live in the remains are still active and that their power goes beyond the site. Higinio Kauil Pat, a ritual expert from Tepich, has performed several ceremonies in the surrounding areas of archaeological remains, including at Tulum. However, Don Higinio does not need to enter the actual site to perform these kinds of ceremonies because he is interacting with livestock believed to be affected by the entities who dwell in the archaeological structures but move around neighboring areas.

Other ceremonies have been performed inside the archaeological site of Tulum, including *jets' meek*, a ceremony in which an infant is presented to the world. During fieldwork, I was told that approximately ten years ago, a ceremony of cleansing of the land took place in front of El Castillo in order to appease the spirits living there. This ceremony is extremely important within

Maya rituality because it allows the living to use the land owned by the spirits and entities. For this reason, it is supposed to be performed to gain permission to carry out any activity on it. However, this permission had apparently never been obtained before. According to the jmeen who performed the ceremony, the spirits were appeased after the ritual in which a chicken, corn tortillas, and *saká* (corn beverage) were offered. This information tells us that in spite of important changes regarding the uses of the site, the Tulum remains are still considered to be the dwelling places of more-than-human entities.

Orality, Rituality, and Reflexivity

Disciplines such as archaeology and anthropology have an influence on present-day interpretations of archaeological sites in Mexico. Sometimes, archaeological and anthropological research and oral history have merged to create new narratives regarding ancient cities, especially in regions where Maya inhabitants have also engaged in these scientific projects. Villa Rojas's *Los elegidos de Dios* contains one of the most interesting examples of the influence of research among local communities, where Tusik's Captain Cituk recalled a narrative that was a direct interpretation of the presence of U.S. archaeologists in the region.

> In the old buildings of Tulum was engraved in hieroglyphics the prophecy that the *americanos* were to join the *mazehualob* to fight the Mexicans. [Captain Cituk] added that these Americans were descendants of remote ancestors of contemporary Indians and that they were the ones who built today's archaeological cities. In support of this idea is the fact that, today, only the Americans are able to decipher what is written on the walls of the old temples. (275–76)[8]

This recollection from a Maya dignitary in the 1930s allows for a better understanding of the impact of research on the interpretation of heritage at a local level.

Archaeology's impact is also observable on the progressive increase of cultural tourism, a type of tourism that feeds on research. During fieldwork, I noticed that landowners from different villages were interested in initiating a process to valorize the archaeological remains present in their lands. This was supposed to consist of research and restoration activities that aimed to include the archaeological remains in community-based ecotourism projects.

Tourism works the other way around too: a large proportion of the Maya residents are migrating to tourist areas in order to work in tourism-related jobs, which has led to important changes in the relationships between the people and their cultural landscape. On the one hand, the highly affluent visitors to archaeological sites such as Coba and Tulum have led to the attribution of economic value to the remains in communities where tourism is considered a viable economic alternative. On the other hand, the diversification of employment opportunities has meant a subsequent decrease in subsistence agriculture, which also means a decrease in the performance of agricultural ceremonies. Additionally, this results in changing interpretations of the remains as the dwelling places for sacred entities related to agriculture. For example, different ritual experts and peasants from the region told me that the lack of rain and the bad harvest can be attributed to the peoples' increasing disinterest in ceremonies related to agriculture.

In these contexts, archaeologists and anthropologists, by dint of their close relations with local communities, are also exposed to local history and knowledge. This affects their belief systems as well. I consulted with several Mexican archaeologists about the importance of ritual in archaeology, especially

FIGURE 10.3 Candle on a pre-Hispanic structure at Tancah, 2018. Photograph by the author.

before beginning fieldwork, largely to avoid potential complications caused by unsatisfied entities. I found that at least three directors of excavations in Quintana Roo usually perform rituals at the beginning of an archaeological campaign or before opening a tomb. During my research in March 2018, I found a candle and some incense on an archaeological structure at Tancah, another pre-Hispanic site located on private land two kilometers from Tulum (see figure 10.3). The guardian told me that the offerings had been left there by archaeologists from another region. He added that it is a "common practice they did in order to ask for protection to the spirits living there."

Interestingly, the guardian of the site, who was Maya, expressed that offering candles to spirits was *"cosa de ellos,"* something that had more to do with the archaeologists' beliefs than with Maya ones (however, in the early 1980s, the archaeologist Arthur G. Miller mentioned that the local community of Tancah usually offered candles to the alux who was believed to dwell in the local cenote cave [88]). The contrast shows that there has been a change in Tancah regarding the sacred value of certain significant archaeological places over the past few decades.

Toward a Political Use of the Sacred?

On 16 December 2018 Tulum witnessed another use of its remains: a ritual in which Mother Earth was asked for permission to build a transregional train project to connect tourist sites—including archaeological remains—associated with the Maya in different Mexican states (Proyecto Tren Maya). The ceremony, called Ritual de los Pueblos Originarios a la Madre Tierra (Ritual from the Indigenous People to the Mother Earth), was celebrated simultaneously in six archaeological sites, including Tulum. This type of initiative is rare in Mexico and likely related to the recent election of President Andrés Manuel López Obrador. His Proyecto Tren Maya, however, has been criticized and questioned by the public and some Maya leaders. Potential ecological damages and the understanding that there would not be actual benefits for the local communities were the main reasons for local opposition.

At Tulum, the Mother Earth ceremony was performed by local politicians, Maya dignitaries, mayapax musicians, and Maya ritual experts.[9] It took place in front of El Castillo. During the speeches, the mayor of Tulum claimed that the project would prove the prophecy of the ancestors and renew the splendor of the Maya civilization, an example of the ongoing prophetical dimension of the remains as well as the use of archaeology as a legitimating tool on both local and national levels (Noticaribe).

Conclusion

My research has shown that the archaeological site of Tulum is evidence of the plurivocality of archaeological heritage. Nowadays, the remains are neither part of a remote past nor a unique social creation. The continuous attribution of ritual use and values to the site highlights a common will among all its users: to legitimate the present through the interpretation of the past. Thus, it can be argued that Tulum is a lived space that allows several kinds of interpretation and representation from colonial to religious or politic. The contacts, invasions, and conflicts between Maya and settlers—both Europeans and Mexicans—have led to changes in the local cultural and religious relations to the site. The scientific colonization of the remains has subsequently converted Tulum into an archaeological project and a nationalist expression of greatness. And, as has been demonstrated, the remains of Tulum have not received much local ritual activity since the late 1970s. Nevertheless, its conversion into a tourist place is the most important change regarding the sacred value attached to the site.

As suggested in this chapter, the remains are still perceived as sacred, especially among elders and ritual experts. Indeed, both the archaeological site itself and its surrounding lands are known to be located beyond the influence of the remains' entities and require the occasional intervention of local ritual experts. Nevertheless, the interpretation of the site as a ceremonial center for the Talking Cross seems to have almost totally vanished. During my fieldwork, I realized that most of my informants did not associate the archaeological remains with the Caste War but with an aesthetic and tourist site. Nonetheless, ethnographic work has shown that Tulum is still part of prophetical imagery related to the "Antiguos," or "Ancient ones." Moreover, the sacredness of the site has also affected other diverse groups, including pan-Maya spiritual groups, New Agers, and Mormons, each interpreting the remains differently according to their beliefs. This diversity confirms the plurivocality of archaeological heritage and questions the assumption that its power as a sacred site is only located in the past.

The common narrative that the INAH closed a path that used to connect different points of Cruzo'ob territory to the remains at Tulum reflects an interruption of the former customs and changes regarding the use of the site. Indeed, this chapter has demonstrated that the dialogues between scientific and local knowledges are reflexive, and that their mutual influences contribute to changes in orality and ritual practice. It is possible to argue that the contacts between both types of knowledge are somehow a resource for intangible heritage preservation and for decolonizing scientific discourses and dissemination.

Notes

I cannot express enough gratitude to all the people in Quintana Roo who have shared their knowledge and time with me. I especially want to thank don Higinio Kauil Pat, don Damaso Pech Cen, don Lázaro Kú and his daughter Magda, don Gregorio Vázquez Canché and the Museo Maya Santa Cruz Xbáalam Naj, don Gaspar Maglah Canul, and the Moure Peña family. I also want to thank María José Con Uribe, Allan Ortega, Darwin Carabeo Barabata, the Zona de Monumentos Arqueológicos de Tulum-Tancah's team, and the Centro INAH Quintana Roo for their support, as well as Margarita Díaz-Andreu, Gemma Celigueta, Amilcar Vargas, my colleagues from Grup d'Arqueologia Pública i Patrimoni (GAPP), and the editors of this volume, Gesa Mackenthun and Christen Mucher. All translations are mine unless otherwise indicated.

1. The Cruzo'ob, also known as Máasewáalo'ob, are the Maya who took up arms during the Caste War and follow the cult of the Talking Cross.

2. The appropriation of the past through archaeology has a rich literature and has been related to Mexican nationalism by several scholars, including Bernal; Breglia; Bueno; Díaz-Andreu; McAnany; Navarrete; and Patterson.

3. Detailed studies such as those by Quintal Avilés et al.; Vapnarsky; and Le Guen provide valuable information about Maya rituality and more-than-human entities.

4. Archaeological research in 2009 identified paintings of three red crosses from the late nineteenth or early twentieth century located within El Castillo (López Portillo Guzmán).

5. Gobierno de México, Estadísticas de Visitantes, "Zonas arqueológicas más visitadas," estadisticas.inah.gob.mx, accessed 7 June 2019.

6. According to Bartolomé and Barabas: "The measures below were made by *Chinan Kaabo*, they are the men of the Itzá. They are the people of Juan Tutul Xiu, currently living beneath the surface of the earth. They are enchanted men" (61).

7. For more information about Maya knowledge of closed paths, see Sullivan.

8. The term *Americans* used by Captain Cituk is a reference to the archaeologists who worked in the Yucatán peninsula in the early twentieth century and who happened to be mostly U.S. citizens. The hegemonic dimension of epigraphy expressed there is reflected in the genealogic relation between the archaeologists who were "able to decipher what is written on the walls of the old temples" and the Maya who knew that the glyphs narrated the history of their ancestors.

9. Mayapax is Maya music from the central region of Quintana Roo.

References

Arden, Traci. "Where Are the Maya in Ancient Maya Archaeological Tourism? Advertising and the Appropriation of Culture." *Marketing Heritage: Archaeology and the Consumption of the Past*, edited by Uzi Baram Yorke Rowan, AltaMira, 2004, pp. 103–13.

Barabas, Alicia M. "Milenarismo y profecía en la etnogénesis de los macehualob de Quintana Roo, México." *Etnografía de los confines: Andanzas de Anne Chapman*, edited by Andrés Medina and Ángela Ochoa, 2008, pp. 163–78.

Bartolomé, Miguel A., and Alicia M. Barabas. *La resistencia maya: Relaciones interétnicas en el oriente de la península de Yucatán*. Colección científica 53. Instituto Nacional de Antropología e Historia, 1977.

Bernal, Ignacio. *A History of Mexican Archaeology*. Thames and Hudson, 1980.

Bracamonte y Sosa, Pedro. *La conquista inconclusa de Yucatán: Los mayas de la montaña, 1560–1680*. Centro de Investigaciones y Estudios Superiores en Antropología Social, 2001.

Breglia, Lisa. *Monumental Ambivalence: The Politics of Heritage*. University of Texas Press, 2006.

Bueno, Christina. *The Pursuit of Ruins: Archaeology, History, and the Making of Modern Mexico*. University of New Mexico Press, 2016.

Castañeda, Quetzil. "Heritage and Indigeneity: Transformations in the Politics of Tourism." *Cultural Tourism in Latin America: The Politics of Space and Imagery*, edited by Michiel Baud and Annelou Ypeij, Brill, 2009, pp. 263–95.

Catherwood, Frederick. *Views of Ancient Monuments in Central America, Chiapas and Yucatan*. New York, 1844.

Con Uribe, María José. "The East Coast of Quintana Roo: A Brief Account of Archaeological Work." *Quintana Roo Archaeology*, edited by Justine M. Shaw and Jennifer P. Mathews, University of Arizona Press, 2005.

Con Uribe, María José. Personal communication. 13 Mar. 2018.

Con Uribe, María José, and Octavio Esparza Olguín. "Recovered History: Stela 11 of Coba." *PARI Journal*, vol. 27, no. 1, 2016, pp. 1–17.

Con Uribe, María José, and Mónica López Portillo Guzmán. "El castillo de Tulum: Historia de un edificio." *Prácticas funerarias y arquitectura en tiempo y espacio*, edited by Antonio Benavides Castillo and Ricardo Armijo Torres, Universidad Autónoma de Campeche, 2014, pp. 114–41.

Díaz-Andreu, Margarita. *A World History of Nineteenth-Century Archaeology, Nationalism, Colonialism, and the Past*. Oxford University Press, 2007.

Dumond, Don E. *El machete y la cruz: La sublevación de campesinos en Yucatán*. Universidad Nacional Autónoma de México, 2005.

Gann, Thomas W. *Maya Cities: A Record of Exploration and Adventure in Middle America*. Duckworth, 1927.

Goñi, Guillermo. *De como los mayas perdieron Tulum*. Instituto Nacional de Antropología e Historia, 1999.

Haber, Alejandro. *Al otro lado del vestigio: Políticas del conocimiento y arqueología indisciplinada*. JAS Arqueología, 2017.

Lefebvre, Henri. *La producción del espacio*. Capitán Swing Libros, 2013.

León Diez, Marco Antonio. *Tuulum: El lugar del resurgimiento*. Selva Libre, 2012.

López Portillo Guzmán, Mónica Alejandra. *Proyecto Norte de Quintana Roo: Tulum, El Meco, El Rey y Xelhá*. Informe de los trabajos realizados en cuatro zonas arqueológicas del norte de Quintana Roo, Temporada 2010. Subproyecto del Programa Nacional de

Conservación de Pintura Mural de la Coordinación Nacional de Conservación del Patrimonio Cultural. Instituto Nacional de Antropología e Historia, 2010.

Lowenthal, David. *El pasado es un país extraño*. Akal Universitaria, 1998.

Maglah Canul, Gaspar. Personal communication. 14 Mar. 2018.

McAnany, Patricia. *Maya Cultural Heritage: How Archaeologists and Indigenous Communities Engage the Past*. Rowman & Littlefield, 2016.

McDannell, Colleen. "Mexicans, Tourism, and Book of Mormon Geography." *Dialogue: A Journal of Mormon Thought*, vol. 50, no. 2, 2017, pp. 55–85.

Miller, Arthur G. *On the Edge of the Sea: Mural Painting at Tancah-Tulum, Quintana Roo, Mexico*. Dumbarton Oaks, 1982.

Navarrete, Federico. "Ruinas y estado: Arqueología de una simbiosis mexicana." *Pueblos indígenas y arqueología en América Latina*, edited by Cristóbal Gnecco and Patricia Ayala Rocabado, Universidad de los Andes, 2009, pp. 65–82.

Noticaribe. "Ceremonia maya en Tulum por el Tren Maya: El proyecto significa el resurgimiento de la cultura, dice Víctor Mas." *Noticaribe*, 16 Dec. 2018, noticaribe.com .mx/2018/12/16/ceremonia-maya-en-tulum-por-el-tren-maya-el-proyecto-significa -el-resurgimiento-de-la-cultura-dice-victor-mas.

Patterson, Thomas C. "Archaeology, History, Indigenismo, and the State in Peru and Mexico." *Making Alternative History*, edited by Thomas C. Patterson and Peter R. Schimdt, School of Americas Research Press, 1995, pp. 69–85.

Peissel, Michel. *The Lost World of Quintana Roo: An Adventurous Quest for Mayan Ruins on the Untamed Coast of Yucatan*. E. P. Dutton, 1963.

Quintal Avilés, Ella F., et al. "U lu'umil maaya wíiniko'ob: La tierra de los mayas." *Diálogos con el territorio: Simbolización sobre el espacio en las culturas indígenas de México*, vol. 1, edited by Alicia M. Barabas, Instituto Nacional de Antropología e Historia, 2003, pp. 273–359.

Redfield, Robert. "Maya Archaeology as the Maya See It." 1932. *Human Nature and the Study of Society: The Papers of Robert Redfield*, edited by Margaret Park Redfield, University of Chicago Press, 1962, pp. 152–60.

Roys, Ralph L. *The Political Geography of the Yucatan Maya*. Kirby Lithographic Company, 1957.

Santana Rivas, Landy, and Georgina Rosado Rosado. *Género y poder entre los mayas rebeldes de Yucatán: Tulum y la dualidad a través del tiempo*. Universidad Autónoma de Yucatán, 2007.

Smith, Linda Tuhiwai. *A decolonizar las metodologías: Investigación y pueblos indígenas*. Txalaparta, 2017.

Stephens, John Lloyd. *Incidents of Travel in Yucatan*. London, 1843.

Sullivan, Paul. *Unfinished Conversations: Mayas and Foreigners During Two Wars*. University of California Press, 1989.

Vapnarsky, Valentina. "The Guardians of Space and History: Understanding Ecological and Historical Relationships of the Contemporary Yucatec Maya to Their Landscape." *Ecology, Power, and Religion in Maya Landscapes*, Verlag Anton Saurwein, 2011, pp. 191–206.

Verdayes Ortiz, Fernando. "Lázaro Cardenas, el primer gran promotor de Quintana Roo."
    Informativo Turquesa, no. 24, 6 Mar. 2017, pp 14–17.

Villanueva Mukul, Eric, and Addy Suárez Méndez. *Los insurrectos: Movimiento indígena maya
    en Yucatán*. Maldonado Editores del Mayab, 2014.

Villa Rojas, Alfonso. *Los elegidos de Dios: Etnografía de los mayas de Quintana Roo*. Instituto
    Nacional Indigenista, 1987.

Webster, David. "The Mystique of the Ancient Maya." *Archaeological Fantasies: How Pseu-
    doarchaeology Misrepresents the Past and Misleads the Public*, edited by G. G. Fagan,
    Routledge, 2006, pp. 129–53.

11

Red Earth, White Lies, Sapiens, *and the Deep Politics of Knowledge*

Philip J. Deloria

MOST BOOKS—AND THEIR IDEAS—FADE WITH time. Others, however, seem marked for constant rebirth; they are zombie books whose assertions take on a kind of deathless influence. One prominent example must surely be Jared Diamond's 1997 volume, *Guns, Germs, and Steel*, which disappears from the shelves for a year or two, only to catch its breath and be resurrected yet again into the world of the airport bookstore and the Barnes and Noble front table. As a result, Diamond's arguments explaining the global dominance of Europe have become a familiar way in which we understand the world and its past.

Among a proliferation of deep-history competitors, the book that seems most likely to join *Guns, Germs, and Steel* is Yuval Noah Harari's *Sapiens: A Brief History of Humankind*. Both authors use powerful storytelling to narrate popular histories that extend across space and time and win the embrace of "big-thinking" public figures such as Bill Gates ("How to Handle"; "What Are"). Both use seemingly cutting-edge syntheses of the deep past to speak loudly to the present and future. As best sellers, they offer commonsense understandings to entire generations of readers and occupy critical locations in the politics of knowledge that shapes political, economic, and social action in the contemporary world. A well-told story rich with philosophical detours, *Sapiens* nonetheless concludes with a turn away from history to a frightening futurism powered by the logics of science and structure that have shaped Harari's picture of the past.

In such books, there is a narrative cost to be paid, invisible to most readers. It falls on Indigenous people, past and present, who are captured by the story, framed by the inevitable coloniality of "prehistory," and mercilessly sacrificed to the big picture. What recourse might be imagined for those people? How might one pursue a critical Indigenous reading of (in this case) *Sapiens* as an exemplar of the deep-history form? What of its tropes and strategies can be made visible and thus contestable? And how might such a reading spur writers to tell better ancient stories, relevant to the future in a moment when genomic science has upended a veritable catalog of the things that the practitioners of history, archaeology, anthropology, and biology thought they knew?

To begin to answer that question, I want to resurrect a different book, much more provocative, which has been in no danger of reappearing in airports—since it never occupied that space in the first place. I am referring to *Red Earth, White Lies: Native Americans and the Myth of Scientific Fact*, published in 1995 by my father, Vine Deloria Jr. My father wrote thirty books during his career, of which a few emerged as important crossovers that carried Native perspectives to non-Native audiences: *Custer Died for Your Sins* (1969), *God Is Red* (1973), and perhaps *Red Earth, White Lies*, the last of which, to be frank, has occasionally presented something of a burden. How, for example, was I to defend something like this, found in the book's concluding chapter, when talking with my scientist friends?

> A number of tribal traditions describe creatures that may have been dinosaurs. . . . The Sioux have a tale about such a monster in the Missouri River. "Its backbone was just like a crosscut saw; it was flat and notched like a saw or a cogwheel." I suspect that the dinosaur in question here must be a stegosaurus. (243)

It would be tempting to think Deloria was just trying to rile people up, and that the statement was of a piece with Harari's provocations concerning (for example) a future ruled by new post-*Sapiens* species created by *Sapiens* intelligent design. But my father was able to entertain the possibility of human-dinosaur interactions because he was also willing to question both uniformitarian geology and evolution.

> It has been very difficult for anyone to get "inside" the fortress of the two incestuous disciplines—evolutionary biology and geology—and raise the relevant questions about either evolution or the stratigraphic column. Yet it is suspected that the stratigraphic column and evolutionary family trees are largely the figment of scholarly imaginations. (179–80)

He embraced Immanuel Velikovsky's theories of catastrophism, suggested that Pleistocene glaciation was likely the result of a comet ice dump, and wondered if humans might have occupied North America as early as 100,000 years ago (Velikovsky, *Earth in Upheaval*, *Worlds in Collision*; see also Gordin; Sagan). Though he loved science, he was at heart an Indigenous creationist who was willing to float a polygenesis argument that blurred the lines between multispecies evolutionary origins and separate divine creations. When my father died, the local newspaper columnist thought it was appropriate to make fun of him, as a crazy Indian, a complete and utter crank (Carroll).

But consider the following conversation, with the Anishinaabeg scholar Michael Witgen:

> *Red Earth, White Lies* was the first piece of writing from Vine Deloria that I ever read. It was this work, rather than the iconic *Custer Died for Your Sins*, that led me to his other published work and into the field of Native Studies literature more generally. What moved me about the book was his ability to use an indigenous perspective and epistemology to push back against the way science, and indeed the academy, framed the history of Native people in North America. (Witgen)

Witgen's recollection points us to the political consequences of deep-time historical narration and the various historicities and knowledge productions embedded in both stories and critiques. Traditional historians have long recognized that we tell stories of the past informed by, and speaking to, the present, and that our narratives thus require a warning label: "Beware! In what follows, I've tried to be an honest broker of knowledge, but there are personal and social contexts that will no doubt get in the way." Deep and big histories might be asked to carry a different label: "Warning! Chronological and global (or galactic) reach may render human action structural and thus comparatively meaningless." In such stories, human action may still be gestured to as contingent and agentic—but how do contingency and agency function in a meaningful way over big chronology? What *kinds* of meanings can be associated with long-frame storytelling? Who wins and who loses in the effort? *Red Earth, White Lies* speaks to these questions, as perhaps the first serious Indigenous critique to engage science and the deep past.

I wholeheartedly wish *Red Earth, White Lies* had been more attentive to evidence, historiography, interpretation, and argument. At the same time, however, the salience of its political/historical voice also opens the door to a reclamation of the text for the present. It's not just that supposedly neutral science-based narratives of the deep past have been wrapped in power and authority, but that—in Vine Deloria's view—they also channeled a frank, on-going, and perhaps "deep" contempt for Indigenous people. To put these two books in dialogue is to rehearse a critical conversation between the popular airport-bookstore writers who relentlessly situate Indigenous people out of time and space and those same Native peoples, very much present in the here and now, and quite determined to resist the stories told about them.

Red Earth, White Lies emerged most directly out of my father's fury at the political consequences for American Indian people of the twinned theories of Bering Strait migration (Hopkins) and the Pleistocene megafauna overkill hypothesis (Martin, "Discovery of America"; Martin, "Prehistoric Overkill").[1] In the first instance, he was arguably prescient in raising issues that are now part of the standard suite of critiques of the classic "ice-free corridor" hypothesis: archaeological remains that pushed the limits of the chronology (Dillehay and Collins; Halligan), geographical analysis of the mountain chains and other physical barriers existing on both sides of the Bering Strait (Arnold; Madsen), ecological analysis of the radical inhospitalities of both Beringia and overland migration paths (Pedersen), the more logical possibilities of coastal seafaring migrations (Anderson et al.; Erlandson et al.; Jett), and the unholy combination of sparse evidence and proliferating speculation that had seen "Clovis First" morph from "theory" to "truth" as it was narrated into orthodoxy by people such as Harari and Diamond.[2]

The consequences were palpable: the Bering Strait narrative turned Indigenous people into immigrants, displacing Aboriginal presence and claims, and encouraged non-Natives to cheerfully suggest: "Well, we're all immigrants from somewhere, aren't we?" (Curry; Deloria, *Red Earth* 83; *Los Angeles Times*; National Park Service).[3] There is an obvious danger in widening the chronological frame to the point that human action becomes structural, abstract, and socially meaningless—even as the supposed lesson remains socially meaningful in the *now*. Over a 200,000-year story—or even 50,000 years—we *could* in fact all be immigrants together; over a 500-year story, not so much. It is important not to confuse the two. Archaeologically inflected deep history is not a big board game or global flow chart but something that places specific demands on the present. Likewise, if one could see Indigenous people as immigrants—just slightly ahead of everyone else—the Bering Strait theory *also* reinvigorated the idea of an untouched continent, barely altered and certainly not owned, and therefore free for the taking. These, Deloria argued, were claims with political content: "Considerable residual guilt remains over the manner in which the Western Hemisphere was invaded and settled by Europeans. Five centuries of brutality lie uneasily on the conscience" (*Red Earth* 81). In his view, the structure of feeling created by "empty continents" and "we are all immigrants" narratives spoke to that guilt and unease for non-Native Americans.

As consequential were the arguments for Pleistocene overkill, and here his annoyance found a clear target in Paul S. Martin, his former colleague at the University of Arizona. If it was bad enough that Indigenous people were just another immigrant population, the suggestion that they had kicked off their immigration by killing every large creature on the continent was worse. It is not just that my father saw political utility in an argument for Indian ecological practice (though that was true); it's that he fundamentally believed in a Native spirituality centering a world that embraced a responsibility to other entities (Cajete; Kimmerer, *Braiding Sweetgrass*; Kimmerer, "Searching for Synergy").

He was willing to admit that that Indigenous world developed over time, and through ecological error. But he saw it as qualitatively distinct, and thus worth defending. Animism—the West's crudely reductive descriptive category—need give no ground to either monotheism or scientific rationalism, in his view. Again, his arguments—now a generation old—anticipated subsequent complications surrounding overkill hypotheses. Where *were* all those other kill sites, both for mammoth and for other prey megafauna? (Grayson and Meltzer). Why insist on parsimony when things were likely just more complicated? Were scientists not supposed to be careful about correlations and causality? Why did Martin (and Diamond, cited often in article form) and others seem to have such a visceral, emotional investment in what should be a disinterested scientific hypothesis? Were their questions methodological or ideological ones?

The arrogant certainty with which overkill was proclaimed has since been complicated by alternative theories—big rival ideas such as climate change (Guthrie; Nogués-Bravo); fringe theories such as hyperdisease (Rothschild and Laub) or a catastrophic comet impact (Firestone); and multifactor complications, including the role of second-order predation (Whitney-Smith), anthropogenic fire (Bird et al.), continentality in climate and vegetation change (Meyer et al.; White et al.), and the unexpected dwarfing of bison (Lyman). As pre-Clovis dates are pushed further back in time (likely to continue happening in North America, as it did in Australia)—and as with the recent identifications of earlier and broader global human migration patterns—it seems likely that both human migration stories and the Pleistocene extinctions will need to be refigured around new timelines and fact sets.

There is a particular historicity at play here. What do I mean by that? Historicity is the *contingent* quality of the unfolding of processes over time that have produced a range of *things*, from ruins and spearpoints to ideas. That assertion immediately suggests that historicity also concerns the nature of our knowledge of such unfolding, such that it's an *epistemological* idea, concerned with ways of knowing—of which there may be several—and the status and source of power for claims to "truth." And that, in turn, suggests that it must contain *ontological* aspects, for such knowledge is surely structured by how one sees and experiences *being*, reality, space, worlding, and—perhaps more than anything else (since we are talking about history)—*time*. Different peoples can in fact produce different historicities—and if we are to take contemporary physics seriously on the question of time, it is hardly clear that one ontological picture ought to take precedence over another. Rather, it seems *very* clear that the seeming superiority of one historicity is the result of uneven relations of force and power.

There is a familiar historicity emerging from a world of linear time, a time that *seems* to produce chronology, and in that chronology (one thing, then another, then another) *seems* to produce not just sequence but also cause and effect; and, if not pure and consistent cause and effect across vast spans of time, then the next best thing: development, evolution, directional change. Such changes over time have begged for narrative. With narrative came a structure of beginnings, middles, and ends; and with beginnings, middles, and ends, the implication of moral lessons, tales of winners and losers (who usually deserved their fates somehow), of one population replacing another, of increasing orders of social complexity over time. Primitive bands turn into tribes, which turn into chiefdoms, which turn into states. Hunters turn into pastoralists, who turn into agriculturalists, who turn into merchants, priests, inventors, and industrialists. This is the arc that structures every big and deep history ever told. What underpinned the anticolonial Indigenous anger that drives *Red Earth, White Lies* was the dangerous relation produced out of these stories, which mingled fact, speculation, narration, and moral, and that then took shape in what Vine Deloria experienced as a clueless, condescending arrogance on the part of "science." That thing that he imagined to be value free—in large part because of science's claims to exactly that—turned out to be anything but.

And so, the supposedly reliable dating of many Clovis sites turns out to be at least partially problematic—supposed *facts* that, it turns out, could not be trusted as such (Dillehay; Waters and Stafford). With only a handful of mammoth kill sites, archaeologists created *speculative* arguments . . . and then arguments that were speculative about their speculations. We cannot reject speculation—it's both good fun *and* the methodological ground for all creative thinking. But speculation should be used to generate questions for further research, not form the framework for confident and assertive narratives.

When Martin, Diamond, or Harari overconfidently narrated a tale of blitz-krieg extinction, they were not only telling hypothetical just-so stories. They were creating beginnings, middles, and ends; settings and characters; and a moral arc that had consequences for the subjects of their stories—which were mapped onto Indigenous peoples.

With these critiques, my father asserted two primary claims that are worth extracting. First, he wanted scholars to understand the ways in which their academic utterances did harm to actual people, politically and epistemolog-ically. He wanted overconfident writers to think harder and smarter about what they said, how they said it, and what kinds of ethical obligations they might incur when they drew implicit or explicit connections between paleo-Indians and Indians, or when they modeled ancient peoples by pointing to contemporary Indigenous cultures and societies. He wanted them, in a word, to stop being so blind to their own privilege and to stop universalizing their own epistemological position.

Second, because despite his protests he still believed in the power of sci-ence, he thought that losing the arrogance and actually engaging Indigenous knowledge could provide additional data that made all that theorizing, hy-pothesizing, and speculating *better*—and not simply by confirming Western scientific ideas but by finding alternative, *Indigenous* historicities (often put-ting temporality in closer dialogue with place) from which to begin. It's not by coincidence that he followed his critiques of the Bering Strait and overkill speculations with a chapter linking up Indigenous memory with scablands floods, Northwest Coast tsunamis, and volcanic eruptions. He wanted writ-ers to see non-Western people *as* people with historical memory rather than as living fossils of archaic forager cultures to be upstreamed back into the distant past.

If Vine Deloria were here today, reading Yuval Noah Harari, would it be crazy to imagine him saying similar things? He might ask: Why do Indig-enous people in *Sapiens* show up so often as relict examples of less complex cultures? What lessons are conveyed about them, even as their existences are pillaged in the service of contemporary and futurist arguments? What, in other words, are the deep politics of ancient history as it is told in this moment, and how different are they from the politics of Jared Diamond or Paul Martin?

Harari uses two narrative modes to frame the relation between the an-cient past and the present. The first locates the Indigenous in ignorance, inferior cognition and inadequate curiosity, condescending humor, and vi-olence. There are many examples. Here is one. Considering the colonial conquest of North America, Harari offers an extended joke, framed as an old Indian "legend." Modern astronauts training in a western desert are observed by a local Indian, who asks them to pass a message to tribal spirits living in the moon. There is much back-and-forth about memorizing exact wording, and the astronauts become curious. When they have the message translated, they see that the Indian has been messing with them: "Don't believe a single word these people are telling you. They have come to steal your lands" (285–86).[4]

When Indians tell that joke to one another, it's kind of funny. When a non-Indian writer uses it to frame colonial conquest, it works to different effect. The Indian—history's loser, bundled up with all the other losers— gets to pull a fast (but harmless) one on modernity, even while being sealed firmly in the past. We might recognize for a split second that the astronaut's very existence is predicated on the Indian's stolen lands, but the possibility of assuming a moral or ethical position on that implication is quickly swept away into harmless humor. History—precisely because it is linear, structural, and deep—has inexorably passed the Indian by.

The joke is one tropic example; the fairy tale offers another. Consider the children's book accent of Harari's account of the Aztec conquest, which turns quickly into a simplistic just-so story: "They came in giant ships, the like of which the Aztecs had never imagined, let alone seen. They rode on the back of huge and terrifying animals, swift as the wind. They could produce light-ning and thunder out of shiny metal sticks. They had flashing long swords and impenetrable armour, against which the natives' wooden swords and flint spears were useless" (293).

Don't the Aztecs—a big, successful, urban, imperial civilization (the kind Harari likes), armed with sharp obsidian swords and thick cotton armor that some Spaniards adopted for themselves, deserve a narrative voice that frames them as something other than frightened children? There is a long and deadly history found in this narrative voice, based in adjective and metaphor— "giant," "flashing," "huge and terrifying," "swift as the wind," "shiny metal sticks," "like lightning and thunder"—that has framed the non-European subject as developmentally impaired, fearful, and doomed.

Harari's second narrative mode uses a rhetorical rhythm that generates an illusion of complexity: first, pose a question; then consider counterarguments, alternative theories, and complications. Then assert an argument. Gesture, at the end of the section, back to complexity—but in such a way as to leave the claim intact. "Were early forager societies more or less prone to war?" he asks. And then responds: "All schools of thought on this are castles in the air" since we cannot really know. But then, he turns to a few studies and asserts that, well . . . yes, sadly, they *were* violent. But then suggests that the answer is probably not yes or no but a diverse range of possibilities. At this point, however, we think we know: they were violent.

An assertion of unknowability—which *might* lead one to simply *stop*—is compromised by a very *sapiens* desire to *narrate*, even when it means speculation from admittedly scant evidence. The power of such narration does *not* lie in the many qualifiers but in the weight of the examples. What's left here, for instance, is the strong aftertaste of violence attached to forager cultures. A claim has been staked but with plausible deniability.

As Gustavo Verdesio has observed, the compulsion to narrate the unknowable is one of the central false premises of archaeology and other deep-time sciences: archaeological evidence is temporally and spatially fragmentary. Its logic is of "affiliations of matter and form," not of event-based history. In this case, it's not Indigenous critique but *Western* logic that says it is wrong, on its face, to produce linear narratives out of discontinuous and insufficient data. Archaeology is, and has always been, in need of a new form of historicity, a different sense of time and the past (Verdesio).

If the evidence of archaeology is discontinuous and fragmentary, Verdesio asks, doesn't it bear a kind of species similarity to the pastness that makes up the present? The past isn't past. It's omnipresent. We create museums to contemplate that fact, though we rarely do so. I can touch that artifact behind the glass, just as many humans have touched it over long spans of time. It turns out that there is a lot more *past* in the present than there is *present* in the present. The present is a brief instant layered on a deep past that coexists in material form in the world of the present. To see that relation—the historical depth of the shallow object—would be to see with a distinct kind of historicity, focused not on developmental stories but on context, contingency, unknowability.

Harari's problematic claims, bolstered by the illusion of serious logic work, are used to contextualize a deep structure of *sapiens* violence that is part of a developmental narrative of equally structural progress. Inevitably, Harari will wrap up the brutality of European conquest in that context. But he's also willing to put some of the blame on Aztecs, Incas, Indians, and Asians for their supposed parochialism and disinterest in their own world—as if they did not know their worlds through their own practices of observation, deduction, experiment, benchmarking, and theorization. The heroes in Harari's story are the curious ones—scientists, who are rhetorically blurred together with conquerors, both willing to *admit their ignorance* and thus to boldly go out in the world, investigate, and discover new things. In *Guns, Germs, and Steel*, the misfortune of the Indigenous was to be born on an island or a disconnected vertical continent rather than a connected horizontal one. The driver of recent history for Harari has been something differently vague, with a Reaganesque ideological touch: "Modern science and modern empires were motivated by the *restless feeling* that perhaps something important awaited beyond the horizon—something that they had better explore and master" (297).

These contextual structures allow Harari to move up quickly to a level of abstraction that steps quickly back from human issues—even as *sapiens* body counts are constantly totted up, usually in the millions. In the case of New World conquest, that means a kind of relativist equivocation: "You can find examples to argue whatever you like: You think that these [European] empires were evil monstrosities that spread death, oppression, and injustice around the world? You could easily fill an encyclopedia with their crimes. You want to argue that they in fact improved the conditions of their subjects with new medicines, better economic conditions and greater security? You could fill another encyclopedia with their achievements" (302).

Neither good nor evil. Complicated. And true, I suppose. But this perfect balance between two alternative frames is hardly becoming, failing to mask the fact that Harari does not really believe in complexity but in *progress*. The human costs of empire, religion, science, and global markets have indeed been high—but for him, all these things must be taken as the locations for indices of progress visible only over long timescales: levels of violence are down over seventy thousand years. Health indicators are up. The deep-past timeframe allows him to argue preemptively against the simplicity of progressivist narratives—all the while offering a deadly metaprogressive narrative of his own.

It produces arguments such as this: Sure, Harari says, "hundreds of millions of people have been killed by the security forces of their own states. Still, from a macro perspective, state-run courts and police forces have probably increased the level of security worldwide. Even in oppressive dictatorships, the average modern person is far less likely to die at the hands of another person than in premodern societies" (368). For an example of this new security, Harari turns to the 1964–85 dictatorship in Brazil, noting that thousands of people were killed or tortured. But when seen in terms of averages and scales across deep time, he says, it was still better to be modern than not. How does he know? The evidence sits right in front of us, in Brazil itself. He seamlessly turns the Indigenous into the prehistoric: "The average Brazilian in Rio de Janeiro was far less likely to die at human hands than the average Wao-rani, Arawete, or Yanomano, indigenous people who live in the depths of the Amazon forest without army, police, or prisons. Anthropological studies have indicated that between a quarter and half of their menfolk die sooner or later in violent conflicts over property, women, or prestige" (368).

This magical Indigenous Other occupies both the present moment—knowable by anthropologists—and the distant past. Indigenous space is both *here*, within a global one-world, and *there*, geographically removed from modernity, buried in the jungle and in time. Missing are any of the historical and contemporary contexts wrought by the incursions of state and capital in the highly contested space that is the Amazon. And missing are the concrete consequences of naming and representing tribal people with exotic names and supposedly exemplary "archaic" customs.

The reality is that the average Indigenous person in Brazil has been much more likely to die at human hands—and the hands are *not* those of other Indigenous people. The Amazon rainforest has long been the site of sustained campaigns of colonization, dispossession, and death. Logging, mining, and land clearance continually rob Indigenous peoples of property and sustenance. Introduced disease—sometimes purposefully introduced—has destroyed countless communities. And the history of sustained and deliberate violence—murder, enslavement, torture, rape—makes clear that Harari's modern state-sponsored "security" rests on the radical insecurity of Indigenous genocide, which is ongoing and structural, extending across and through dictatorships and democracies (Amnesty International; Moran; Watts and Rocha).[5]

Red Earth, White Lies would also wish to press Harari on the question of science. Though Harari reveals himself to be a serious Buddhist, science is really his God: there is no meaning in the universe outside chemical reactions in the brain and the cold logic of natural selection. Meaning, in every case, is a human construct only. And science and scale, in this telling, allow an observer to get outside the problems of *meaning*: of the temptations of shallow history, cultural blinders, political correctness, liberal humanism, and all the rest.

It is difficult for Indigenous people to see Western science as optimistically as Harari does, as some kind of truth machine built on a foundation of humility and caution. "Physicists readily admit they don't know what caused the Big Bang," he observes, "or how to reconcile quantum mechanics with the theory of general relativity" (252). True, but one might observe that he has picked rather low-hanging fruit for an example of scientific uncertainty. He points confidently to vigorous scientific debates (note, though, that his example is from economics, the most dubious of sciences). "In other cases," he observes, "particular theories are supported so consistently by the available evidence, that all alternatives have long since fallen by the wayside. Such theories are accepted as true—yet everyone agrees that were new evidence to emerge that contradicts the theory, it would have to be revised or discarded" (253).

Actually, not everyone does agree. As Thomas S. Kuhn pointed out almost six decades ago, "science" is an institutional and cultural formation capable of erecting significant barriers to challenges to its theories—and can be vicious in smacking down heterodoxy. This was a key caution articulated in *Red Earth, White Lies*, given ironic shape in a long and deliberate accounting of geologist J. Harlen Bretz's struggles and censures as he tried to convince the scientific establishment of the geological record left behind by the scablands floods of Washington State.

We need not see sinister academic conspiracy theories to understand that "science" is a functional culture, with interests—and thus the potential to be compromised—even as it claims to be uncompromised. The following passage from *Red Earth, White Lies* sounded aggressive and paranoid in 1995.

> Scientific theories are often built on the most tenuous of evidential foundations and survive only because of the gentleman's agreement within scientific peer groups not to embarrass colleagues. One theory with dubious validity serves to provide the platform for articulating another theory which has even less to recommend itself and a third theory assumes that the first two are correct. By relying on outmoded general theories and doctrines, a scholar can skate out onto the pond of fictional enterprise, promulgate nonsense, and be taken seriously by his colleagues. (108)

Today, the passage seems only mildly critical, when viewed in light of the current crises in the natural and social sciences around falsification of data, inability to replicate, and academic politics.[6]

If new historicities—not so deeply beholden to linear time and progressive narrative—were to focus on contingency, humility, and an archaeology of possibility, they would pose one final challenge to Harari's narrative form, which is framed around an unarticulated quality of *inexorability*. Agriculture might not have happened—here is a head fake in the direction of contingency—but according to Harari, once certain system conditions opened the door, it became, in effect, inexorable. Structural patterns gave shape to individual human decisions, which then created the structure for further action. Likewise, at the end of the book, the human creation of future generations of superhumans is basically read as inevitable and inexorable, for the same reasons. If the specific *form* of action is possibly open to contingency, the basic *process* is already locked and loaded.

Readers can visualize his post-*sapiens* future in precision medicine, genetic manipulation, technological mind and body replacement, and the over-the-top computer modeling of the brain.

There seem to be no insurmountable technical barriers preventing us from producing superhumans. The main obstacles are the ethical and political objections that have slowed down research on humans. And no matter how convincing the ethical arguments may be, it is hard to see how they can hold back the next step for long, especially if what is at stake is the possibility of prolonging human life indefinitely, conquering incurable diseases, and upgrading our cognitive and emotional abilities. (403–4)

Here, the inexorability argument is on full display. Possibilities turn into inevitabilities under the banner of progress—prolonging life, curing disease, upgrading the posthuman. The only thing slowing them are certain ethical humanist dimensions, those things we might once have associated with humility, uncertainty, contingency, and a moral stance on historical forces such as violent colonialism and imperialism.

Inexorability cannot help but do harm to Indigenous people—and to all people, as human beings (not species-level *sapiens*) trying to craft a sustainable future in the moment of climate change and pandemic disease. If, as Harari suggests, *connections*—and thus seemingly higher levels of complexity—are inevitable trajectories for the human world, then Indigenous peoples are necessarily framed with a familiar fate: assimilate into the global one-world or *die*. Emergent local cultures are meaningless distractions in the inexorable world of *Sapiens*; residual and adaptive cultures are useful rhetorically but nowhere else.

Red Earth, White Lies was not ready to give in to all that. Perhaps my father so wanted deep-time scholarship—geology, archaeology, paleobiology—to challenge its own orthodoxies that he got a little carried away with the dinosaurs and the over-the-top catastrophism. Part of his challenge required a critical attack on the academic structure of science. But perhaps the more important part was a challenge to scholars to see Indigenous peoples as peoples—not as *objects* "good to think with" or think about but as *intellectuals and historians* in their own right, good to think *with*, in partnerships borne out of respect. Can we imagine new stories—equally deep and big— that step outside the narrative inevitabilities so visible in books like *Sapiens*? That decolonize prehistory? And might we imagine the twinned question: Can Indigenous peoples *also* imagine new Indigenous stories, deeply engaged with scientific knowledge, that place *them* in the narrative driver's seat when contemplating the deep past, that use science to corroborate *Native* stories?

My father's motives in *Red Earth, White Lies* were transparently clear: it was a love/hate letter to scientists crafted on the grounds where science met up with politics, ethics, and morality. Yuval Noah Harari's motives in

Sapiens—particularly his use of the past to propose an idiosyncratic, cavalier, reckless, irresponsible futurism—are much less clear. Scientists lined up to hate *Red Earth, White Lies* (or more often, to ignore it). I wonder where they are on the same questions today, and why they leave their field to be defined as an amoral caricature. And I wonder whether asking those questions might allow them, too, to think about where they—and the Indigenous—might sit together in the uneven world of *Sapiens* today.

Notes

1. Succinctly put, the Bering Strait migration theory states that the first inhabitants of North America traveled from Asia across a land bridge approximately twelve thousand years ago during periods of glaciation in which much of the Earth's water was frozen in glaciers, therefore lowering sea levels and exposing the Bering Strait land bridge. Humans then traveled through the "ice-free corridor" below the Strait to populate the rest of the American continent.

2. Thomas D. Dillehay and Michael B. Collins suggest that migration to the Americas may have taken place thousands of years prior to the generally accepted figure, 12,000 years. Jessi J. Halligan et al. locate stone tools and mastodon bones at the Page-Lasdon site in Florida that were found to be approximately 14,550 years old, and suggest that hunter-gatherers in the Gulf Coastal Plain coexisted with and used megafauna for approximately 2,000 years before the megafauna became extinct. Mikkel Pedersen et al. conclude that the first Americans were unlikely to have used the "ice-free corridor" as a migration route because of its inhospitable climate and terrain at the time.

3. *Los Angeles Times* readers responding to a name change from Columbus Day to Indigenous Peoples Day make clear the pervasiveness of the "immigrant" argument, summarized best by reader James Willis, who writes, "It is scientific fact that there is no such thing as 'indigenous people' in the Western Hemisphere. We are all descendants of immigrants, whether by boat, plane or Alaskan land bridge. Hackel's references to 'indigenous people who immigrated here from other regions' and 'the first indigenous settlers to arrive in the L.A. Basin' are linguistic and factual nonsense. Like descendants of French, Portuguese or Chinese migrants, his 'indigenous people' or 'Native Americans' are also descendants of earlier migrations from other continents. These residents of the Americas are no more indigenous than kudzu vine or tumbleweed."

    The National Park Service's webpage about the Bering Land Bridge National Preserve casually describes Native Americans as "America's first immigrants." Even well-meaning comments can sometimes go awry. In an August 2019 *National Geographic* article about the first Europeans that argues against the concept of "pure" Europeans (a concept that has long fed racist rhetoric), Harvard paleogeneticist David

Reich—working from a deep-time perspective—proclaimed, "There are no indigenous people" (qtd. in Curry).

4. Deloria employs similar humor in *Custer Died for Your Sins*, describing a cartoon that circulated in Indian country that showed a flying saucer landing while a Native watched, captioned, "Oh, no, not again" (148).

5. Profit-driven environmental degradation has had a profound and deadly effect on Brazil's Indigenous peoples. In 2013 a report (originally believed to be "lost" since its submission to the Brazilian government in 1967) surfaced, detailing the genocide, enslavement, torture, and rape of Indigenous peoples in the Brazilian Amazon. The report recounted widespread and systematic abuse by Brazil's Indian Protection Service (originally SPI, Service for the Protection of Indians), a government organization created to protect the country's Indigenous peoples but used as a mechanism to wipe them off their land. One hundred thirty-four officials were originally charged in the crimes, but no one was jailed. Among hundreds of crimes, the report alleged that some tribes were completely wiped out when officials intentionally introduced smallpox to the village, donated sugar mixed with strychnine, and in one case dropped dynamite from airplanes onto isolated villages (Watts and Rocha). In 2019 Amnesty International predicted widespread violence if Brazil's government did not protect Indigenous peoples from illegal land seizures and logging. Many Indigenous leaders have reported receiving death threats from loggers and miners for defending their land, and fear more armed intruders in the dry season, when easier access to the forest facilitates clearing and burning.

6. I remind readers of these crises of verifiability *not* to join in the transparently ideological discourses that attach the word *fake* to anything—including science—that runs counter to simplistic political loyalties but to invoke a long-standing intellectual discussion in science, technology, and society scholarship, which seems usefully joined to parallel critiques offered by Native intellectuals. At the end of the day, *Red Earth, White Lies* sought a *better* and more self-aware Western science, which was itself suggested by the critical perspective on knowledge formation characteristic of the scientific method.

References

Amnesty International. "Brazil: Risk of Bloodshed in the Amazon Unless Government Protects Indigenous Peoples from Illegal Land Seizures and Logging." *Amnesty International*, 7 May 2019, amnesty.org/en/latest/news/2019/05/brazil-risk-of-bloodshed-in-the-amazon-unless-government-protects-indigenous-peoples-from-illegal-land-seizures-and-logging.

Anderson, A., et al. "Prehistoric Maritime Migration in the Pacific Islands: An Hypothesis of ENSO Forcing." *The Holocene*, vol. 16, no. 1, 2006, pp. 1–6.

Arnold, Thomas G. "Radiocarbon Dates from the Ice-Free Corridor." *Radiocarbon*, vol. 44, no. 2, 2002, pp. 437–54.

Bird, R. Bliege, et al. "Fire Stick Farming Hypothesis: Australian Aboriginal Foraging Strategies, Biodiversity, and Anthropogenic Fire Mosaics." *Proceedings of the National Academy of Sciences of the United States of America*, vol. 105, no. 39, 30 Sep. 2008, pp. 14796–801.

Bretz, J. Harlen. "The Channeled Scabland of the Columbia Plateau." *Journal of Geology*, vol. 31, no. 8, 1923, pp. 617–49.

Cajete, Gregory. *Native Science: Natural Laws of Independence*. Clear Light, 2000.

Carroll, Vincent. "Vine Deloria's Other Side." *Rocky Mountain News* (Denver), 18 Nov. 2005.

Curry, Andrew. "The First Europeans Weren't Who You Might Think." *National Geographic*, Aug. 2019.

Deloria, Vine, Jr. *Custer Died for Your Sins: An Indian Manifesto*. Macmillan, 1969.

Deloria, Vine, Jr. *God Is Red*. Grosset & Dunlap, 1973.

Deloria, Vine, Jr. *Red Earth, White Lies: Native Americans and the Myth of Scientific Fact*. Scribner, 1995.

Diamond, Jared. *Guns, Germs, and Steel: The Fate of Human Societies*. W. W. Norton, 1997.

Dillehay, Thomas D. "Probing Deeper into First American Studies." *Proceedings of the National Academy of Sciences of the United States of America*, vol. 106, no. 4, 27 Jan. 2009, pp. 971–78.

Dillehay, Thomas D., and Michael B. Collins. "Early Cultural Evidence from Monte Verde in Chile." *Nature*, vol. 332, no. 6160, 1988, pp. 150–52.

Erlandson, Jon M., et al. "Paleoindian Seafaring, Maritime Technologies, and Coastal Foraging on California's Channel Islands." *Science*, vol. 331, no. 6021, 2011, pp. 1181–85.

Firestone, R. B., et al. "Evidence for an Extraterrestrial Impact 12,900 Years Ago That Contributed to the Megafaunal Extinctions and the Younger Dryas Cooling." *Proceedings of the Natural Academy of the Sciences of the United States of America*, vol. 104, no. 41, 9 Oct. 2007, pp. 16016–21.

Gates, Bill. "How to Handle a National Crisis." *GatesNotes* (blog), 20 May 2019, gatesnotes.com/Books/Upheaval.

Gates, Bill. "What Are the Biggest Problems Facing Us in the 21st Century?" *New York Times Book Review*, 4 Sep. 2018.

Gordin, Michael D. *The Pseudoscience Wars: Immanuel Velikovsky and the Birth of the Modern Fringe*. University of Chicago Press, 2012.

Grayson, Donald K., and David J. Meltzer. "A Requiem for North American Overkill." *Journal of Archaeological Science*, vol. 30, 2003, pp. 585–93.

Guthrie, R. Dale. "New Carbon Dates Link Climatic Change with Human Colonization and Pleistocene Extinctions." *Nature*, vol. 441, no. 7090, 2006, pp. 207–9.

Halligan, Jessi J., et al. "Pre-Clovis Occupation 14,550 Years Ago at the Page-Ladson Site, Florida, and the Peopling of the Americas." *Science Advances*, vol. 2, no. 5, May 2016, pp. 1–8.

Harari, Yuval Noah. *Sapiens: A Brief History of Humankind*. Translated by the author with the help of John Purcell and Haim Watzman, Harvill Secker, 2014.

Hopkins, David M. *The Bering Land Bridge*. Stanford University Press, 1967.

Jett, Stephen C. *Ancient Ocean Crossings: Reconsidering the Case for Contacts with the Pre-Columbian Americas*. University of Alabama Press, 2017.

Kimmerer, Robin Wall. *Braiding Sweetgrass: Indigenous Wisdom, Scientific Knowledge and the Teachings of Plants*. Milkweed, 2013.

Kimmerer, Robin Wall. "Searching for Synergy: Integrating Traditional and Scientific Ecological Knowledge in Environmental Science." *Journal of Environmental Studies and Sciences*, vol. 2, no. 4, 2012, pp. 317–23.

Kuhn, Thomas S. *The Structure of Scientific Revolutions*. 3rd ed., University of Chicago Press, 1996.

Los Angeles Times. "Opinion: Christopher Columbus Was No Saint—and Neither Were the Indigenous Americans." 11 Oct. 2017.

Lyman, Lee. "Late-Quaternary Diminution and Abundance of Prehistoric Bison (*Bison* sp.) in Eastern Washington State, U.S.A." *Quaternary Research*, vol. 62, no. 1, July 2004, pp. 76–85.

Madsen, David B. "Colonization of the Americas Before the Last Glacial Maximum: Issues and Problems." *Entering America: Northeast Asia and Beringia Before the Last Glacial Maximum*, University of Utah Press, 2004, pp. 1–26.

Martin, Paul S. "The Discovery of America." *Science*, vol. 179, no. 4077, 1973, pp. 969–74.

Martin, Paul S. "Prehistoric Overkill." *Pleistocene Extinctions: The Search for a Cause*, edited by Paul S. Martin and H. E. Wright Jr., Yale University Press, 1967, pp. 75–120.

Meyer, Hanno, et al. "Long-Term Winter Warming Trend in the Siberian Arctic During the Mid- to Late Holocene." *Nature Geoscience*, vol. 8, 2015, pp. 122–25.

Moran, Emilio. "Deforestation in the Brazilian Amazon." *Tropical Deforestation: The Human Dimension*, edited by Leslie E. Sponsel et al., Columbia University Press, 1996, pp. 149–64.

National Park Service. "Bering Land Bridge National Preserve." nps.gov/articles/bering .htm. Accessed 6 Nov. 2020.

Nogués-Bravo, David, et al. "Climate Change, Humans, and the Extinction of the Woolly Mammoth." *PLOS Biology*, vol. 6, no. 4, Apr. 2008, e79.

Pedersen, Mikkel, et al. "Postglacial Viability and Colonization in North America's Ice-Free Corridor." *Nature*, vol. 537, no. 7618, 2016, pp. 45–51.

Rothschild, Bruce M., and Richard Laub. "Hyperdisease in the Late Pleistocene: Validation of an Early 20th Century Hypothesis." *Naturwissenschaften*, vol. 93, no. 11, Nov. 2006, pp. 557–64.

Sagan, Carl. *Broca's Brain: Reflections on the Romance of Science*. Random House, 1979.

Velikovsky, Immanuel. *Earth in Upheaval*. Doubleday, 1955.

Velikovsky, Immanuel. *Worlds in Collision*. Macmillan, 1950.

Verdesio, Gustavo. "Towards a New Production of Time: Rethinking Indigenous and Collaborative Archaeologies." Paper delivered at the Symposium on Deep Historicities, Harvard University, 15 Apr. 2019.

Waters, Michael R., and Thomas W. Stafford Jr. "Redefining the Age of Clovis: Implications for the Peopling of the Americas." *Science*, vol. 315, no. 5815, 2007, pp. 1122–26.

Watts, Jonathan, and Jan Rocha. "Brazil's 'Lost Report' into Genocide Surfaces After 40 Years." *The Guardian*, 29 May 2013.

White, J. M., et al. "An 18-Million-Year Record of Vegetation and Climate Change in Northwestern Canada and Alaska: Tectonic and Global Climate Correlates." *Palaeogeography, Palaeoclimatology, Palaeoecology*, vol. 130, no. 1, 1997, pp. 293–306.

Whitney-Smith, Elin. "Late Pleistocene Extinctions Through Second-Order Predation." *The Settlement of the American Continents*, edited by C. Michael Barton et al., University of Arizona Press, 2004, pp. 177–88.

Witgen, Michael. Email communication with author. 25 May 2019.

Epilogue

Kirsten Matoy Carlson

I TEACH FEDERAL INDIAN LAW—THE unique law that has developed over the past five centuries to govern the relationships among Indians and non-Indians in the United States—predominately to non-Indian students at a university in a moderately sized urban center. I start my class with an acknowledgment that a century ago, no one envisioned my class being taught. For close to three centuries, European colonists and later the United States treated Indian nations as if they would eventually disappear (see Carlson and McHalsie in this volume). But Indigenous peoples are still here. As the interdisciplinary chapters in this volume attest, Indigenous peoples not only remain but they continue to resist marginalization and to offer alternative narratives about ancient American history. On the first day of class, I challenge my students with a question similar to the one Philip J. Deloria and his father have asked: How do we find space where both Indigenous and non-Indigenous peoples might sit together in the world today?

This question, in various forms, resonates through the chapters in this book. Read together, the chapters question what deep history is, who makes it, how they make it, and what its political implications are. Some authors use prehistory as a lens for seeing how settlers and scientists have dismissed, ignored, and degraded Indigenous peoples' historical connections and intimate knowledge of places and spaces (Budhwa, Carlson and McHalsie, Deloria, Gniadek, Kolodny, Mucher, Picas). They emphasize the need to think critically about how the stories being told are informed by Western science and settler colonialism (Deloria, Mucher, Thrush). Other chapters reveal the hidden and changing nature of Indigenous perspectives on and relationships to deep history (Picas, Christie). They propose how Indigenous narratives may

249

inform and complement Western science (Budhwa, Picas). Yet other chapters raise thoughtful concerns about how archaeologists, anthropologists, and historians respond to the alternative narratives presented by Indigenous peoples and have served both to legitimate and undermine Indigenous perspectives (Budhwa, Deloria, Kolodny, Mucher, Oliver). Some authors go even further, raising and considering the practical implications of prehistory on law and politics (Carlson and McHalsie, Deloria, Kolodny, Thrush). They note how the erasure of Indigenous peoples from deep history has undermined their legal and political claims and emphasize how Indigenous peoples have continuously contested this marginalization.

As these chapters suggest, the law serves as a poignant example of how, when, and where contestations over prehistory occur and have practical impacts. Law is not the only space in which such controversies unfold. But the law is all about winners and losers. It can be used by Indigenous and non-Indigenous peoples to privilege and validate particular views of deep history and affect power relations among Indigenous peoples, the settler state, and Western science (Carlson and McHalsie, Kolodny, Oliver, Thrush).

Both Indigenous and non-Indigenous groups make legal claims related to or dependent upon their respective views of deep history (Carlson and McHalsie, Kolodny, Oliver, Thrush). Native claims to governance, land and resources, and even identity stem from their precontact history. These claims are fundamentally about the connection between people and the land and the ability of Indigenous peoples to govern or control that relationship (Carlson and McHalsie, Kolodny, Oliver, Thrush). Look behind many Native claims and you find prehistory. Seemingly "objective" scientists make claims too, and many of their claims have undermined the claims made by and experiences of Indigenous peoples (Deloria, Kolodny, Mucher).

These clashing views have historically played out and currently still play out in Western courts and legislatures. Settlers first legally defined their relationships with Native peoples through treaties and later through statutes and court decisions. Because of the legal nature of relationships among Natives and non-Natives, Western courts and legislatures are often asked to resolve these issues. Western institutions turn to the familiar—Western law—and struggle with the unfamiliar (Kolodny, Carlson and McHalsie). Western courts are rarely cognizant of and often not open to the deep histories of Native peoples as they know and experience them. Recent examples include the 2015 *Penobscot Nation v. Mills* decision to deny the Penobscot's historical claims to the bed of the Penobscot River, which privileged Western views of deep history over Penobscot ones (Kolodny), and Justice William Rehnquist's decision in *Oliphant v. Suquamish Indian Tribe*, 435 U.S. 191 (1978), which manipulated history to deprive tribes of criminal jurisdiction over non-Indians. Ignorance of the prehistory underlying tribal claims undermines the ability of the law to mediate contested terrains effectively. It also influences the stories that are told (and not told). As a result, there is no question that Indigenous peoples historically lost in this arena. The real-world impact of these losses continues to be felt.

Deep history has occasionally been used to help Indigenous peoples win or at the very least to level the playing field (Thrush, Oliver, Carlson and McHalsie). Important recent legal changes include the U.S. Congress's creation of a nationwide process for the repatriation of cultural materials to federally recognized Indian nations in the Native American Graves Protection and Repatriation Act (NAGPRA) of 1990; the U.S. Supreme Court's faithful application of the canons of treaty construction to uphold Anishinaabek off-reservation hunting, fishing, and gathering rights in *Minnesota v. Mille Lacs Band of Chippewa Indians*, 526 U.S. 172 (1999); and the Supreme Court of Canada's decision to acknowledge the importance of Aboriginal perspectives on Aboriginal title in *Delgamuukw v. The Queen*, (1997) 3 SCR 1010. These changes in the law have increased consultations with Indigenous peoples about prehistory, and they illustrate how rethinking the stories told about the deep past may alter power relations in the present.

Judicial and legislative ambivalence about how to accommodate Indigenous perspectives has produced laws that structure relationships among Natives and non-Natives in contradictory ways. These laws accentuate the continued, practical need to find space where both Indigenous and non-Indigenous peoples might sit together in the world today. I have learned from my students that many Americans have yet to contemplate this question. Finding an answer is hard because we have to grapple with vastly different perspectives of the past and how they shape present and future relationships.

Contributors

Rick Budhwa is an applied anthropologist who has worked within the realm of Indigenous cultural resource management for twenty-five years. Budhwa received a BA (honors) in anthropology from the University of Western Ontario as well as a Post Baccalaureate Diploma and an MA in anthropology / First Nations studies / archaeology at Simon Fraser University. From his experiences, Rick envisioned Crossroads Cultural Resource Management as a company to ensure transdisciplinary projects beyond conventional archaeology to reflect the complexities and intangible aspects of culture for past, present, and future generations. In his present position, Budhwa works closely with multiple stakeholders (First Nations, industry, government, communities, and academia) to identify gaps resulting from differing worldviews and to establish common ground for meaningful dialogue. He is also a professor at Coast Mountain College in northern British Columbia, where he teaches anthropology, archaeology, history, and sociology. He is the publisher of *Culturally Modified: The Journal of Cultural Resource Management*. Budhwa has been formally adopted into the Gitdumden Clan of the Wet'suwet'en peoples in the traditional territories where he lives.

Keith Thor Carlson holds the Tier One Canada Research Chair in Indigenous and Community-Engaged History at the University of the Fraser Valley, British Columbia. Born and raised in Powell River on British Columbia's west coast, his scholarship focuses on the Salish people of British Columbia and Washington State. He was adopted as an honorary member of the Stó:lō Nation in a potlatch ceremony in 2001. Another research interest remains in mid-twentieth-century Philippine peasant history, and in particular in the history of the Hukbalahap. Carlson considers community engagement fundamental to both his and his graduate students' research. Outside academia, he continues to receive ongoing education from Salish knowledge keepers and knowledge interpreters. Among his major publications are *You Are Asked to Witness: The Stó:lō in Canada's Pacific Coast History* (1997), *A Stó:lō-Coast Salish Historical Atlas* (2001), and *The Power of Place, the Problem of Time: Aboriginal Identity and Historical Consciousness in the Cauldron of Colonialism* (2010). His most recent book, co-edited with John Lutz, Dave Shaepe, and Naxaxalhts'i, is *Towards a New Ethnohistory: Community-Engaged Scholarship Among the People of the River* (2018).

Kirsten Matoy Carlson is an associate professor at Wayne State University Law School. Her research focuses on legal advocacy and law reform, with particular attention to the various strategies used by Indian nations and Indigenous groups to reform federal Indian law and policy effectively. Carlson's research integrates traditional legal analysis with social science methodologies for studying legal and political advocacy. Carlson earned her JD cum laude and a PhD in political science from the University of Michigan; an MA degree with distinction in Māori studies from the University of Wellington, New Zealand; and a BA in international studies from Johns Hopkins University. Prior to joining Wayne Law, she advocated nationally and internationally to protect the rights of Indian nations as a staff attorney at the Indian Law Resource Center. She led the center's advocacy efforts to restore criminal jurisdiction to Indian nations to end violence against women in Indian country. Carlson has been a visiting research scholar at the University of Ottawa and a visiting associate professor at the University of Minnesota Law School. Carlson's articles have been published in the *Michigan Law Review, University of Colorado Law Review, Indiana Law Journal, American Indian Law Review*, and *Michigan State Law Review*. She serves on the State Bar of Michigan Standing Committee on American Indian Law and is a fellow of the American Bar Foundation.

Jessica Christie is a professor of art history at East Carolina University. She specializes in the visual culture of the ancient and contemporary Maya and Inka as well as rock art in the Americas. She has conducted field investigations at precontact Maya sites for more than twenty years and observed contemporary Maya ceremonies for ten years. Since 1997, her field research has focused on the Andes, although she also recently completed a field investigation of el-Amarna in Egypt. Christie has edited or co-edited two volumes about Maya and ancient American palace architecture, *Maya Palaces and Elite Residences* (2003) and *Palaces and Power in the Americas: From Peru to the Northwest Coast* (2006), as well as edited *Landscapes of Origin in the Americas* (2009). Her monograph *Memory Landscapes of the Inka Carved Outcrops: From Past to Present* (2016) investigates the social agency of Inka rock shrines/*wak'a*. Her current book, *Earth Politics of Cultural Landscapes and Intangible Heritage: Three Case Studies in the Americas* (forthcoming), reconstructs the historical layers of Canyon de Chelly on the Navajo Reservation, one Yucatec Maya site, and an Andean community and interweaves them with contemporary practices and traditions. This work links Indigenous and Western knowledge systems regarding land values to draw lessons for a regenerative planet.

Philip J. Deloria is the Leverett Saltonstall Professor of History at Harvard University, where his research and teaching focus on the social, cultural, and political histories of the relations among American Indian peoples and the United States as well as the comparative and connective histories of Indigenous peoples in a global context. Deloria previously taught at the University of Colorado and the University of Michigan. His first book, *Playing Indian* (1998), traces the tradition of white "Indian play" from the Boston Tea Party to the New Age movement, while his book *Indians in Unexpected Places* (2004) examines the ideologies surrounding Indian peoples in the early twentieth century and the ways Native Americans challenged them through sports, travel, automobility, and film and musical performance. Deloria is the co-editor of *A Companion to American Indian History* (with Neal Salisbury, 2004). His co-authored *American Studies: A User's Guide* (with Alexander Olson, 2017) offers a comprehensive treatment of the historiography and methodology of the field of American studies. His most recent book, *Becoming Mary Sully: Toward an American Indian Abstract* (2019), addresses American Indian visual arts of the mid-twentieth century.

Melissa Gniadek is an assistant professor in the Department of English at the University of Toronto, where she teaches early and nineteenth-century American literature and culture. Her current book project investigates temporal concepts within settler colonialist discourse. Her forthcoming monograph, *Oceans at Home: Maritime and Domestic Fictions in Nineteenth-Century American Women's Writing*, examines how oceanic regions, particularly the Pacific, and stories circulated in writing by women in the first half of the nineteenth century. Her work has appeared in numerous journals, including *American Literature, Early American Literature, New Global Studies, J19: The Journal of Nineteenth-Century Americanists, Legacy: A Journal of American Women Writers*, and *Lateral: The Journal of the Cultural Studies Association*.

Annette Kolodny (d. 9 Sep. 2019) was College of Humanities Professor Emerita of American Literature and Culture at the University of Arizona in Tucson. While at the University of British Columbia (1970–74), Kolodny was instrumental in creating the first academically accredited women's studies program in Canada. She was Dean of Humanities at the University of Arizona, Tucson, from 1988 to 1993. Kolodny has received awards from the Guggenheim, Rockefeller, and Ford Foundations, and a fellowship from the National Endowment for the Humanities. Among her books are *The Lay of the Land: Metaphor as Experience and History in American Life and Letters* (1975), *The Land Before Her: Fantasy and Experience of the American Frontiers,*

1630–1860 (1984), *Failing the Future: A Dean Looks at Higher Education in the 21st Century* (1998); an annotated new edition of Joseph Nicolar's 1893 *The Life and Tradition of the Red Man* (2007), and *In Search of First Contact: The Vikings of Vinland, the Peoples of the Dawnland, and the Anglo-American Anxiety of Discovery* (2012).

Gesa Mackenthun is a professor of American studies at Rostock University. Her publications include *Fictions of the Black Atlantic in American Foundational Literature* (2004), *Metaphors of Dispossession: American Beginnings and the Translation of Empire, 1492–1637* (1997), and *Sea Changes: Historicizing the Ocean* (co-edited with Bernhard Klein, 2004). She was the initiator and first spokesperson of the PhD program "Cultural Encounters and the Discourses of Scholarship," funded by the German Research Foundation (2006–15). She is the co-editor of eight conference volumes on various aspects of that topic, including *Entangled Knowledge: Scientific Discourses and Cultural Difference* (2012), *Agents of Transculturation* (2014), *Fugitive Knowledge: The Loss and Preservation of Knowledge in Cultural Contact Zones* (2015), and *DEcolonial Heritage: Natures, Cultures and the Asymmetries of Memory* (with Aníbal Arregui, 2018). She is currently finalizing a book on imperial archaeology and colonial and transcultural constructions of the American deep past.

Christen Mucher is an associate professor of American studies at Smith College (Massachusetts), where she teaches courses on early North America, Native and Indigenous studies, U.S. empire, and museums. Mucher's forthcoming monograph addresses archaeology, historiography, and Indigenous dispossession in the United States and Mexico from the 1780s to the 1830s. Her co-translation and critical edition of Haiti's first novel, *Stella* (1859) by Émeric Bergeaud, was published in 2015. Mucher's work has received support from the Newberry Library, New York Historical Society, American Antiquarian Society, and the National Endowment for the Humanities.

Naxaxalhts'i (aka Sonny McHalsie), LLD Hon., is a widely respected and published Stó:lō knowledge keeper from Canada's South Pacific Coast. He works as cultural advisor/historian for the Stó:lō Research and Resource Management Centre, where he provides advice and cultural guidance to the Stó:lō Xwexwilmexw treaty negotiation team. He and Keith Thor Carlson have collaborated extensively over the past three decades. Together they wrote *I Am Stó:lō: Katherine Explores Her Heritage* (1997), which focused on Naxaxalhts'i's family and especially his daughter. Naxaxalhts'i authored chapters in the multi-award-winning publication *A Stó:lō-Coast Salish Historical Atlas* (2001). He also wrote the extended foreword to Carlson's *The Power of Place, the Problem of Time* (2010). He was the author of the chapter "We Have to Take Care of Everything That Belongs to Us" in *Be of Good Mind* (2007). His areas of expertise include Halq'eméylem place-names, fishing, and Stó:lō oral history. He is a member of the Shxw'ow'hamel First Nation, is the proud father of two girls and six boys, and has a growing number of grand-children. He continues to fish at his ancestral fishing ground at Aseláw in the lower Fraser River canyon.

Jeff Oliver is a senior lecturer in archaeology at the University of Aberdeen, Scotland. While born and raised on the west coast of Canada, he has lived and worked for the past twenty years in the United Kingdom. He is a his-torical landscape archaeologist interested in the colonial history of western Canada and improvement-period Britain. His work addresses issues such as cultural interaction, historiography, and interdisciplinarity. Recent projects have focused on the archaeologies of migrant communities in the Canadian Prairies and crofting colonies within the Lowlands of Scotland. He is the au-thor of *Landscapes and Social Transformations on the Northwest Coast* (2010) and is co-editor of three volumes, including *Wild Signs: Graffiti in Archaeology and History* (with Tim Neal, 2010), *Historical Archaeologies of Cognition: Explorations into Faith, Hope and Charity* (with James Symonds and Anna Badcock, 2013), and *Contemporary and Historical Archaeology of the North* (with Neil Curtis, 2015), a special issue of the journal *Historical Archaeology*.

Mathieu Picas is a cultural heritage management PhD candidate at the Uni-versity of Barcelona. He is a member of the Grup d'Arqueologia Pública i Patrimoni research group. His research focuses on the sacred values of ar-chaeological heritage and the relationships between local communities and cultural landscapes in Mexico and Guatemala. He holds a bachelor's and mas-ter's degree in foreign literature, languages, and culture from the University of Pau (France) and another MA in intercultural relations and international cooperation from the Université de Pau et des Pays de l'Adour and a mas-ter's degree in intercultural relations and international cooperation from the Université Lille 3 Charles de Gaulle. From 2011 to 2012, he was an assistant professor at the University of Quintana Roo. From 2015 to 2018, he worked and volunteered for different organizations related to natural and cultural heritage in Mexico, Nicaragua, and Spain (UNDP, UNESCO, INAH, EAA). From 2018 to 2020, he was a research assistant for the ERC Artsoundscapes project at the University of Barcelona.

Daniel Lord Smail is the Frank B. Baird, Jr. Professor of History at Harvard University, where he works on deep human history and the history and anthropology of Mediterranean societies between 1100 and 1600. His current research approaches transformations in the material culture of later medieval Mediterranean Europe using household inventories and inventories of debt collection from Lucca and Marseille. Among other subjects, he has written on the practice of compulsive hoarding. His books include *Legal Plunder: Households and Debt Collection in Late Medieval Europe* (2016), *Deep History: The Architecture of Past and Present* (with Andrew Shryock and others, 2011), *On Deep History and the Brain* (2008), and *The Consumption of Justice: Emotions, Publicity, and Legal Culture in Marseille, 1264–1423* (2003).

Coll Thrush is a professor of history at the University of British Columbia in Vancouver in unceded Musqueam Coast Salish territory, and affiliate faculty at UBC's Institute for Critical Indigenous Studies. He is also a visiting professor at the University of Kent in the UK. Thrush is the author of *Native Seattle: Histories from the Crossing-Over Place* (2007; 2nd ed., 2017) and the co-editor of *Phantom Past, Indigenous Presence: Native Ghosts in North American History and Culture* (with Colleen Boyd, 2011). His most recent book is *Indigenous London: Native Travelers at the Heart of Empire* (2016), which examines that city's history through the experiences of Indigenous travelers—willing or otherwise—from territories that became the United States, Canada, Australia, and New Zealand. Thrush's current project is a critical cultural and environmental history of shipwrecks, settler colonialism, and Indigenous survivance on the northwest coast of North America.

Index